DATE DUE

MY 12			
AP 26 '00			
JE 9 '03			
NO 2 5 '09			

DEMCO 38-296

The
U.S. Constitution
and the
Power to Go to War

Recent Titles in
Contributions in Military Studies

"Mad Jack": The Biography of Captain John Percival, USN, 1779–1862
David F. Long

Military Helicopter Doctrines of the Major Powers, 1945–1992: Making
Decisions about Air-Land Warfare
Matthew Allen

Joint Military Operations: A Short History
Roger A. Beaumont

Iron Brigade General: John Gibbon, A Rebel in Blue
Dennis S. Lavery and Mark H. Jordan

Looking Back on the Vietnam War: A 1990s Perspective on the Decisions,
Combat, and Legacies
William Head and Lawrence E. Grinter, editors

The Search for Strategy: Politics and Strategic Vision
Gary L. Guertner, editor

Paying the Premium: A Military Insurance Policy for Peace and Freedom
Walter Hahn and H. Joachim Maitre, editors

Imperial Spies Invade Russia: The British Intelligence Interventions, 1918
A. J. Plotke

Uneasy Coalition: The Entente Experience in World War I
Jehuda L. Wallach

Peacekeepers and Their Wives: American Participation in the Multinational
Force and Observers
David R. Segal and Mady Wechsler Segal

The American Revolution, Garrison Life in French Canada and New York
Translated by Helga Doblin and edited with an introduction by Mary C. Lynn

In Caesar's Shadow: The Life of General Robert Eichelberger
Paul Chwialkowski

THE
U.S. CONSTITUTION
AND THE
POWER TO GO TO WAR

Historical and Current Perspectives

Edited by GARY M. STERN
and MORTON H. HALPERIN

Prepared Under the Auspices of
The Center for National Security Studies

Contributions in Military Studies, Number 150

GREENWOOD PRESS
Westport, Connecticut • London

Library of Congress Cataloging-in-Publication Data

The U.S. Constitution and the power to go to war : historical and current
 perspectives / edited by Gary M. Stern and Morton H. Halperin, under
 the auspices of the Center for National Security Studies,
   p. cm.—(Contributions in military studies, ISSN 0883–6884;
 no. 150)
   "The chapters in this book were originally commissioned for the
 September 18–19, 1992 CNSS conference on Constitutional Government
 and Military Intervention after the Cold War, held at and
 cosponsored by the Georgetown University Law Center"—
 Acknowledgments.
   Includes bibliographical references and index.
   ISBN 0–313–28958–1 (alk. paper)
   1. War and emergency powers—United States—History—Congresses.
 2. Executive power—United States—History—Congresses. 3. United
 States. Congress—Powers and duties—History—Congresses.
 4. United States—Constitutional history—Congresses. I. Stern,
 Gary M. II. Halperin, Morton H. III. Center for National Security
 Studies (Washington, D.C.). IV. Georgetown University. Law Center.
 V. Series.
 KF5060.A75U8   1994
 342.73′062347.30262—dc20   93–15840

British Library Cataloguing in Publication Data is available.

Library of Congress Catalog Card Number: 93–15840
ISBN: 0–313–28958–1
ISSN: 0883–6884

First published in 1994

Greenwood Press, 88 Post Road West, Westport, CT 06881
An imprint of Greenwood Publishing Group, Inc.

Printed in the United States of America

The paper used in this book complies with the
Permanent Paper Standard issued by the National
Information Standards Organization (Z39.48–1984).

10 9 8 7 6 5 4 3 2 1

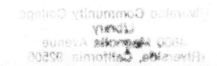

Contents

Acknowledgments

This book could not have been written without the generous support of the Ford Foundation, which provided the primary funding for the Center for National Security Studies' Project on Constitutional Government and Military Intervention After the Cold War.

The chapters in this book were originally commissioned for the September 18–19, 1992 CNSS conference on Constitutional Government and Military Intervention After the Cold War held at and cosponsored by the Georgetown University Law Center. In planning for the conference, we were greatly assisted by an Advisory Committee composed of Barry Blechman, Harold Koh (who is also a contributor to this book), Edward Luttwak, and Eugene Rostow. Georgetown Law Professor Barry Carter ably served on our planning committee, and Molly Jackson, the Administrator for International Programs at the Law Center, provided fantastic logistical support in organizing the conference. Georgetown law students Kenneth Rexford, Stefanie Sanderman, and Megan Smith served as conference rapporteurs, and their notes were helpful in preparing this book.

Very special thanks goes to Sally Householder at CNSS for her constant and cheerful support at every stage of the project and book. Thanks also to Penny Bevis and Lynthia Gibson of CNSS for their assistance.

Introduction

Gary M. Stern and Morton H. Halperin

This book examines the "war powers" of the President and Congress in light of the end of the Cold War. After 45 years, the principal motivator of U.S. foreign policy abruptly disappeared. But the dissolution of the Soviet Union did not mean that the United States would no longer be fighting wars; indeed, just as the U.S.S.R. was taking its final gasps, the United States amassed and engaged the largest military force since World War II when it attacked Saddam Hussein's Iraq. Nor did the end of the superpower rivalry give the United States a green light to initiate wars without any fear of international recrimination; rather, the United Nations has begun to emerge as a control on international military action. These factors thus compel a new look at a very old subject.

The drafters of the Constitution understood the critical importance of the decision to go to war. They recognized that war and the government's fear of foreign enemies posed a threat to individual liberty here at home. They also believed that in a democratic nation, the decision to go to war should be preceded by public debate and should only be made if there was a consensus in support of the use of force. At the same time, they recognized that the President had to be able to act decisively in genuine emergencies.

The War Clause represents their effort to incorporate these goals into the governmental structure. It hinges the decision to go to war on the cooperation of both political branches, which must act on the public record, yet allows the President to respond militarily to immediate threats to the nation and grants him or her full command authority. In this way it sought to cure the defects experienced under both the British monarchy and the Continental Congress.

During the Cold War, the government assumed that these principles could no longer be applied in the face of a potentially overwhelming adversary "whose avowed objective is world domination by whatever means and at whatever cost."[1] On this rather newfound rationale, Presidents took the nation into armed combat with no intention of seeking prior congressional approval; they also used the mechanism of covert action to involve the United States in foreign military operations without the public's, or sometimes even Congress's, knowledge or consent. These actions led to a number of military and political debacles, both at home and abroad.

Beginning in the 1970s, Congress sought to reassert its war power authority and to establish statutory restraints on the President. It passed the War Powers Resolution and the Intelligence Oversight Act and put greater controls on arms transfers.[2] Subsequent events, however, have shown that these statutes have not been wholly effective. The Executive branch was able either to ignore them or find loopholes to evade compliance, while Congress was lax in enforcing its own regulatory schemes.

The result has been a constitutional stand-off between the two political branches over how the government should proceed with respect to future decisions to use military force—each side feeling both entrenched and resentful of the other's motives and intents. Although there is a general consensus that the laws and practices of the government are in need of revision, there is little agreement on what to do and how to do it.

In this volume we examine the war powers of the United States government from revolutionary times to the present, and then look at ways to develop a new post–Cold War consensus on appropriate criteria for deciding when to use military or paramilitary force and on the executive and legislative procedures that should preceed such action.

This book is the outgrowth of an ongoing project of the Center for National Security Studies (CNSS) on the U.S. Constitution and the Power to Go to War in the Post-Cold War Era. Following the fall of the Berlin Wall in late 1989, CNSS received a grant from the Ford Foundation to study anew the process by which a constitutional democracy commits itself to military action abroad. In September 1992, CNSS cosponsored a two-day conference on Constitutional Government and Military Intervention After the Cold War with the Georgetown University Law Center. The chapters of this book are based on papers commissioned for that conference and were revised subsequently. (A list of the conference participants appears in the appendix.)

When CNSS began planning the conference in 1990, we still lived in a two superpower world in which the possibilities of true international multilateralism had not yet materialized. Accordingly, the original paper topics focused exclusively on the domestic conflict between Congress and the President over the war power. At that time we paid scant attention to U.S. involvement in U.N.- sponsored military actions or other international law considerations. Moreover, while Congress continued to study and complain about the President taking unilateral military action, not since World War II had it inserted itself into the decision-making process of going to war. With a new world just upon us, we were still operating under old world assumptions.

Almost immediately after the project began, changing world events forced us to rethink many of our initial assumptions, although they reinforced certain aspects. The Soviet Union disintegrated, eliminating not only the military threat, but also the superpower rivalry and international bipolarism that had characterized the Cold

War. This change significantly undermined the principal justifications for the Executive branch's legal aggrandizement of the war power.

Then in the summer of 1990, Iraq invaded Kuwait. President Bush immediately deployed U.S. troops into a potential war situation without congressional authorization. Indeed, the Bush Administration continued to act on the presumption that it had inherent power to use force whenever it saw fit, thus making the constitutional provision granting to Congress alone the power to declare war a virtual nullity. Congress, on the other hand, demonstrated by its last minute vote authorizing the Persian Gulf War that it would not let its war power responsibilities completely lapse. Indeed, Congress engaged in an extensive debate and then voted to authorize the use of force by only a narrow margin—52–47 in the Senate, and 250–183 in the House.[3] In addition, the House also passed, by an overwhelming margin—302–131—a general resolution declaring that

The Congress finds that the Constitution of the United States vests all power to declare war in the Congress of the United States.

Any offensive action taken against Iraq must be explicitly approved by the Congress of the United States before such action may be initiated.[4]

Although the invasion of Kuwait engendered essentially a Cold War response from President Bush, the international community responded in an unprecedented fashion. For the first time since its inception, the U.N. Security Council was poised to exercise its Article 42 peacekeeping function—involving the use of force—without the threat of a permanent member veto.

Such a possibility raised, most significantly, the question of what role domestic constitutional procedures play in a U.N.–sanctioned military action. A new debate began to unfold, one in which traditional Cold War political inclinations were shifting. Some scholars who supported congressional war power authority but also favored empowering the U.N. argued that any military action sanctioned by the Security Council was by definition a "police action" not subject to the normal constitutional war power constraints; even if this was not explicit in the U.N. Charter and the U.S. implementing legislation, they stated, it was the clear intent of the Charter and should now become the norm.[5] Others responded that there was nothing in the U.N. or subsequent U.S. legislation that overrides the constitutional procedures concerning the war power.[6]

The impending Iraq war also brought renewed focus on the Declaration of War Clause of the U.S. Constitution. Since the Vietnam War, debates over presidential military action focused almost exclusively on the War Powers Resolution, a 1973 statute designed to establish procedures by which the President and Congress are supposed to interact when the use of military force is anticipated or initiated. Several lawsuits had been brought by Members of Congress in the 1980s seeking to enforce the statute. The courts had universally rejected the suits on the ground that the issue was a nonjusticiable political question that could only be settled by the political branches of the government.[7]

In 1990, however, 54 Members of Congress brought a lawsuit in federal court against the President solely under the Constitution, arguing that the initiation of force against Iraq by the President meets the standards of the Declaration of War Clause and therefore requires advance congressional authorization; they sought an injunction against the President from engaging in offensive military action without such congressional authorization. The unique factual posture of this case allowed the court to consider the issue prior to the actual engagement of U.S. forces into hostilities. Because all previous cases had been brought after the conflict had begun, leaving as the only possible remedy a court order that the President withdraw the forces, courts had been extremely reluctant to intervene.

Yet the federal district court took up the challenge and for the first time in U.S. history issued a formal judicial interpretation of the Declaration of War Clause in the case *Dellums v. Bush*.[8] The court did so while denying the plaintiffs' requested injunction on the ground that the case was not yet "ripe"; the court, however, suggested that an injunction might be appropriate if the President intended to initiate offensive military action in actual defiance of an express congressional resolution opposing the use of force. The case was subsequently dismissed as moot after Congress voted in support of the war; but the opinion of the court stands as an important precedent supporting congressional war power and, in light of the earlier cases rejecting similar claims, leaves the legal status of this issue unsettled.

Accordingly, the paper topics and the conference format were reconceived along the lines presented in this book to account for the dramatic changes in the post–Cold War world situation. After a brief historical review, this book focuses on the various legal constraints that define and limit the war power—the Constitution, statutes, treaties, international law, and the courts. It also considers "covert" paramilitary action as a tangent of the war power. Finally, the book offers two perspectives on how to proceed in the future.

Due to space limitations, we were unable to include in this book one important topic of the conference—the domestic impact of war on individual rights. J. Gregory Sidak, a Resident Scholar at the American Enterprise Institute, addressed this issue in his paper on "War, Liberty, and Enemy Aliens."[9] Sidak focused specifically on the Alien Enemy Act of 1798, a statute that gives the President vast powers to arrest, intern, and remove "enemy aliens," but only during a "declared war." He applied an economic analysis akin to the Coase Theorem[10] in arguing that the constitutional formality of "declaring war can help to safeguard individual liberty in the United States when Congress decides to authorize the President to pursue our foreign policy objectives through the use of military force." In his view, a formal declaration serves the purpose of alerting the electorate to the dangers posed not only by a foreign enemy, but also by the expanding power of the U.S. government during wartime: "To eschew declaring war when we wage war is to encourage the federal government to expand at the expense of individual liberty."[11]

Chapter One presents an historical survey of the war power and the use of force. Louis Fisher outlines the constitutional framework and the intent of the framers. He points out that the framers rejected John Locke's model that would have put the power of war and peace among the President's "federative" powers. Fisher succinctly recites the very familiar debate at the constitutional convention over the War Clause, and notes that "legislative control over the deployment of military forces was widely supported by the Framers."[12] Fisher recounts the early experience of actual military engagements. He concludes that such practice was "fully consistent with the expectations of the framers," whereby the decision to use force whether in declared or undeclared wars was reserved to Congress.

Fisher then walks through the period from the mid-19th to the mid-20th centuries, a time when congressional war powers remained dominant, if not sometimes in the breach. President Polk, for example, instigated a military clash that precipitated the Mexican-American War. Even though Congress subsequently declared war on Mexico, it also censured the President for "unnecessarily and unconstitutionally" causing it to begin. President Lincoln also took military action and denied the writ of habeas corpus in the Civil War without congressional approval. But as Fisher points out, not only did Lincoln face a domestic rebellion that truly threatened the life of the nation, he also conceded to Congress his possible constitutional transgression, stating that he did only what he considered "a public necessity, trusting then, as now, that Congress would readily ratify them."

Fisher describes how Harry Truman was the first President to conduct a major war without seeking at least tacit support from the Congress; although justified under the imprimatur of the United Nations, the Korean War was essentially a U.S. war. Four decades later, President Bush followed Truman's lead in arguing that he has "the authority to fully implement the United Nations Resolutions" without congressional authorization. Bush strongly implied that he could have and would have gone to war even without that U.N. support, and even if Congress had explicitly opposed him.

In analyzing the constitutional constraints on the power to go to war, Peter Raven-Hansen takes us back once again through what he describes as the all too familiar history of the War Clause, positing six major conclusions from that record: (1) the Framers intended it to be harder to initiate war than to achieve or continue peace; (2) Congress's power to "declare" war was not merely ceremonial, but rather the power to commence war when it had not already been commenced against us by an enemy; (3) the President has clear power to repel sudden attacks; (4) the President has sole power as Commander-in-Chief to conduct all wars; (5) Congress's appropriation power with respect to the military was designed to keep "the means of carrying on the war" in the Legislative, not the Executive branch; (6) Congress's power to grant letters of marque and reprisal applies in the same manner to uses of force less than war.

Raven-Hansen then considers to what extent "customary national security law" has affected the original design. He finds that through custom the President has acquired unilateral power to use armed forces in the "rescue, evacuation, and protection of American nationals and their property, and hot pursuit of attackers." Although Raven-Hansen has constructed a legal model that seems closer to reality, does it rise to the level of constitutional norm? In the conference, Harold Koh suggested that if Raven-Hansen's model could be overridden by statute, then it would by necessity be of "sub-constitutional stature."[13] Such a statute would presumably have to impose stricter limits on presidential action than Raven-Hansen currently concedes. The War Powers Resolution was one such statute that attempted to override past Executive branch practice. But aside from its non-binding section on "purpose and policy," no such explicit limitations are made.[14]

The War Powers Resolution gets thorough treatment in Chapter 3 as the major statutory constraint on the war power. Following a brief history of its enactment, Ellen Collier provides a detailed analysis of each substantive section and the constitutional questions raised. She then runs through the record of presidential compliance, discussing many of the 25 instances that were reported under the statute, and 19 that were not. The rest of this chapter focuses on the limitations of the law in practice, as seen through several major War Powers Resolution cases. Collier concludes with a discussion of possible amendments.

Jane Stromseth sets out the principal treaty constraint upon the war power—the U.N. Charter—and its statutory corollary—the U.N. Participation Act. She posits and compares three prevailing models concerning the proper division of constitutional war powers with respect to the use of military force authorized by the United Nations: the "political accommodation" model, the "police power" model, and the "contract" model. Decisively rejecting the police power model, defended most recently by Thomas Franck and Faiza Patel as essentially nullifying the War Clause,[15] Stromseth vigorously promotes the contract approach, whereby Congress would give the President preauthorization to use a limited number of U.S. military forces in certain defined circumstances in accordance with Article 43 of the U.N. Charter.

Stromseth's approach engendered widespread support at the conference, with most participants agreeing that the time had arrived to implement the dictates of the Charter and the Participation Act. However, several persons, most notably John Hart Ely and Jules Lobel, questioned whether the War Clause permitted Congress to make a general preauthorization of war without designating a specific enemy. In their view, congressional authorization of military force must by definition include the target against whom it is being authorized.

The legal support for that view, however, is not at all clear. Supreme Court authority suggests otherwise. Justice Jackson's category 1 in the *Steel Seizure* case, that when "the President acts pursuant to an express or implied authorization of Congress, his authority is at its maximum,"[16] combined with the dicta in *United States v. Curtiss-Wright Export Co.*,[17] ceding broad foreign affairs powers to the federal government as a whole, would seem to support congressional preauthorization in accordance with the U.N. Charter. Stromseth also notes that there are various ways to accommodate this concern if it were indeed a barrier.[18]

Interestingly, in Chapter 5 Lobel himself acknowledges such joint authority in the context of international law constraints on the war power. He argues convincingly that the President's foreign affairs power is constitutionally limited by international law when acting alone. But he also concedes that many norms of customary international law are dynamic and therefore subject to change based on contrary state practice; he also acknowledges that the United States must be able to participate in this method of developing international law. Accordingly, Lobel proposes that when the United States chooses to violate international law, it must, at a minimum, follow "separation of powers restraints to ensure that any such violation is agreed to by both Congress and the President."

In Chapter 6 Harold Koh argues that the courts have a "constitutionally required" role to play in war powers cases. Koh argues that, notwithstanding the "collective amnesia" that judges have suffered about their historical role in war powers cases, the issues of judicial competence and appropriate legal standards should now be conclusively settled by Judge Greene's opinion in *Dellums v. Bush*. He then focuses the debate on the relatively few issues on which there is major disagreement—congressional standing, scope of judicial review, and injunctive relief. In his view, the *Dellums* opinion judiciously settled these issues as well, in large part by promoting political dialogue and, eventually, resolution between Congress and the President of their war power dispute over the Iraq War.

In Chapter 8, we argue that the procedures for authorizing so-called "covert" paramilitary actions, which in today's world are covert in name only, should be incorporated into the war powers rubric. The War Clause includes the power to grant letters of marque and reprisal. As Jules Lobel has also argued, this constitutional authority is the historical antecedent to what is now overt/covert lethal support of foreign military forces. Our scheme would not undermine the desired effectiveness of using clandestine means; it only requires congressional authorization of the policy objective, much as a declaration of war is only a generalized goal established by Congress that does not specify the means by which to achieve it.

Greg Treverton counters in Chapter 7 that our proposal would invariably lead to disclosures of operational details that should remain secret. In his view, a limited authority to use covert action should remain, otherwise Presidents would simply seek circumventions as occurred in the Iran-Contra affair. On the whole, however, Treverton argues that under the current procedures governing covert action, Congress and the President interact and cooperate much more effectively than they do with respect to overt war.

The last two chapters consider how to proceed in the post–Cold War future. John Norton Moore offers his view on emergency war powers, arguing that "[t]here is broad presidential authority to use the armed forces, at home and abroad, in emergency or immediate engagement settings, in response to aggressive attack."[19] Moore bases his conclusion in part on modern necessity in the nuclear age and on what he considers the nature of aggression in the 20th century. He attributes such aggression largely to a combination of totalitarian regimes and "deterrence failure." He then suggests that the United States adopt a war powers model that gives the President broad authority to respond to such emergencies, while acknowledging "that there are *major* potential congressional checks on presidential authority to engage the nation in war other than the check of requiring *prior* congressional authorization."[20]

Finally, we offer a proposal to help establish a new working consensus between Congress and the President on war powers issues. What we envision is that there should be full and public debate any time the use of military force, whether overt or clandestine, is contemplated and that the two political branches will work together to discuss, formulate, and enact an appropriate authorizing resolution prior to the actual engagement of such forces. Congress should also preauthorize a limited number of forces for the President to use unilaterally in accordance with U.N. Security Council authorization. Our proposal attempts to bypass the never-ending legal standoff over which branch has what power, in order to establish effective working guidelines for war power decision making in the post–Cold War world.

NOTES

1. Quoted in S. Rep. No. 755, 94th Cong., 2d Sess., Book I, at 9 (Apr. 26, 1976) (Church Committee Report). *See also* Chapter 5.

2. War Powers Resolution, 50 U.S.C. §§ 1541–48; Intelligence Oversight Act, 50 U.S.C. §§ 413–15 (amended in 1991); Arms Export Control Act, 22 U.S.C. § 2795.

3. Pub. L. No. 102–1, 105 Stat. 3, Authorization for Use of Military Force Against Iraq Resolution (1991).

4. Cong. Rec. H405 (daily ed. Jan. 12, 1991), Vol. 137, No. 8.

5. Thomas Franck & Faiza Patel, *UN Police Action in Lieu of War: 'The Old Order Changeth'*, 85 Am. J. Int'l L. 63 (1991).

6. Michael J. Glennon, *The Constitution and Chapter VII of the United Nations Charter*, 85 Am. J. Int'l L. 74 (1991).

7. *See, e.g.*, *Conyers v. Reagan*, 765 F.2d 1124 (D.C. Cir. 1985) (U.S. invasion of Grenada); *Crockett v. Reagan*, 558 F. Supp. 893 (D.D.C.), *aff'd per curiam*, 720 F.2d 1355 (D.C. Cir. 1983), *cert. denied*, 467 U.S. 1251 (1984) (U.S. military aid to El Salvador); *Lowry v. Reagan*, 676 F. Supp. 333 (D.D.C. 1987) (naval escorts of Kuwaiti ships in the Persian Gulf).

8. 752 F. Supp. 1141 (D.D.C. 1990).

9. This paper has been published in 67 N.Y.U. L. Rev. 1402 (1992).

10. *See* Ronald H. Coase, *The Problem of Social Cost*, 3 J. Law. & Econ. 1 (1960); *see also* J. Gregory Sidak, *To Declare War*, 41 Duke L. J. 27 (1991) and *The Inverse Coase Theorem and Declarations of War*, 41 Duke L. J. 325 (1991); *but see* Harold H. Koh, *The Coase Theorem and the War Clause: A Response*, 41 Duke L. J. 122 (1991).

11. 67 N.Y.U. L. Rev. At the conference, Sidak argued that the harshness of the Alien Enemy Act may encourage Congress not to declare war and therefore recommended that the statute be amended. Although such formalism may put the people on notice, it may not serve the interests of individual liberty. For example, Harold Koh responded that by not declaring war, there are actually more restrictions on the government and therefore greater protections of civil liberties; Koh also asserted that, contrary to Sidak's contention, governmental accountability is lower under a formal declaration.

12. Chapter 1.

13. In Chapter 6, Koh refers to "quasi-constitutional custom," defined as "informal accommodations between two or more branches on the question of who decides with regard to particular foreign affairs matters."

14. Senator Joseph Biden and John Ritch outlined a legislative proposal that presages Raven-Hansen's views. *See The War Power at a Constitutional Impasse: A 'Joint Decision' Solution*, 77 Geo. L. J. 367 (1988).

15. *See* Franck & Patel, *supra* note 5; *but see* Glennon, *supra* note 6.

16. *Youngstown Sheet & Tube Co. v. Sawyer*, 343 U.S. 579, 635–37 & n.2 (1951).

17. 299 U.S. 304 (1936).

18. *See* Chapter 4, n.83.

19. Chapter 9.

20. Chapter 9. In contrast, Moore argues that legal models which restrict presidential authority, "such as the War Powers Resolution, may have the opposite effect of what was intended. That is, they may increase the risk of American involvement in major war." *Id.*

1   Historical Survey of the War Powers and the Use of Force

Louis Fisher

Under the Constitution, the ultimate authority to control the deployment of military forces lies with Congress. That principle is bedrock to our governmental system. Yet we all know that the conditions of the 20th century, including the availability of a standing army, have shifted much of that power to the President. The war-making power of the President constantly erodes the war-declaring power of Congress. Nevertheless, the contemporary growth of presidential power does not take from Congress any of its original powers—powers which may at any time place limits on the extent to which the President can deploy armed forces.

Congressional acquiescence, of course, expands the scope of presidential power and may invite additional executive encroachments. It is tempting to suggest that presidential initiatives may be tolerable for short-term military commitments, but that long-term involvements require congressional approval. To some extent the historical record supports that dichotomy, but much depends on the nature of the action and its location. For example, given the explosive conditions of the Middle East, it was important for President Bush to obtain congressional approval before going to war against Iraq, regardless of the war's duration.

THE CONSTITUTIONAL FRAMEWORK

The framers were quite deliberate about placing with Congress the fundamental power to deploy armed forces. Had they wanted to vest that control with the President, they had many models to choose from. John Locke, in his *Second Treatise of Government*, delegated foreign policy (the "federative" power) to the Executive. The federative power consisted of "the power of war and peace, leagues and alliances, and all the transactions with all persons and communities without the commonwealth." To Locke, the federative power was "almost always united" with the Executive. Any attempt to separate that power from the Executive would invite "disorder and ruin."[1]

Sir William Blackstone, in his *Commentaries*, was even more explicit on the scope of executive power. The King had absolute power over foreign affairs and war: the right to send and receive ambassadors, make treaties and alliances, make war or peace, issue letters of marque and reprisal, command the military, raise and regulate fleets and armies, and represent the nation in its intercourse with foreign nations.[2]

These theories, fully accessible to the framers, were unacceptable in America. After the American colonies declared their independence from England, all executive powers passed to the Continental Congress. That same principle was incorporated in the first national constitution, the Articles of Confederation. The Philadelphia Convention adopted a separation of powers, but the framers took many of Locke's federative powers and Blackstone's royal prerogatives and gave them either to Congress exclusively or assigned them on a shared basis to Congress and the President.

Given the governmental systems operating worldwide in 1787, the scope of power granted to Congress is remarkable. Under Article I, Section 8, not only does Congress have the power "to declare war, grant letters of marque and reprisal, and make rules concerning captures on land and water," it has the general power "to raise and support armies" and "to provide and maintain a navy." Moreover, it has the power "to make rules for the government and regulation of the land and naval forces"; "to provide for calling forth the militia to execute the laws of the union, suppress insurrections and repel invasions"; and "to provide for the organizing, arming, and disciplining of the militia, and for governing such part of them as may be employed in the Service of the United States."

The intent of the framers is clear. The delegates at the Philadelphia Convention repeatedly emphasized that the power of peace and war associated with the monarchy would not be given to the President. Charles Pinckney supported a vigorous executive, but "was afraid the Executive powers of [the existing] Congress might extend to peace & war &c which would render the Executive a Monarchy, of the worst kind, to wit an elective one."[3] John Rutledge endorsed a single executive, "tho' he was not for giving him the power of war and peace."[4] Roger Sherman looked upon the President as an agent of Congress, and considered

the Executive magistracy as nothing more than an institution for carrying the will of the Legislature into effect, that the person or persons ought to be appointed by and accountable to the Legislature only, which was the depositary of the supreme will of the Society.[5]

James Wilson endorsed a single executive, but did not consider "the Prerogatives of the British Monarch as a proper guide in defining the Executive powers. Some of these prerogatives were of a Legislative nature. Among others that of war & peace &c."[6]

In Federalist No. 69, Alexander Hamilton differentiated between presidential power and the power of the monarchy. Under the Constitution, the President has "concurrent power with a branch of the legislature in the formation of treaties," whereas the British King "is the *sole possessor* of the power of making treaties."

The royal prerogative in foreign affairs was shared with Congress, he noted. He compared the distribution of war powers in England and in the American Constitution. The power of the King "extends to the *declaring* of war and to the *raising* and *regulating* of fleets and armies." Unlike the King of England, the President "will have only the occasional command of such part of the militia of the nation *as by legislative provision may be called into the actual service of the Union*" (emphasis added). No such tether restricted the King.

Legislative control over the deployment of military forces was widely supported by the framers. James Madison emphasized that the Constitution "supposes, what the History of all Govts demonstrates, that the Ex. is the branch of power most interested in war, & most prone to it. It has accordingly with studied care, vested the question of war in the Legisl."[7]

The debates at the Philadelphia Convention reveal the framers' understanding of the need for presidential initiative in defensive actions. Pinckney objected to the draft language giving Congress the power to "make war," because legislative proceedings "were too slow" in an emergency for the safety of the country. He expected Congress to meet only once a year. Madison and Elbridge Gerry then recommended that "declare" be substituted for "make," leaving to the President "the power to repel sudden attacks." Their motion carried.[8]

This grant of power here was carefully limited. The framers empowered the President to repel sudden attacks in an emergency when Congress was not in session. That power covered attacks against the mainland of the United States and on the seas. The President never received a general power to deploy troops whenever and wherever he thought best. When Congress came back in session, it could reassert whatever control on military activity it considered necessary.

Comments on the Madison-Gerry amendment reinforce the narrow grant of authority to the President. Sherman was explicit: "The Executive shd. be able to repel and not to commence war."[9] Gerry said he "never expected to hear in a republic a motion to empower the Executive alone to declare war."[10] George Mason spoke "agst giving the power of war to the Executive, because not [safely] to be trusted with it; . . . He was for clogging rather than facilitating war."[11] At the Pennsylvania ratification convention, James Wilson expressed the prevailing sentiment that the system of checks and balances

will not hurry us into war; it is calculated to guard against it. It will not be in the power of a single man, or a single body of men, to involve us in such distress; for the important power of declaring war is vested in the legislature at large.[12]

The concept of keeping presidential power separate from the power to take the nation to war was well understood. Madison insisted that constitutional liberties could be preserved only by reserving the power of war to Congress:

Those who are to *conduct a war* cannot in the nature of things, be proper or safe judges, whether *a war ought* to be *commenced, continued*, or *concluded*. They are barred from the latter functions by a great principle in free government, analogous to that which separate the sword from the purse, or the power of executing from the power of enacting laws.[13]

Upon seeing the draft constitution, Thomas Jefferson praised the decision to transfer the war power "from the executive to the Legislative body, from those who are to spend to those who are to pay."[14] As a delegate to the Philadelphia Convention, George Mason drove home the same point by stating that the "purse & the sword ought never to get into the same hands [whether Legislative or Executive.]"[15]

The framers gave the President the title Commander in Chief for a number of reasons. The direction of war, Hamilton said in Federalist No. 74, "most peculiarly demands those qualities which distinguish the exercise of power by a single head." The power of directing war and emphasizing the common strength "forms a usual and essential part in the definition of the executive authority." This clause of the Constitution also protected the principle of civilian supremacy. The person leading the armed forces would be the civilian President, not a military officer.[16]

Other than emergency actions to defend the country while Congress is in recess, the power of Commander in Chief exists to carry out legislative, not executive, power. Consider the language in the Constitution: "The President shall be Commander in Chief of the Army and Navy of the United States, and of the Militia of the several States, when called into the actual Service of the United States." Congress, not the President, does the calling. Article I gives to Congress the power to provide "for calling forth the Militia to execute the Laws of the Union, suppress Insurrections and repel invasions."

EARLY EXPERIENCES UNDER THE WAR POWERS

Precedents established during the first few decades after the Philadelphia Convention are fully consistent with the expectations of the framers. The decision to go to war or to deploy military forces was reserved to Congress. Presidents accepted that principle for all wars: declared or undeclared.

The Quasi-War with France in 1798–1800 was clearly authorized by Congress. President John Adams asked Congress to put the country on a war footing. Although he pledged to pursue peaceful negotiations, political conditions abroad compelled him "to recommend to your consideration effectual measures of defense."[17] Congress carefully debated these bills, enacting several dozen to prepare for war. A series of statutes granted supplemental funds for a naval armament, increased the number of ships, authorized another regiment of artillerists and engineers, reinforced the defense of ports and harbors, funded additional cannons, arms, and ammunition, empowered the President to raise a provisional army and seize French ships, and suspended commerce with France. Though war was never formally declared, no one doubted that Congress had authorized war. During the debates in 1798, Congressman Edward Livingston considered the country "now in a state of war; and let no man flatter himself that the vote which has been given is not a declaration of war."[18]

The Quasi-War with France clarified the prerogatives of Congress over war and the deployment of military force. The war prompted several important judicial decisions. In 1800 and 1801 the Supreme Court twice recognized that Congress could authorize hostilities in two ways: either by a formal declaration of war or by statutes that authorized an undeclared war, as had been done against France. In the first case, the Court stated that military conflicts could be "limited," "partial," and "imperfect," without requiring Congress to make a formal declaration.[19] In the second case, Chief Justice Marshall wrote for the Court: "The whole powers of war being, by the constitution of the United States, vested in congress, the acts of that body can alone be resorted to as our guides in this inquiry."[20]

Those cases do not imply that once Congress authorizes war the President is at complete liberty to choose the time, location, and scope of military activities. In authorizing war, Congress may place limits on what Presidents may and may not do. Part of the legislation passed by Congress during the Quasi-War authorized the President to seize vessels sailing *to* French ports. President Adams acted contrary to this statute by issuing an order directing American ships to capture vessels sailing *to or from* French ports. Captain George Little followed Adams' order by seizing a Danish ship sailing from a French port. He was later sued for damages and the case came to the Supreme Court. Chief Justice Marshall wrote the decision.

Marshall admitted that the case gave him much difficulty. He confessed that the "first bias" of his mind was very strongly in favor of the opinion that although the instructions from President Adams "could not give a right, they might yet excuse [a military officer] from damages." Initially, Marshall assumed an "implicit obedience, which military men usually pay to the orders of their superiors, which indeed is indispensably necessary to every military system." That system of military hierarchy seemed to Marshall to justify the actions of Captain Little, "who is placed by the laws of his country in a situation which in general requires that he should obey them." On second thought, Marshall decided that Captain Little could be sued for damages:

I have been convinced that I was mistaken, and I have receded from this first opinion. I acquiesce in that of my brethren, which is, that the instructions cannot change the nature of the transaction, or legalize an act which, without those instructions, would have been a plain trespass.[21]

Presidential orders, even those issued by the Commander in Chief, are therefore subject to restrictions placed by Congress. The policy of Congress necessarily prevails over presidential orders and military actions that are taken pursuant to statutory authority. In the case of Captain Little, Congress later decided that he should not have been liable for following a presidential order. In 1807 it passed a private bill to reimburse him for the damages awarded against him.[22] The legislative history gives no reasons for the congressional action.[23] However, Congress may have concluded that federal law failed to adequately distinguish between lawful orders and unlawful orders. In 1789, Congress had directed military officers "to observe and obey the orders of the President of the United States."[24] Legislation in 1799 provided that any officer "who shall disobey the orders of his superior . . . on any pretence whatsoever" shall be subject to death or other punishment.[25] It wasn't until 1800, after Captain Little had seized the French ship, that Congress narrowed the duty of military officers. They were prohibited from disobeying the "lawful orders" of superior officers.[26]

At about this same time, the federal courts decided a Neutrality Act case that further restricted presidential war power. President Washington issued his Proclamation of Neutrality in 1793 because he was concerned that military initiatives by private citizens might embroil the United States in the war between France and England.[27] The constitutional powers of Congress and the President would be undermined through such actions.

Congress passed the Neutrality Act of 1794 to curb private activities in foreign military adventures. A Department of Justice analysis in 1979 concluded that the legislative history of the Act "clearly shows that the evil it proscribed was precisely and exclusively one which threatened the ability of the Government to carry on a coherent foreign policy."[28] The foreign policy at issue here was not a presidential monopoly. Congress defined the policy and enacted criminal penalties.

The Neutrality Act prohibited the exportation of any articles of war. Prohibited articles found on board a vessel would be forfeited. If articles of war were exported to a foreign country, the vessel could be seized and the captain fined.[29] Congress also prohibited American citizens from accepting a commission to serve "a foreign prince or state in war by land or sea."[30] Nor could persons within the United States provide ships of war to be used by a foreign prince or state "to cruise or commit hostilities upon the subjects, citizens or property of another foreign prince or state with whom the United States are at peace."[31] Furthermore, persons within the territory or jurisdiction of the United States were prohibited from providing assistance to "any military expedition or enterprise to be carried on from thence against the territory or dominions of any foreign prince or state with whom the United States are at peace."[32]

President Jefferson recognized the extreme danger of allowing private citizens to decide by themselves to deploy armed forces. In his Fourth Annual Message, he referred to complaints that persons residing within the United States had armed merchant vessels and forced a commerce in defiance of the laws of other countries: "That individuals should undertake to wage private war, independently of the authority of their country, can not be permitted in a well-ordered society."[33] The tendency, he said, was "to produce aggression on the laws and rights of other nations and to endanger the peace of our own."[34]

Numerous violations of the Neutrality Act were brought before the federal courts. In one of the significant cases, decided in 1806, a circuit court in New York reviewed the indictment of Colonel William S. Smith for engaging in military actions against Spain. He claimed that his military enterprise "was begun, prepared, and set on foot with the knowledge and approbation of the executive department of our government."[35] The court gave no credence to his claim that a President or his assistants could somehow authorize military adventures that violated congressional policy. The court described the Neutrality Act as "declaratory of the law of nations; and besides, every species of private and unauthorized hostilities is inconsistent with the principles of the social compact, and the very nature, scope, and end of civil government."[36]

As to Smith's claim that he acted with the knowledge and approbation of the executive branch, the court rejected the proposition that the Neutrality Act allowed executive officials to waive statutory provisions: "if a private individual, even with the knowledge and appropriation of this high and preeminent officer of our government [the President], should set on foot such a military expedition, how can he expect to be exonerated from the obligation of the law?" The court continued:

Supposing then that every syllable of the affidavit is true, of what avail can it be on the present occasion? Of what use or benefit can it be to the defendant in a court of law? Does it speak by way of justification? The President of the United States cannot control the statute, nor dispense with its execution, and still less can he authorize a person to do what the law forbids. If he could, it would render the execution of the laws dependent on his will and pleasure; which is a doctrine that has not been set up, and will not meet with any supporters in our government. In this particular, the law is paramount. Who has dominion over it? None but the legislature; and even they are not without their limitation in our republic. Will it be pretended that the President could rightfully grant a dispensation and license to any of our citizens to carry on a war against a nation with whom the United States are at peace?[37]

Jefferson understood the prerogatives of Congress over military options. As Secretary of State he set forth for Congress the alternatives in dealing with the demands of Algiers, Tunis, and Tripoli for tributes:

Upon the whole, it rests with Congress to decide between war, tribute, and ransom, as the means of re-establishing our Mediterranean commerce. If war, they will consider how far our own resources shall be called forth, and how far they will enable the Executive to engage, in the forms of the constitution, the cooperation of other Powers. If tribute or ransom, it will rest with them to limit and provide the amount; and with the Executive, observing the same constitutional forms, to make arrangements for employing it to the best advantage.[38]

In his First Annual Message on December 8, 1801, Jefferson informed Congress of the arrogant demands of the Pasha of Tripoli. Unless the United States paid tribute, the Pasha threatened to seize American ships and citizens. Jefferson responded by sending a small squadron of frigates to the Mediterranean to protect against the threatened attack. He then asked Congress for further guidance, stating that it was "[u]nauthorized by the Constitution, without the sanction of Congress, to go beyond the line of defense." It was up to Congress to authorize "measures of offense also." Jefferson gave Congress all the documents and communications it needed so that the legislative branch, "in the exercise of this important function confided by the Constitution exclusively," could consider the situation and act in the manner it considered most appropriate.[39]

In defensive operations, Jefferson retained the right to act first and seek congressional approval later. After Congress had recessed in 1807, a British vessel fired on the American ship *Chesapeake*. Jefferson ordered military purchases for the emergency, reporting his action to Congress after it convened. "To have awaited a previous and special sanction by law," he said, "would have lost occasions which might not be retrieved."[40] He later observed that fidelity to the written law is "doubtless *one* of the high duties of a good citizen, but it is not the *highest*." The laws of necessity, self-preservation, and "of saving our country when in danger" deserved a higher priority. He concluded: "To lose our country by a scrupulous adherence to written law, would be to lose the law itself, with life, liberty, property, and all those who are enjoying them with us; thus absurdly sacrificing the end to the means."[41]

Jefferson was not opening the door to any and all presidential initiatives. He had something specific in mind: presidential actions in response to emergencies that threatened the survival of the nation. His words cannot be interpreted to sanction more recent U.S. interventions in such places as Grenada, Iraq, Libya, Nicaragua, and Panama.

WAR POWERS IN THE NINETEENTH CENTURY

With access to troops and ships, Presidents were always in a position to deploy forces to precipitate a war before Congress had a chance to deliberate and decide national policy. The potential for engaging the country in war was demonstrated by President Polk's actions in 1846, when he ordered General Zachary Taylor to occupy disputed territory on the Texas-Mexico border. His initiative provoked a clash between American and Mexican soldiers, allowing Polk to tell Congress a few weeks later that "war exists." Although Congress formally declared war on Mexico, Polk's actions were censured by the House of Representatives in 1848 because the war had been "unnecessarily and unconstitutionally begun by the President of the United States."[42] One of the members voting against Polk was Congressman Abraham Lincoln, who later wrote to a friend:

Allow the President to invade a neighboring nation, whenever *he* shall deem it necessary to repel an invasion, and you allow him to do so, *whenever he may choose to say* he deems it necessary for such purpose—and you allow him to make war at pleasure. . . . This, our Convention understood to be the most oppressive of all Kingly oppressions; and they resolved to so frame the Constitution that *no one man* should hold the power of bringing the oppression upon us.[43]

Lincoln's statement may appear to be insincere or cynical, in view of his later actions as President during the Civil War. On his own initiative he deployed military forces without first obtaining authority from Congress. While Congress was in recess, he issued proclamations that called forth the state militia, suspended the writ of habeas corpus, and placed a blockade on the rebellious states. Yet the nature of Lincoln's actions was different. Polk's initiatives led to war with a foreign nation; Lincoln faced a domestic crisis that threatened the nation's survival. Second, Lincoln had genuine doubts about the legality of his actions, particularly the suspension of the writ of habeas corpus, and therefore sought authority from Congress. He told Congress that his actions, "whether strictly legal or not, were ventured upon under what appeared to be a popular demand and a public necessity, trusting then, as now, that Congress would readily ratify them."[44] Lincoln never justified his actions solely on the grants of presidential power found in the Constitution. In fact, he implied that he probably encroached upon the powers of

Congress. He merely asserted that his actions were not "beyond the constitutional competency of Congress."[45]

Lincoln therefore invoked each stage of the executive prerogative: acting in the absence of law and sometimes against it; explaining to the legislature what he had done, and why; and requesting the legislative body to authorize his actions. The superior law-making body was Congress, not the President. Congress debated his request at length, eventually passing legislation "approving, legalizing, and making valid all the acts, proclamations, and orders of the President, etc., as if they had been issued and done under the previous express authority and direction of the Congress of the United States."[46]

Other than Polk's initiatives in Mexico and Lincoln's emergency actions during the Civil War, the war power in the nineteenth century stayed essentially in the hands of Congress. During the war between the United States and Mexico, U.S. authorities acting under presidential orders conquered the port of Tampico. The Supreme Court identified this important check on presidential power: "As commander-in-chief, he is authorized to direct the movements of the naval and military forces placed by law at his command, and to employ them in the manner he may deem most effectual to harass and conquer and subdue the enemy."[47] Notice: "placed *by law* at his command." The power of Commander in Chief is necessarily broad, but it must follow the policy declared by Congress in law.

The congressional power to decide the scope of war and the disposition of armed forces is discussed in a Supreme Court case in 1889. England had called upon the United States to supply naval forces in a military action against China. The commitment of offensive force, said the Court, remained a judgment call for Congress:

As this proposition involved a participation in existing hostilities, the request could not be acceded to, and the Secretary of State in his communication to the English government explained that the war-making power of the United States was not vested in the President but in Congress, and that he had no authority, therefore, to order aggressive hostilities to be undertaken.[48]

Significantly, the Court spoke not merely of the congressional power to declare war but of a broader power: *war-making*. The decision to commit the nation's blood and treasures was left to Congress, not the President. In his concurring opinion in the *Steel Seizure* case, Justice Jackson warned that no judicial doctrine "would seem to me more sinister and alarming than that a President whose conduct of foreign affairs is so largely uncontrolled, and often even is unknown, can vastly enlarge his mastery over the internal affairs of the country by his own commitment of the Nation's armed forces to some foreign venture."[49]

The Spanish-American War of 1898, World War I, and World War II were all formally declared by Congress. Of course Presidents used force on many lesser occasions, often without authorization from Congress. A list of such actions probably contains over two hundred actions. Anyone examining this list will conclude, as did the presidential scholar Edward S. Corwin, that they consist largely of "fights with pirates, landings of small naval contingents on barbarous or semi-barbarous coasts, the dispatch of small bodies of troops to chase bandits or cattle rustlers across the Mexican border, and the like."[50] They are not precedents that justify unilateral threats by President Bush to make war against Iraq in 1991.

WAR POWERS AFTER WORLD WAR II

In the aftermath of World War II, the United Nations was established in an effort to redefine the law of war by limiting the ability of member nations to use force and requiring them to respond against breaches of the peace. Article 43 of the U.N. Charter provides that all members of the United Nations shall undertake to make available to the Security Council, "on its call and in accordance with a special agreement or agreements," armed forces and other assistance. The purpose of these agreements was to spell out the numbers and types of forces, their degree of readiness and general location, and the nature of the facilities and assistance to be provided. Could the President on his own enter into special agreements? Definitely not. Article 43 provides that they shall be ratified by each nation "in accordance with their respective constitutional processes."

Congress determined the meaning of "constitutional processes" in Section 6 of the U.N. Participation Act of 1945, which requires that the agreements "shall be subject to the approval of the Congress by appropriate Act or joint resolution."[51] Two qualifications are included in Section 6, but they do not eliminate the need for congressional approval. Presidents could commit armed forces to the United Nations only after Congress approved.

The legislative history of the U.N. Participation Act leaves no doubt about that. In his appearance before the House Committee on Foreign Affairs, Under Secretary of State Dean Acheson explained that only after the President receives the approval of Congress is he "bound to furnish that contingent of troops to the Security Council; and the President is not authorized to furnish any more than you have approved of in that agreement."[52] When Congresswoman Edith Rogers remarked that Congress "can easily control the [Security] Council," Acheson agreed unequivocally: "It is entirely within the wisdom of Congress to approve or disapprove whatever special agreements the President negotiates."[53] Congressman John Kee wondered whether the qualifications in Section 6 of the U.N. Participation Act permitted the President to provide military assistance to the Security Council without consulting or submitting the matter to Congress. Acheson firmly denied that possibility. No special agreement could have any "force or effect" until Congress approved it.[54]

Other parts of the legislative history support this understanding.[55] It was agreed that "military agreements could not be entered into solely by executive action."[56] A few Senators argued that congressional approval might be satisfied by obtaining only the approval of the Senate, through the treaty process, but it was widely recognized that the decision to go to war must be made by both Houses of Congress. A Senate amendment to permit approval of military agreements through the treaty process was defeated overwhelmingly, 57 to 14.[57]

The restrictions on the President's power under Section 6 to use armed force were clarified by amendments adopted in 1949, allowing the President on his own initiative to provide military forces to the United Nations for "cooperative action." However, presidential discretion to deploy these forces were subject to stringent conditions: they could serve only as observers and guards, could perform only in a noncombatant capacity, and could not exceed one thousand.[58]

In 1990 Professor Thomas M. Franck of New York University Law School argued that a U.N. decision to use force preempted any role for Congress. In his view, a congressional declaration or authorization of war was no longer possible. The title of his article, printed in the *New York Times*, was eye-catching: "Declare War? Congress Can't."[59] Franck claimed that the U.N. Charter "does not leave room for each state, once the Council has acted, to defer compliance until it has authority from its own legislature."

In a subsequent article, Franck and a colleague elaborated on this view. They conceded that the framers adopted the war-declaring clause "to ensure that this fateful decision did not rest with a single person." But instead of accepting the rest of the framers' decision—that the President would have to seek the approval of Congress—they concluded that action by the Security Council would suffice. The crucial responsibility for checking presidential initiatives and assuring joint action somehow fell to the United Nations, not to Congress. Through this reasoning the legislative branch could be completely circumvented: "The new system vests that responsibility in the Security Council, a body where the most divergent interests and perspectives of humanity are represented and where five of fifteen members have a veto power. This Council is far less likely to be stampeded by combat fever than is Congress."[60]

In arguing that Presidents need authorization only from the U.N. Security Council, not from Congress, Franck and Patel seriously misread the legislative history of the U.N. Charter and the U.N. Participation Act. Nothing supports the notion that Congress, by endorsing the structure of the United Nations, amended the Constitution by reading itself out of the war-making power. Congress did not, and could not, do that.

Mutual Defense Treaties

The discussion about the "constitutional processes" required for Article 43 actions under the U.N. Charter also applies to mutual defense treaties entered into by the United States. Those treaties—NATO, SEATO, ANZUS, etc.—do not empower the President to use armed force abroad without congressional consent. The treaties merely authorize armed force. The principle of an attack on one nation being considered an attack on all does not require an immediate presidential response. There is no automatic commitment to war. Force is to be used only after following constitutional processes, which includes Congress (both Houses).[61] Mutual defense treaties do not "transfer to the President the Congressional power to make war."[62] The Senate and the President cannot use the treaty process to take from the House of Representatives its constitutional role in the war power.[63]

The Korean War

In 1950, President Truman took the country to war against Korea. He acted on his own, without congressional authority; he claimed as legal authority vague sanctions from the United Nations, notwithstanding statutory safeguards put in place by the U.N. Participation Act and fortified by unambiguous legislative history. It is thus extraordinary that President Truman could act militarily in Korea under the U.N. umbrella without any congressional approval. The reason is clear: he never used the procedure of special agreements that assured congressional involvement. With the Soviet Union absent, the Security Council voted 9 to 0 to call upon North Korea to cease hostilities and to withdraw their forces. Two days later the Council requested military assistance from U.N. members to repel the attack, but by that time Truman had already ordered U.S. air and sea forces to assist South Korea.

Two observations about Truman's legal authority are appropriate. First, it is absurd to argue that the President's constitutional powers vary with the presence or absence of Soviet delegates to the Security Council. As Robert Bork noted in 1971, "the approval of the United Nations was obtained only because the Soviet Union happened to be boycotting the Security Council at the time, and the President's Constitutional powers can hardly be said to ebb and flow with the veto of the Soviet Union in the Security Council."[64]

Second, the Truman Administration did not act pursuant to U.N. authority, even though it strained to make that case. On June 29, 1950, Secretary of State Acheson claimed that all U.S. actions taken in Korea "have been under the aegis of the United Nations."[65] He said that President Truman had done his "utmost to uphold the sanctity of the Charter of the United States and the rule of law," and that the administration was in "conformity with the resolutions of the Security Council of June 25 and 27, giving air and sea support to the troops of the Korean government."[66] Yet Truman committed U.S. forces a day before the Council called for military action, as Acheson later admitted in his memoirs.[67] Although President Truman continued to call the war a U.N. police action, the United Nations exercised no authority over the conduct of the war. Other than token support from a few nations, it was a U.S. war.

President Dwight D. Eisenhower believed that Truman had made a serious mistake, politically and constitutionally, by going to war in Korea without congressional approval. Eisenhower thought that national commitments would be stronger if entered into jointly by both branches. Toward that end he asked Congress for specific authority to deal with crises in the Formosa Straits and in the Middle East. Congress passed joint resolutions authorizing him to act in those areas.[68] He stressed the importance of collective action by Congress and the President: "I deem it necessary to seek the cooperation of the Congress. Only with that cooperation can we give the reassurance needed to deter aggression."[69]

Eisenhower's theory of government and international relations invited congressional support for area resolutions. On New Year's Day in 1957, he met with Secretary of State John Foster Dulles and congressional leaders of both parties. House Majority Leader John McCormack asked Eisenhower whether he, as Commander in Chief, already had sufficient constitutional authority to act in the Middle East without congressional approval. Eisenhower replied that he might have that power, in theory, but "greater effect could be had from a consensus of Executive and Legislative opinion. . . . I reminded the legislators that the Constitution assumes that our two branches of government should get along together."[70] Eisenhower knew that lawyers and policy advisers in the executive branch could always discover precedents for unilateral presidential action, but that did not satisfy him. It was his seasoned judgment that a commitment by the United States would impress allies and enemies more if it represented the collective judgment of the President and Congress.

Unlike Eisenhower, President John F. Kennedy was prepared to act solely on his own constitutional authority in the Cuban missile crisis. He claimed that as Commander in Chief "I have full authority now to take such action" militarily against Cuba.[71] Congress passed the Cuba Resolution of 1962, but it did not authorize presidential action. It merely expressed the sentiments of Congress.[72]

The Vietnam War

Next came the fateful Tonkin Gulf Resolution of 1964, which approved and supported "the determination of the President, as Commander in Chief, to take all necessary measures to repel any armed attack against the forces of the United States and to prevent further aggression." The United States was "prepared, as the President determines, to take all necessary steps, including the use of armed force."[73]

At the beginning, President Lyndon B. Johnson made it easy for Congress. Instead of asking that funds for Vietnam be included in an omnibus defense appropriation bill, which might be difficult for members of Congress to vote against, he requested that appropriations be placed in a supplemental bill set aside exclusively for Southeast Asia.[74] Later, when Congress funded the war through regular appropriations bills, federal courts were uncertain whether those statutes authorized the war. Some judges, after initially accepting that theory, found it unpersuasive. Judge Wyzanski made this observation in a 1973 decision:

This court cannot be unmindful of what every schoolboy knows: that in voting to appropriate money or to draft men a Congressman is not necessarily approving of the continuation of a war no matter how specifically the appropriation or draft act refers to that war. A Congressman wholly opposed to the war's commencement and continuation might vote for the military appropriations and for the draft measures because he was unwilling to abandon without support men already fighting. An honorable, decent, compassionate act of aiding those already in peril is no proof of consent to the actions that placed and continued them in that dangerous posture. We should not construe votes cast in pity and piety as though they were votes freely given to express consent.[75]

While it is true that the congressional power of the purse is an important check on presidential power, that check is most potent when the President is seeking funds. Congress can control that decision by a simple majority in either House. But when

Congress is attempting to use an appropriations bill to terminate funding, the President may veto that bill and force Congress to locate a two-thirds majority in each House for an override. That is what happened in 1973. A congressional cutoff of funds was vetoed by President Nixon, forcing Congress to enter into a compromise that allowed the administration to bomb Southeast Asia for an additional 45 days.[76]

In 1969, by passing the National Commitments Resolution, the Senate returned to Eisenhower's principles. The resolution defined a national commitment as the use of U.S. armed forces on foreign territory, or a promise to assist a foreign country by using U.S. armed forces or financial resources "either immediately or upon the happening of certain events." The resolution provides that "it is the sense of the Senate that a national commitment by the United States results only from affirmative action taken by the executive and legislative branches of the United States Government by means of a treaty, statute, or concurrent resolution of both Houses of Congress specifically providing for such commitment."[77] Passed in the form of a Senate resolution, it had no legal effect. However, it marked a significant expression of constitutional theory by a bipartisan Senate. The Democrats supported it 43–3; the Republicans voted in favor 17–13. The final tally: 70–16.

The War Powers Resolution

From 1970 to 1973, the House and the Senate drafted legislation to curb the President's power to initiate war. As enacted, the War Powers Resolution calls for the "collective judgment" of both Congress and the President before U.S. troops are sent into combat. The text of the statute is inconsistent on what Presidents may do based on their own independent authority. Section 2(c) offers a very narrow definition of presidential power. Presidents may introduce U.S. forces into hostilities or imminent hostilities only pursuant to a declaration of war, specific statutory authorization, or a national emergency created by attack upon the United States, its territories or possessions, or its armed forces. Yet subsequent sections seem to suggest that the President may use military force without prior congressional consent for up to 90 days—certainly greater leeway for presidential power than the framers ever imagined.

As would be expected from broad legislation that emanated from Congress over a period of years, the War Powers Resolution has its share of inconsistencies and structural deficiencies. As a general framework for reconciling legislative and executive interests, however, it is remarkably sound. It recognizes that Presidents may need to act militarily without congressional authorization for limited periods; it contemplates close consultation and cooperation between the branches; and it requires explicit congressional approval if the President intends to engage the country in a long-term military commitment.

The latter proposition has received a broad endorsement from both parties, liberals and conservatives alike. Writing in 1975, Secretary of State Henry Kissinger said that the decade-long struggle over executive dominance in foreign affairs "is over." The "dominant fact" of national politics was that Congress "is a coequal branch of government" and must have "both the sense and the reality of participation."[78] In testimony before the Senate Foreign Relations Committee in 1988, Abraham Sofaer, legal adviser to the State Department, said that the Reagan Administration recognized that Congress has "a critical role" to play in determining when the United States commits armed forces to actual or potential hostilities. No presidential policy in this area can have "any hope of success in the long term unless Congress and the American people concur in it and are willing to support its execution."[79]

Robert F. Turner, who recognizes greater latitude for presidential power than I do, nevertheless appreciates the need for executive-legislative cooperation. In testimony before the House Foreign Affairs Committee in 1988, he expressed this position very eloquently. Although from "a purely constitutional perspective" the President possesses a great deal of independent power in the making and conduct of foreign policy, "in the long run those policies are almost guaranteed to fail if the Congress and the American people do not understand and support them." Regardless of legal analysis, Turner said it is a "political imperative" that Congress and the President cooperate in a spirit of mutual respect and comity.[80]

Experience under the War Powers Resolution has supported the soundness of that legislation. Presidents have been able to respond to short-term emergencies without seeking prior congressional approval: the *Mayaguez* capture in 1975, Grenada in 1983, and Libya in 1986. Long-term engagements, including Lebanon in 1983 and Iraq in 1991, have required explicit congressional approval.

The Persian Gulf War

Notwithstanding the War Powers Resolution, the Bush Administration harkened back to the Korean War precedent to argue that it was constitutionally sufficient for the President to obtain authority from the U.N. Security Council, not from Congress. That proposition is wholly without merit.

In preparing for an offensive war against Iraq, President Bush initially devoted his time and energy in seeking support from other nations and the U.N. Security Council. On November 29, 1990, the Security Council passed a resolution authorizing the use of force. The resolution did not *require* the United States to use force. It merely "authorized" member states to take all necessary means, including force, to implement the Security Council resolutions. U.S. actions after that point were entirely permissive, to be guided by its constitutional processes.

Until its eleventh-hour decision to seek legislation from Congress, the Bush Administration said it could act unilaterally. In testimony before the Senate Armed Services Committee on December 3, 1990, Secretary of Defense Dick Cheney said that President Bush did not require "any additional authorization from the Congress" before attacking Iraq.[81] On January 8, 1991, President Bush decided to ask Congress to pass legislation supporting his policy in the Persian Gulf. A day later reporters asked him whether he needed a resolution from Congress. He replied: "I don't think I need it. . . . I feel that I have the authority to fully implement the United Nations resolutions."[82]

The confrontation with Iraq in 1991 reopened the debate on presidential war powers. In *Dellums v. Bush*, the Justice Department took the position that President Bush did not need prior authorization from Congress. According to its analysis, Bush could have independently taken the nation from a defensive posture in Saudi Arabia to an offensive operation against Iraq. The Justice Department advanced a number of sweeping interpretations of presidential power, all of which Judge Harold Greene systematically challenged and rejected. Judge Greene remarked that if the President has

the sole power to determine that any particular offensive military operation, no matter how vast, does not constitute war-making but only an offensive military attack, the congressional power to declare war will be at the mercy of a semantic decision by the Executive. Such an "interpretation" would evade the plain meaning of the Constitution, and it cannot stand.[83]

Perhaps that interpretation cannot stand in court, as I hope is the case. But it may prevail if Congress fails to use the constitutional powers at its command. When it acquiesces to presidential initiatives, the record clearly shows that legislative passivity will not be corrected by judicial activism. A handful of legislators going to court will be told (appropriately) to return to their chambers and use the ample legislative tools that are available to check the President.[84] As Justice Powell once warned Congress, if it "chooses not to confront the President, it is not our task to do so."[85] Congress does not function in a vacuum. Citizens and scholars must pressure Congress constantly to discharge the responsibilities given it by the Constitution.

NOTES

1. John Locke, *Second Treatise of Civil Government* §§ 146–148 (1962).
2. William Blackstone, 2 *Commentaries on the Laws of England* 237–80 (William Young Birch & Abraham Small eds., 1803).
3. 1 *Records of the Federal Convention* 65 (Max Farrand ed., 1937).
4. Id.
5. Id.
6. Id. at 65–66.
7. 6 *The Writings of James Madison* 312 (Gaillard Hunt ed., 1900–1910) (letter of April 2, 1798 to Thomas Jefferson).
8. 2 Farrand, *supra* note 3, 318–19.
9. Id. at 318.
10. Id.
11. Id. at 319.
12. 2 *The Debates in the Several State Conventions, on the Adoption of the Federal Constitution* 528 (J. Elliot ed., 1836–1845).
13. 6 *The Writings of James Madison, supra* note 7 at 148.
14. 5 *The Writings of Thomas Jefferson* 123 (Paul L. Ford ed., 1892–1899).
15. 1 Farrand, *supra* note 3, 139–40.
16. 10 Op. Att'y Gen. 74, 79 (1861).
17. 1 *A Compilation of the Messages and Papers of the Presidents* 226 (J. Richardson ed., 1897–1925).

18. 8 *Annals of Cong.* 1519 (1798).

19. *Bas v. Tingy*, 4 U.S. (4 Dall.) 37 (1800); *Talbot v. Seeman*, 5 U.S. (1 Cranch) 1 (1801).

20. *Talbot v. Seeman*, 5 U.S. at 28.

21. *Little v. Barreme*, 6 U.S. (2 Cranch) 169, 179 (1804).

22. 6 Stat. 63 (1807).

23. *Annals of Cong.*, 9th Cong., 2d Sess. 29–32, 230–31, 253, 260–61 (1806–1807).

24. 1 Stat. 96, § 3 (1789).

25. 1 Stat. 711, § 24 (1799).

26. 2 Stat. 47 (1800) (Art. XIV).

27. 32 *The Writings of George Washington* (J. Fitzpatrick ed., 1937–1944) (letter to Secretary of the Treasury Alexander Hamilton, April 12, 1793).

28. Office of Legal Counsel, U.S. Department of Justice, "Applicability of the Neutrality Act to Activities of the Central Intelligence Agency," memorandum from Larry L. Sims to Philip B. Heymann, Assistant Attorney General, Criminal Division, Oct. 10, 1979, at 5.

29. 1 Stat. 369–70 (1794).

30. Id. at 381–82.

31. Id. at 382, § 3.

32. Id. at 384, § 5.

33. 1 Richardson, *supra* note 17, at 358.

34. Id.

35. *United States v. Smith*, 27 F. Cas. 1192, 1229 (C.C.N.Y. 1806) (No. 16,342).

36. Id.

37. Id.

38. 1 *American State Papers: Foreign Relations* 105 (W. Lowrie & M. Clarke eds., 1882), cited in Gehard Casper, *An Essay in Separation of Powers: Some Early Versions and Practices*, 30 Wm. & Mary L. Rev. 211, 245 (1989).

39. 1 Richardson, *supra* note 17, at 315.

40. Id. at 416.

41. 5 *The Writings of Thomas Jefferson* 542 (Washington ed., 1861).

42. *Cong. Globe*, 30th Cong., 1st Sess. 95 (1848).

43. 1 *The Collected Works of Abraham Lincoln* 451–52 (R. Basler ed., 1953).

44. 7 Richardson, *supra* note 17, at 325.

45. Id.

46. 12 Stat. 361 (1861).

47. *Fleming v. Page*, 50 U.S. 603, 615 (1850).

48. *The Chinese Exclusion Case*, 130 U.S. 581, 591 (1889).

49. *Youngstown Sheet & Tube Co. v. Sawyer*, 343 U.S. 579, 642–43 (1952) (Jackson, J., concurring) (footnote omitted).

50. Edwin Corwin, *The President's Power*, The New Republic, Jan. 29, 1951, at 16; *see also* Francis D. Wormuth & Edwin B. Firmage, *To Chain the Dog of War: The War Power of Congress in History and Law* 135–53 (2d ed. 1989).

51. 22 U.S.C. § 287d; *see generally* Chapter 4.

52. Hearings on Participation by the United States in the United Nations Organization before the House Committee on Foreign Affairs, 79th Cong., 1st Sess. 23 (1945).

53. Id.

54. Id. at 25–26.

55. *See, e.g.,* S. Rep. No. 717, 79th Cong., 1st Sess. 5 (1945); 91 Cong. Rec. 12267 (1945).

56. S. Rep. No. 717, 79th Cong. 1st Sess. 8 (1945).

57. 91 Cong. Rec. 11303 (1945); *see also* H. Rep. No. 1383, 79th Cong., 1st Sess. 7 (1945).

58. 22 U.S.C. § 287d-1; 63 Stat. 735–36, § 5 (1949).

59. N.Y. Times, Dec. 11, 1990, at A27.

60. Thomas Franck & Faiza Patel, *UN Police Action in Lieu of War: 'The Old Order Changeth'*, 85 Am. J. Int'l. L. 63, 74 (1991). *But see* Michael J. Glennon, *The Constitution and Chapter VII of the United Nations Charter*, 85 Am. J. Int'l L. 74 (1991); Chapter 4.

61. Richard H. Heindel, et al., *The North Atlantic Treaty in the United States*, 43 Am. J. Int'l. L. 633, 649 (1949).

62. Id. at 650.

63. Michael J. Glennon, *United States Mutual Security Treaties: The Commitment Myth*, 24 Colum. J. Transnat'l L. 509 (1986).

64. Robert Bork, *Comments on the Articles on the Legality of the United States Action in Cambodia*, 65 Am. J. Int'l. L. 79, 81 (1971).

65. 23 Dept. of State Bull. 43 (1950).

66. Id. at 46.

67. Dean Acheson, *Present at the Creation* 408 (1969).

68. 69 Stat. 7 (1955); 71 Stat. 4 (1957).

69. Public Papers of the Presidents, 1957, at 11.

70. Dwight Eisenhower, *Waging Peace* 179 (1965).

71. Public Papers of the Presidents, 1962, at 674, 679.

72. 76 Stat. 697 (1962).

73. 78 Stat. 384 (1964).

74. 79 Stat. 109 (1965).

75. *Mitchell v. Laird*, 476 F.2d 533, 538 (D.C. 1973). For earlier conclusions by federal courts that appropriations constituted legislative support for a presidential war policy, see *Orlando v. Laird*, 317 F. Supp. 1013, 1018–1019 (E.D. N.Y. 1970); *aff'd*, 443 F.2d 1039, 1042 (2d Cir. 1971); *Berk v. Laird*, 317 F. Supp. 715, 724, 728, 730 (E.D.N.Y. 1970), *aff'd*, 429 F.2d 302, 305 (2d Cir. 1970); and *DaCosta v. Laird*, 448 F.2d 1368, 1369 (2d Cir. 1971).

76. Louis Fisher, *Constitutional Conflicts between Congress and the President* 270–71 (1991).

77. 115 Cong. Rec. 17245 (1969).

78. 72 Dept. of State Bull. 562 (1975).

79. Hearings on the War Power After 200 Years: Congress and the President at a Constitutional Impasse before the Senate Committee on Foreign Relations, 100th Cong., 2d Sess. 144 (1988).

80. Hearings on War Powers: Origins, Purposes, and Applications before the House Committee on Foreign Affairs, 100th Cong., 2d Sess. 56 (1988).

81. Hearings on Crisis in the Persian Gulf Region: U.S. Policy Options and Implications before the Senate Committee on Armed Services, 101st Cong., 2d Sess. 701 (1990).

82. 27 Wkly Comp. Pres. Doc. 25 (1991).

83. *Dellums v. Bush*, 752 F. Supp. 1141, 1145 (D.D.C. 1990).

84. *Lowry v. Reagan*, 676 F. Supp. 333 (D.D.C. 1987); *Conyers v. Reagan*, 578 F. Supp. 324 (D.D.C. 1984), *dism'd as moot*, 765 F.2d 1124 (D.C. Cir. 1985); *Sanchez-Espinoza v. Reagan*, 568 F. Supp. 596 (D.D.C. 1983), *aff'd*, 770 F.2d 202 (D.C. Cir. 1985); *Crockett v. Reagan*, 558 F. Supp. 893 (D.D.C. 1982), *aff'd*, 720 F.2d 1355 (D.C. Cir. 1983).

85. *Goldwater v. Carter*, 444 U.S. 996, 998 (1979).

2   Constitutional Constraints: The War Clause

Peter Raven-Hansen

The history of the Constitution's War Clause[1] is familiar to anyone who has read one of the more than fifty books or 250 scholarly articles written to date on the constitutional war powers. "Mr. Madison and Mr. Gerry moved to insert 'declare,' striking out 'make' war; leaving to the Executive the power to repel sudden attacks."[2] This snippet from the records of the Constitutional Convention is quoted or paraphrased in every one of these writings. Almost as many note that the President has used armed force abroad on _____ (fill in the blank) occasions over 200 years without a declaration of war.[3]

Yet, with obligatory cites to this familiar history, professors, politicians, and pundits recently reached widely different conclusions about President Bush's constitutional authority to order Operation Desert Storm without a congressional go-ahead. President Bush himself invoked custom, when he brushed off questions about the law with the observation that "history is replete with examples where the President has to take action."[4] Others argued from the "repel-sudden-attack" notes of the Convention that the Constitution gives Congress the decision to fight offensive war and gives the President the decision to fight defensive war, but they disagreed about which was which. At least one scholar, echoing claims made during the Vietnam War, suggested that the President lacked authority to launch Operation Desert Storm even *after* Congress's resolution of approval because the Constitution requires formal declaration.[5]

This diversity of conclusions no doubt confirms the gloomy prognosis of John Quincy Adams: "The respective powers of the President and Congress of the United States in the case of war with foreign powers are yet undetermined. Perhaps they can never be defined."[6] But it may also reaffirm the old adage that "familiarity breeds contempt." Over-familiarity with the history of the making and execution of the War Clause may have generated unconscious contempt for its details; the history is more often cited than examined.

In this chapter I therefore briefly summarize the familiar history of both the making and execution of the War Clause, and then use it to test diverse conclusions about the War Clause voiced during the Persian Gulf War.[7] I conclude that they all either overstate or understate the President's authority, and that even the President's customary, and arguably evolving, war power of self-defense, rescue, and protection would not have authorized Operation Desert Storm without prior congressional approval.

THE TOO FAMILIAR HISTORY OF THE WAR CLAUSE

The Framing and Ratification of the Constitution

It is easy at first glance to see why everyone is familiar with the history of the framing of the War Clause: it covers a scant two pages of the records of the Constitutional Convention.[8] The ratification debates (including *The Federalist*) add relatively little to its length. Nevertheless, this history permits some conclusions that I only summarize here in the interests of space.[9]

The first is indisputable: the Framers arranged an institutional process to make it harder to initiate war than to achieve or continue peace. Second, they vested Congress not just with the ceremonial and then-already obsolete power of formal declaration of war, but also with the power to commence war when it had not already been commenced against us by an enemy. Third, the Framers impliedly but necessarily gave the President the power to repel sudden attacks. To be sure, the "repel-sudden-attacks" language is not constitutional text, but it is logically doubtful that any text, or even legislative history, is necessary to anchor a right of self-defense, lest the Constitution operate as a suicide pact. As Justice and Framer Paterson said, "[a]bstractly from . . . [the Constitution], the right to repel invasions arises from self-preservation and defense, which is a primary law of nature, and constitutes part of the law of nations."[10] Fourth, and correlatively, the Framers empowered the President as Commander in Chief to conduct any war authorized by Congress or thrust upon us by attack. Fifth, they assigned Congress the specific power of appropriation for military forces[11] in order to assure that "the means of carrying on the war would not be in the hands of the President, but of the Legislature."[12]

Last, the Framers also gave Congress the power to grant letters of marque and reprisal. This power merits a longer look because it is generally overlooked.[13] Even though technical letters of marque and reprisal are long since obsolete, in 1789 they formed an important part of the nation's armament.[14] Originally governmental licenses for the private use of force,

"letters of marque" came to refer to the authorization both of armed trading vessels to attack ships of foreign nations during peace or war and of private vessels, outfitted with armaments and called privateers, to fight in place of or alongside public naval vessels. The term "reprisals" came to refer to any utilization of force with the sovereign's consent in retaliation for an injury caused by the sovereign of another state or his subjects. Thus, by the eighteenth century, letters of marque and reprisal referred primarily to sovereign utilization of private forces, and sometimes public forces, to injure another state. . . . [T]he term "letters of marque and reprisal" lost much of its technical meaning and came to signify any intermediate or low-intensity hostility short of declared war that utilized public *or* private forces.[15]

The framers knew that general reprisals, or "imperfect war," could easily lead to general or "perfect war," as it had for England in 1652, 1664, 1739, and 1756.[16] This gave them added reason to vest control over reprisals in the same body which had control over declarations of war.

Any power to commence undeclared war that was not granted to Congress by the Declaration Clause was therefore arguably granted by the Marque and Reprisal Clause (excepting the defensive war power). Lofgren's cautious conclusion that this "clause . . . could easily have been interpreted as serving as a kind of shorthand for vesting in Congress the power of *general* reprisal outside the context of declared war"[17] is reinforced by Lobel's independent conclusion that by this clause the framers "referred to the power to commence a broad spectrum of armed hostilities short of declared war."[18] Secretary of State Thomas Jefferson, Secretary of War James McHenry, and Hamilton all agreed, in Hamilton's words, that "anything beyond . . . [repelling force with force—self-defense] must fall under the idea of reprisals and requires the sanction of that Department which is to declare or make war."[19]

Practice Under the War Clause and the Evolution of Customary National Security Law[20]

Of course, the history of the War Clause did not end with the framing and ratification. It includes our practice—the use of U.S. armed forces abroad on at least 215 occasions through 1989.[21] Many of these uses were made without express prior statutory authorization. Yet an action is not constitutional just because the President takes it, even repeatedly; "one cannot derive an *ought* from an *is*."[22] If a presidential use of armed force without declaration is constitutional, it must be because it satisfies a plausible theory of constitutional interpretation, a theory which fits the reality. This section explores such a theory.

Justice Frankfurter articulated a theory of authorization based upon practice in the *Steel Seizure* case when he wrote that "[a] systematic, unbroken, executive practice, long pursued to the knowledge of the Congress and never before questioned, . . . making as it were such an exercise of power part of the structure of government, may be treated as a gloss on 'executive Power' vested in the President by § 1 of Art. II."[23] The resulting law has been called "quasi-constitutional custom."[24]

The Supreme Court applied the theory of customary law to uphold President Carter's suspension of pending claims against Iran in *Dames & Moore v. Regan*.[25] The Court first found that neither the International Emergency Economic Powers Act (IEEPA)[26] nor the "Hostage Act"[27] specifically authorized the suspension of claims in American courts. Emphasizing the impossibility of legislating in advance with respect to every action a President might have to take in a national security emergency, however, the Court endorsed the theory of customary law, "[a]t least . . . where there is no contrary indication of legislative intent and when, as here, there is a history of congressional acquiescence in conduct of the sort engaged in by the President."[28] It then traced the 180-year history of executive claims settlements, noting that no fewer than eighty executive agreements to liquidate claims had been made between 1817 and 1917 and at least ten since 1952.[29] It also found that Congress was on notice of the practice of executive claims settlement and had "implicitly approved" of it by enacting collateral legislation regarding procedures for distribution of settlement funds, by indicating in IEEPA and the Hostage Act "congressional willingness that the President have broad discretion when responding to the hostile acts of foreign sovereigns," by holding hearings on the Iranian agreement itself without acting to disapprove or modify it, and by consistently "fail[ing] to object to this longstanding practice . . . even when it had an opportunity to do so."[30]

Dames & Moore also shows, however, that customary law is not created by just any "series of essentially random acts that happen to form a pattern of usage."[31] Justice Frankfurter's articulation of the theory of customary law in the *Steel Seizure* case suggests three strong predicates for the creation of customary constitutional war authority in the President.

First, the executive practice of using armed force abroad must be "systematic, unbroken" and long-pursued.[32] Satisfaction of the first predicate enables us to identify a custom in the practice and to articulate and delimit the authority that it establishes.

By giving notice to Congress of the claim of authority by the executive, consistent practice also helps satisfy the second predicate: knowing acquiescence by Congress.[33] If Congress has had notice through its established information-gathering channels (hearings or required reports to committees) of the practice *and* the corresponding claim of authority to use armed force even without a declaration, then its failure to object when it has a practical opportunity to do so,[34] its re-enactment of general legislation, or its enactment of collateral, but consistent legislation, may be taken as acquiescence in the practice sufficient to establish customary constitutional law.[35] Absent notice to Congress of the practice and a presidential claim of authority, however, neither Congress's inaction nor collateral or general legislation—including lump-sum appropriations—can be taken as acquiescence in the practice and claim.[36]

Finally, the Supremacy Clause and the Constitution's provision for amendment suggest a third, typically unstated but universally assumed predicate of customary law: that the executive practice must not violate any unambiguous constitutional command[37] or statute.[38] "Illegality," Justice Frankfurter wrote, "cannot attain legitimacy through practice."[39]

BREEDING CONTEMPT? CONTEMPORARY WAR POWERS CLAIMS

It remains to apply the familiar history of the War Clause and the theory of its customary evolution, as summarized above, to recently voiced conclusions about the President's unilateral war power.

The President Goes First: General Customary Authority to Use Force Before Congressional Approval

President Bush was not alone in asserting a general customary constitutional authority in the President to use force without prior congressional approval. In defense of the Vietnam War, Leonard Meeker, Legal Adviser to the Department of State, also invoked custom to claim a presidential "power to deploy American forces abroad and commit them to military operations when . . . [he] deems such action necessary to maintain the security and defense of the United States."[40] This claim of customary war authority satisfies none of the predicates for customary law. Furthermore, its constitutionality is not saved by its proponents' lip-service to the ex post congressional power to pull the appropriations plug on a President's military adventure.

The theory of general customary authority starts on the wrong foot by invoking bad or at least unexamined history.[41] Meeker, for example, cites "at least 125 instances in which the President has ordered the armed forces to take action or maintain positions abroad without obtaining prior congressional authorization, starting with the 'undeclared war' with France (1798–1800)."[42] The naval war with France, however, was authorized by a series of hotly-debated, carefully-crafted, incrementally escalating statutes.[43] Subsequently, the Supreme Court not only expressly found that Congress had authorized a limited naval war, but emphasized that the statutory limits set the bounds of lawful hostilities.[44] Indeed, when the President issued orders which exceeded the limits set by Congress, the Court held the execution of those orders by an obedient naval captain to be unlawful.[45] Here then is a classic case of over-familiarity; examination of the precedent hardly justifies its inclusion on the President's side of the ledger.

The precedents which can be so included, moreover, do not satisfy the first predicate for customary law: a systematic, unbroken, and long-pursued practice. The only previous unilateral presidential deployment on the 500,000-man scale of the Persian Gulf War was the Korean War. Even under the most relaxed theory of customary law, a single executive action does not a custom make. Rather, in *United States v. Midwest Oil Co.*,[46] cited by Justice Frankfurter in the *Steel Seizure* case to illustrate his theory, the practice involved 252 actions spanning eighty years;[47] in *Dames & Moore*, the Court cited more than ninety actions over 200 years, including ten since 1952.[48]

The claim of general customary authority also fails to satisfy the second predicate of knowing acquiescence by Congress. Whenever the President has acted under claim of only some colorable statutory authority, Congress's acquiescence signified at most its agreement with that claim and not with some unasserted claim of inherent constitutional authority of the President to wage war without congressional approval. In another example of bad or at least incomplete history, one of the early list-makers identified only at most "a dozen or two" instances in which the President "sought or got Congressional authority."[49] By contrast, a list prepared for Congress in 1973 finds more than thirty instances of statutory authorization over the same time period,[50] and it omits instances in which Congress ratified the use of force after the event. Neither of these lists attempts to identify those instances in which Congress was presented with a fait accompli, or was misled about the use of force and therefore denied the opportunity to acquiesce knowingly and voluntarily. Yet Sofaer found that Presidents in the early-19th century repeatedly and deliberately issued vague instructions to adventurous agents and then withheld from Congress the information needed to determine the agents' authority.[51] In addition, the history cited in support of the claim of general customary war-making authority omits numerous instances in which Congress refused to grant all or part of the authority sought by or on behalf of an Administration.[52] Sofaer identifies six examples in the first thirty years of the republic alone,[53] and Wormuth and Firmage add many more.[54]

A claim of general customary authority also fails to satisfy the third predicate for customary law, because it would violate the spirit, if not the letter, of the War Clause if the claim is extended to large-scale and potentially sustained hostilities like the Gulf War. The federal court in *Dellums v. Bush* had no difficulty finding that, even before the war began, the U.S. forces deployed in the Gulf were "of such magnitude and significance as to present no serious claim that a war would not ensue if they became engaged in combat. . . . "[55] If the President can start such a war without prior congressional approval, then the power to declare war is strictly ceremonial, existing for a dwindling number of domestic and international purposes[56] that have not prompted any nation to declare war since 1948.[57] The claim of general customary authority to initiate war therefore effectively reads the Declaration Clause, not to mention the Marque and Reprisal Clause, out of the Constitution.

In mitigation of this result, proponents of a general customary war power for the President often emphasize that Congress still retains the "ultimate" check of denying appropriations, pulling the financial plug on hostilities commenced by the President.[58] Under their theory the President only goes first; Congress has the last word via the power of the purse.

Congress's power to pull the plug on disfavored hostilities does not save their theory for two reasons. First, their theory assumes that by merely failing to appropriate, Congress *can* pull the plug. This may be true in the long run, but as William Banks and I have shown elsewhere, customary and statutory spending authority to transfer and reprogram funds and to spend from emergency and contingency accounts effectively gives the President a healthy spending cushion, sufficient to support sizeable military adventures for a period without further appropriations.[59] Moreover, some of the same persons who argue that the President can go first also argued during the Iran-Contra Affair that he has the constitutional authority to raise and spend third-party funds without appropriation.[60] It is beyond the scope of this chapter to show why this is surely wrong,[61] but the very fact that defenders of presidential power have asserted it robs the "pull-the-plug" concession of any mitigating effect it might otherwise have.

Of course, Congress could also use appropriations riders to prohibit spending from any source for a presidential military adventure of which it disapproves, as it eventually did to end the Vietnam War. But this alternative is no substitute for control over a war's commencement because it is subject to veto by the President. The constitutional rule the Framers enacted was that peace continues *until* Congress speaks, not that war goes forward *unless* Congress speaks; inertia favors peace. The opposite rule shifts the burden of going forward from the President to Congress and presents at least the mathematical possibility that just thirty-four Senators (the number necessary to uphold a presidential veto) and the President could make war. That is not the constitutional arithmetic.

Second, pulling the plug may pose serious political problems. Thus, Chief Judge Bazelon and Judge Wyzanski observed, in refusing to find ratification of the Vietnam War from appropriations, that "[a] Congressman wholly opposed to the war's commencement and continuation might vote for military appropriations and for draft measures because he was unwilling to abandon without support men already fighting."[62] This observation was echoed in the recent complaint of a Congressman who explained that he was voting for a $1.9 billion appropriation for the U.S. deployments in Operation Desert Shield only because he did not want to jeopardize lives of Americans already sent to the Gulf region, adding that he thought they should be brought home right away.[63] Although Banks and I have argued that these political complaints are exaggerated,[64] and that Congress can often fine-tune its appropriations cut-offs to permit orderly withdrawals and de-escalation, such fine-tuning is itself constitutionally vulnerable if it intrudes unduly on the Commander in Chief's inherent power of command while the war still continues.[65]

The President May Fight Defensive War Without Prior Congressional Approval

Even the most ardent advocates of presidential war power do not contend that he has the power to launch "offensive war" without prior congressional approval.[66] But does he have the power to make "defensive war"? Anyone familiar with the old adage that the best defense is a good offense would hesitate before answering because "defensive war" is hardly a term of art. The answer may depend on whether a President is repelling sudden attack or fighting a de facto war started by an enemy, rescuing or protecting American nationals, defending and enforcing international law by a "police action," or defending U.S. allies and inchoate American security interests.

The Core Defensive War Power: Repelling Attack. As noted above, the history of the framing and ratification supports an implied constitutional authority of the President to repel a sudden attack. But nothing in that history suggests that this authority extends beyond literally repelling the attack. As we have seen, even Hamilton writing privately in 1798 (i.e., not as a publicist trying to sell the Constitution to a suspicious citizenry) declared that the constitutional power does not extend beyond repelling force with force, leaving any further response to Congress under the "idea of reprisals."[67] Early customary law was not to the contrary; presidents conceded the need for congressional authority to go beyond immediate self-defense.[68]

In *United States v. Smith*,[69] Justice Paterson, author of the New Jersey Plan at the Convention, explained why. When the nation is not already at war or under direct attack, it may be

more prudent to submit to certain acts of a hostile nature, and to trust to negotiations for redress, than to make an immediate appeal to arms. Various considerations may induce to a measure of this kind; such as motives of policy, calculations of interest, the nature of the injury and provocation, the relative resources, means and strength of the two nations, &c. and, therefore, the organ entrusted with the power to declare war, should first decide whether it is expedient to go to war, or to continue in peace. . . .[70]

The relevant considerations in such a case, in other words, are policy considerations suitable for legislative, not just executive appraisal. Once an attack short of de facto war has been repelled, "nothing is lost by resorting to diplomacy and delaying a military response until Congress has acted."[71]

On the other hand, if the attack involves invasion of the United States or is otherwise on a scale that creates a de facto general war, Justice Paterson reasoned, it would be "not only lawful for the president to resist such invasion, but also to carry hostilities into the enemy's own country; and for this plain reason, that a state of complete and absolute war exists between the two nations."[72] As Senator Hunter put it in 1813, "[d]efensive war explains and declares itself."[73] In *The Prize Cases*,[74] a majority of the Court endorsed Paterson's reasoning in upholding Lincoln's unilateral proclamation of a naval blockade of the Confederacy. When war is made by invasion or massive insurrection, the Court asserted, "the President is not only authorized but bound to resist force by force. He does not initiate the war, but is bound to accept the challenge without waiting for any special legislative authority."[75] By commencing de facto war against us, an enemy makes the choice otherwise assigned to Congress by the Constitution, and the choices that remain are questions of command assigned to the Commander in Chief.

This is not to say that the President's resulting authority is unlimited. The Court did say in *The Prize Cases* that whether an insurrection amounts to de facto war is for the President to decide in the first instance, but it did not thereby leave him to make that decision without regard to the facts. The predicate for this defensive war power is an actual state of de facto war. "The only case in which the Executive can enter a war, undeclared by Congress," Madison said, "is when a state of war has 'been *actually*' produced by the conduct of another power, and then it ought to be made known as soon as possible to the Department charged with the war power."[76] No such actual war, for example, resulted from Panama's declaration in December 1989 that it was in a "state of war" with the United States while U.S. economic "aggression" persisted,[77] and the President derived no defensive war power from that declaration alone. "Such empty declarations still leave open the decision whether to turn the 'paper war' into an actual war and hence, theoretically remain candidates for congressional, rather than presidential war making."[78]

Moreover, Congress retains the power of the purse even in defensive war and may use it both to end the war and arguably to control its escalation. Although the latter use is subject to separation-of-powers limits,[79] most legal scholars would agree that Congress could at least use the power of the purse to prevent extension of a defensive war to a country with which we are not at war. Some would also allow Congress to prevent military initiatives during a defensive war that pose "a grave risk of escalation and unnecessary suffering,"[80] effectively commencing a new war.

The Customary Defensive War Power: Rescuing and Protecting American Nationals. Does the defensive war power thus far sketched extend further to the defense of American nationals abroad? Neither the framing nor the ratification debates supply an answer. Is the defensive war power exhausted when the attack is complete? The phrase "sudden attacks" in Madison's notes suggests an affirmative answer, but they are not constitutional text. Some legal scholars have asserted that rescue missions after attack, and "protective interposition" before attack, lie beyond the President's defensive war power and require statutory authorization.[81] Others have claimed "that the Executive has unlimited authority to use the armed forces . . . for protective purposes abroad in any manner. . . ."[82] This is a debate, however, that may be partly settled by customary law suggesting that neither of these conclusions is correct.

Presidents have repeatedly used armed force since at least 1790 for the stated purpose of rescuing or protecting American nationals and their property. As early as 1804 Jefferson advised Congress that he had unilaterally ordered troops "to protect our citizens from violence . . . and, when necessary, to repel an inroad, *or to rescue a citizen or his property*," but, by contrast, would await congressional approval for "offensive action."[83] Although a complete analysis would require individualized examination, the lists of uses of force suggest a few generalizations about them. Many involved naval landings to protect Americans from hostile mobs when the local authorities could not. Others involved hostilities against Native Americans, including some sustained Native American suppression campaigns, though war was never declared. Others involved hostilities against pirates who preyed on American shipping. A few involved border crossings in pursuit of bandits. Wormuth and Firmage estimate that no fewer than 77 of the 137 instances that they examined fell into these categories, although they draw finer distinctions among them.[84]

These incidents have important characteristics in common, however. Although many of the hostilities against Native Americans, pirates, or bandits did not involve the direct protection of American nationals, they were usually ordered on a protective rationale following attacks on American seamen or settlers, and they indirectly had some protective effect. They also posed little risk of loss to the nation or of escalation to general war because of their scale and the nature of the enemy,[85] and for these reasons, had more in common with domestic police enforcement than with international war (hence the phrase "police actions"). Except for some Native American campaigns, few of these uses of force involved sustained hostilities (although some of the early twentieth century deployments in Latin America and the Caribbean turned into relatively sustained occupations). In a large number, the hostilities were terminated with the evacuation or securing of American nationals or their property. Neither "pirates," "bandits," "aborigines" or other primitive peoples, nor warring "mobs" or "factions" in states where the government had broken down, were regarded as sovereigns, capable of organizing sustained armed opposition.[86] While racism and parochialism contributed in part to such characterizations, the terms used also signified reasonably accurate assessments of the risks to the nation posed by these uses of force.

So numerous had such uses of force become by 1860, that Justice Nelson, sitting on circuit, could write in *Durand v. Hollins* that, "as respects the interposition of the executive abroad, for the protection of the lives or property of the citizen, the duty must, of necessity, rest in the discretion of the president."[87] He held that the exercise of that duty was a nonjusticiable political question in a legal challenge to a naval captain's shelling of Greytown, Nicaragua. Although the facts of the case strongly suggest that the shelling was an unauthorized reprisal rather than a protective intervention, President Pierce justified it by mischaracterizing Greytown as "a marauding establishment . . . incapable of being treated in any other way than as a piratical resort of outlaws or camp of savages depredating on emigrant trains or caravans and the frontier settlements of civilized states,"[88] thus neatly collecting every contemporary epithet but "aborigine" in a single sentence. Thirty years later, Justice Miller, speaking for the Court in *In re Neagle*, endorsed the same view in dicta tracing the executive power of protection to the Take Care Clause, in the assumed absence of legislation on point.[89] Neither case held the President's power of rescue and protection to be exclusive nor purported to rule on its scope when Congress has legislated on the subject. Both, by referring to the Take Care Clause as a source of the power, implied that such legislation could limit the power.

Apart from this judicial sanction of a concurrent constitutional power in the President to use armed force on a small scale for rescue and protection in circumstances posing little risk of escalation or sustained engagement, history suggests customary law authority. The frequency and consistency of such uses of force seem sufficient, although more individualized examination of the instances is necessary for a firm conclusion. But did Congress knowingly and voluntarily acquiesce in the practice, and is it consistent with the Marque and Reprisal Clause?

Almost invariably, as noted, Presidents justified these uses of force to Congress as protective and characterized the subjects of the force as disorganized and nonsovereign, and thus, by implication, incapable of sustained hostilities or escalation to general war. They also invariably asserted statutory authority and/or international law authority on the theory that rescue and protective intervention did not amount to acts of war.[90] This pattern continued until well into the 20th century. On notice then of the protective rationale, low risk of sustained hostilities or escalation, and asserted statutory and international law justifications, Congress almost always acquiesced.[91] But it never acquiesced in any claim of inherent constitutional authority by the President, because, until well into the 20th century, one was never made.[92]

While Congress sometimes acquiesced by doing nothing, it also enacted affirmative legislation approving many of these uses of force. Anti-piracy legislation dating from 1790, at first impliedly and after 1819, expressly authorized naval operations against pirates.[93] It did not expressly authorize naval landings in pursuit of pirates, but neither did it prohibit them, although Congress knew of them.[94] As early as 1789, too, Congress authorized the President to call the militia into service "for the purpose . . . of protecting the inhabitants of the frontiers . . . from the hostile incursions of the Indians."[95] Although Congress also on occasion failed to authorize requested action against Native Americans,[96] this was the exception, not the rule. On notice of Native American suppression operations that went beyond repelling attacks, Congress either expressly or impliedly, by making necessary appropriations, authorized many of the operations.

In and after 1865, the Secretary of Navy also used legislative rulemaking authority delegated to him by Congress to issue regulations authorizing naval commanders to act at the behest of U.S. diplomatic agents abroad for the protection of American nationals and their property against actual or impending violence.[97] Wormuth and Firmage conclude that naval landings which meet the strict requirements of these regulations were statutorily authorized.[98]

Finally, in 1868 Congress enacted what the Supreme Court has somewhat inaccurately called "the Hostage Act," authorizing and requiring the President to "use such means, not amounting to acts of war, as he may think necessary and proper to obtain or effectuate the release" of American citizens "unjustly deprived of . . . [their] liberty by or under the authority of any foreign government. . . . "[99] The legislative history of the Act clearly shows that Congress intended to prohibit the President from taking reprisals against foreign governments because these constituted acts of war within Congress's war power.[100] Instead, it authorized acts (including negotiation and threats) not amounting to acts of war under international law. To the degree that rescue operations were not regarded as acts of war under international law,[101] the 1868 Congress can be said to have authorized the President to use armed force for rescue and protective intervention even against foreign sovereigns.

Whether or not any particular statute thus authorized a particular use of force for such purposes, the entire mass of legislation is "highly relevant in the looser sense of indicating congressional acceptance of a broad scope for executive action," as the Supreme Court said of the not directly apposite legislation in *Dames & Moore*.[102] The legislation may be taken at least as collateral evidence of congressional acquiescence in the executive practice.

The availability of colorable statutory authority for many of these uses of force also satisfies the third predicate for customary law: they did not violate the clear requirements of the Constitution. The Marque and Reprisal Clause does not forbid such uses of force; it only requires congressional approval. Moreover, if the primary concern of the War Clause in general, and the Marque and Reprisal Clause in particular, is to assure congressional control over acts that risk escalation to general war, most of the uses of force for rescue and protection of American nationals would appear to lie beyond it.

The rescue/protection authority, however, must be confined to cases of actual or reasonably imminent risk to Americans. In addition, its logical limit is its immediate object: rescue and protection. Once American nationals are evacuated out of harm's way or otherwise secured, the authority is exhausted. Neither customary law, as demarcated by the practice that Congress understood and acquiesced to, nor international law as incorporated into the Hostage Act, permits the President to order reprisals on his own initiative.[103]

The Customary Defensive War Power: Defending and Enforcing International Law by "Police Actions."[104] The argument that the use of U.S. armed forces abroad for rescue or protection of American nationals was permitted because it was not an act of war under international law has recently been adapted to anchor a broader claim. Franck and Patel have argued that President Bush needed no prior approval from Congress for the Gulf War because it was merely a "police action" to enforce international law declared by the U.N. Security Council, and not war or an act of war subject to the Declaration Clause at all.[105] The same rationale was offered by the congressional reports accompanying the U.N. Participation Act[106] in 1945 to explain why U.S. forces made available to the Security Council by congressionally-approved "special agreements" could be used by the Council in unforeseen hostilities without reapproval by Congress. "Preventive or enforcement action by these forces on the order of the Security Council would not be an act of war," they asserted, "but would be international action for the preservation of the peace and for the purpose of preventing war. Consequently, the provisions of the Charter do not affect the exclusive power of the Congress to declare war."[107] In other words, international sanction through the Security Council is all that is necessary to make the use of U.S. armed force a police action within the President's inherent executive power, instead of a war or act of war within the congressional war power.

The legal analysis that helped lay the groundwork for this argument was a 1944 memorandum by former Solicitor General John W. Davis and Professors Phillip C. Jessup and Quincy Wright, among others. They began their analysis of the President's power to deploy force to enforce international law by distinguishing sharply between war in the domestic constitutional sense and war in the international sense: "It must be emphasized that this problem is one of American constitutional law. So far as international law is concerned any employment of constitutional 'war' powers by the U.S., if authorized by the international organization to enforce international obligations, would not be 'war.' "[108] Yet such employment might be "war" in the constitutional sense. The fundamental flaw in the police action theory is that it overlooks this distinction and erroneously equates the constitutional and international definitions of war.

For these scholars, it was not the appellation "police action" that constitutionally justified the use of special agreement forces, but their *size*. The special agreements would provide "forces limited in size, and their use, while adequate to deal with minor disturbances of international peace, would not create a situation of war in *either* the constitutional or international sense."[109] It would not be war in the international sense because it would be a U.N.-approved use of force to enforce an international law obligation—a police action. It would not be war in the constitutional sense, according to the 1944 memorandum, because small-scale forces had historically been deployed by presidents on their own constitutional authority "to protect American citizens abroad, to prevent an invasion of the territory, or to suppress insurrection."[110]

"If, however, the world is faced by a serious aggression," they added, "[w]hile these [limited special agreement] forces would be immediately available to the international council, it would be understood that in the United States the President would immediately call upon the Congress to examine the situation and to make available further forces or to authorize the full use of war powers. . . ."[111] Consequently, no matter how such fuller uses of force are properly characterized in the international sense, they are war in the constitutional sense because of the risk of loss they pose to the United States. They are therefore subject to the War Clause, and the President must obtain prior congressional approval for them.

In short, by the theory of the 1944 memorandum, there are small-scale or "retail" police actions, and there are large-scale or "wholesale" police actions. Retail international police actions are not war in either the international sense or, by its authors' extrapolation from customary law, in the constitutional sense, and the President may order them without prior congressional approval. But wholesale police actions are war in our constitutional sense and therefore subject to prior congressional authorization, absent attack on the United States or its nationals.

The retail/wholesale theory is flawed or, at best, ahead of its and our time. By resting the argument for retail force on practice, it takes us full circle back to customary constitutional law and the core defensive war powers of the President. Stressing the size of U.S. forces committed to U.N. use, the authors of the 1944 memorandum isolated the factors of small scale and low risk in the President's customary authority to rescue and protect Americans and the fact that rescue and protection operations were sometimes justified partly by reference to international law. But it is doubtful whether the executive practice can *yet* support an extrapolation from the customary law of hostile deployment for rescue and protection of *Americans* to rescue and protection of *foreigners*, although the trend may be favorable to it.[112] The practice of rescue and protection of Americans, after all, was justified not only by reference to international law, but by colorable claims of statutory authority. Moreover, international law was usually invoked for rescue deployments to support the right of the United States as sovereign to use the force, not the right of the President to use it without congressional approval. Finally, to the extent that international law set the parameters of the President's rescue authority vis-a-vis foreign governments, it was because Congress incorporated it into the Hostage Act by authorizing actions "not amounting to acts of war." No comparable legislation authorizes rescue or protection of non-citizens.

Even if scale of force and risk of escalation, and not statutory authority, are the sole criteria for the President's customary rescue/protection power, there remains the thorny question of where the line should be drawn between retail and wholesale uses of force. The authors of the 1944 memorandum conceded that the line is "not easy to define precisely. . . ."[113] But it is not necessary to define it for the Persian Gulf War. No matter where you draw the line, the deployment of more than 500,000 U.S. troops with the greatest per capita firepower in military history does not fall on the retail side. This was no "retail police action" that can fit within *any* fairly-drawn contour of even the President's evolving customary authority.

The Customary Defensive War Power: Defending Allies and Inchoate U.S. Security Interests. The most extreme variant on the claim of defensive war power for the President is the assertion that it extends to the defense of allies and inchoate U.S. security interests anywhere in the world as the President sees them.[114] For example, one scholar rebutted the claim that President Bush needed prior congressional approval for the Gulf War by asserting that "collective defense to expel an invader, rescue hostages or otherwise confront aggression initiated by another is not 'offensive war.'"[115] Another wrote that "[t]he precedents" show that President Bush may order American armed forces to defend another nation if that nation is already at war, so long as he does not start an "offensive war."[116] These claims of presidential authority are refuted by the history of both the making and execution of the War Clause.

There is utterly no support in the history of the framing and ratification of the War Clause for any claim that the framers intended the implied repel-sudden-attack power of the President to include attacks on other nations. The Articles of Confederation assigned the war power to the Continental Congress and prohibited any state from waging war, "unless such state be actually invaded by enemies. . . ."[117] The exception "did not extend to invasion of even a contiguous sister state in the 'league of friendship,' " Berger observes.[118] Madison described the congressional war power conferred by the Constitution by reference to the Articles of Confederation.[119] It is therefore hardly likely that he and his colleagues at the Convention intended to extend the President's defensive war power to invasions of noncontiguous *foreign* states, whether or not they are in alliance with the United States. Indeed, fear of entangling alliances was a persistent theme of the times. In the preface to his famous remarks explaining that the Constitution created a "system [that] will not hurry us into war," James Wilson reminded the Pennsylvania ratifying convention that "we are happily removed from . . . [the commotions of Europe], *and are not obliged to throw ourselves into the scale with any.*"[120]

Nor does the logic of the core defensive power to repel sudden attack support this extension. When the nation itself is attacked, resort to Congress is both impractical and superfluous; war is at hand and the decision to resist is a foregone conclusion. But "[t]hat decision, where a foreign state is attacked, will depend on a variety of factors—proximity to the United States; the value of the country as an ally; other United States interests involved, such as military bases and sites; and the nature of the aggression and the aggressor."[121] These factors point to a classically legislative policy judgment and evoke the factors assigned by Justice Paterson in *United States v. Smith*[122] to legislative appraisal.

Because "presidentially-authorized hostilities are always ostensibly 'defensive,' "[123] the claim that the President may unilaterally use force to defend allies or inchoate security interests is ultimately no more than a variant on the claim that the President has general customary authority to use force without prior congressional approval. As shown above, however, no such authority is established by practice. While isolated interventions to shore up friendly foreign governments in distress, some of Franklin Roosevelt's initiatives in anticipation of our entry into World War II and the Korean War may supply precedents, they are at once too few, too dissimilar, and too ambiguous to constitute the kind of systematic, unbroken and long-pursued practice, or to give the kind of clear notice to Congress, necessary to establish customary law.

Finally, practically the whole war power would be swallowed by a presidential power that is triggered by nothing more substantial or restricted than the President's own perception of a threat to a U.S. ally, inchoate security interest, or "the fundamental rights of the nation," including but not limited to "the stability of worldwide economies, the freedom of shipping in international sea lanes, and the avoidance of escalating . . . [the] limited conflict [between Iraq and Kuwait] into a larger religious or cultural war."[124] Nothing is left Congress but the never used nor likely to be used power to declare offensive war and the politically problematical power to end a war by pulling the plug. In short, merely stating the "inchoate security interest" claim in all its boldness refutes it. We have not come so far, nor could we without a constitutional amendment.

Formal Declaration of War Is Required

Resurrecting a claim many thought interred by the Vietnam War, Sidak asserted that "[t]o commence warfare on the scale witnessed against Iraq, the President needed to receive a formal declaration of war," and, consequently, that Congress's joint resolution of approval in January 1991 "was a legal nullity, a merely precatory or hortatory gesture."[125] This conclusion is not only inconsistent with the probable contemporaneous understanding and usage of "declare,"[126] but also with the assignment of "imperfect" war powers to Congress by the Marque and Reprisal Clause.

The conclusion is contrary to history and case law, too.[127] It is a serious blow to the formal declaration claim that our first major war was the undeclared, but congressionally authorized, naval war with France. Congress subsequently statutorily authorized war with several Barbary states without declaration, as well as the Seminole War in 1837–1838, the Vietnam War, the Gulf War, and dozens of lesser military ventures. Although the larger-scale authorizations are probably too few to make a custom, they demonstrate that neither Congress, nor the presidents who accepted these authorizations without demanding a declaration, have read the Declaration Clause as narrowly as Sidak.

The practice in the naval war with France is particularly instructive because it was so close in time to the Constitutional Convention and was subsequently approved by the Supreme Court. In *Bas v. Tingy*,[128] Justice Washington acknowledged that the war was not a "perfect war . . . declared in form," but he found it nonetheless a "public," "imperfect" war between the United States and France, "*authorised by the legitimate authority of the two governments*."[129] To the argument that Congress had passed no act saying that we are at war, he responded, "This is true; but . . . [this was not] necessary to be done: because . . . as to America, the degree of hostility meant to be carried on, was sufficiently described without declaring war, or declaring that we were at war."[130] Justice Chase added pointblank that "Congress is empowered to declare a general war, or congress may wage a limited war. . . ."[131] Justice Paterson also found that "this modified warfare is authorised by the constitutional authority of our country," "*in the manner prescribed by the constitutional organ of our country.*"[132] Finally, in a companion case growing out of the war with France, Chief Justice Marshall asserted that "[t]he whole powers of war being, by the constitution of the United States, vested in congress, the acts of that body can *alone* be resorted to as our guides in this enquiry."[133]

The claim that formal declaration is required is also wholly at odds with the Vietnam-era cases upholding the legality of that war. In *Orlando v. Laird*, the Second Circuit Court of Appeals asserted that "[t]he Congress and the Executive have taken mutual and joint action in the prosecution and support of military operations," citing not just the Tonkin Gulf Resolution but also the fact that "Congress has ratified the executive's initiatives by appropriating billions of dollars to carry out military operations in Southeast Asia. . . ."[134] The First Circuit Court of Appeals also rejected any contention that formal declaration was the only legislative modality for going to war, noting the Marque and Reprisal Clause, and finding that the "joint accord" of the political branches satisfied the Constitution.[135] These modern cases cannot be distinguished; if the formal declaration claim is right, they and their predecessors from the naval war with France must all be wrong.

The formal declaration claim fares little better when "characterized as a principle of constitutional governance rather than constitutional law."[136] In the first place, there is no historical evidence that formal declarations are attended by more serious deliberation than less formal legislation. Quite the contrary, every U.S. declaration of war but one was passed with little or no debate.[137] Of course, several of these followed attacks on the United States, and all were preceded by indirect debate about the appropriate U.S. response to developing foreign crises. But the same may be said of many less formal authorizations for military force.

Nor are declarations necessarily "more specific" in stating war objectives and their rationale.[138] Historically, declarations have been terse.[139] Of course, declarations have been focused and given specific meaning by the President's request for them. But this is no less true of less formal legislative approvals for the use of military force enacted at the President's request. Less formal legislation is likely to be more ambiguous than a declaration, but the joint resolution approving the use of force against Iraq[140] shows that it need not be. In any event, the formal declaration claim overrates the clarity of declaration in defining the scope of hostilities. "The scope of hostilities is derived not from a verbal formula," Ratner observes, "but from the context and purpose of the resolution."[141]

Finally, any practical accounting of principles of constitutional governance must take into account the costs as well as the benefits of formality. Sidak argues for formal declaration partly on the grounds of its irreversibility, on the theory that war is a "discrete" rather than a "continuous variable."[142] This theory would have baffled Clausewitz, who taught that "war is nothing more than the continuation of politics by other means."[143] Congress avoided formally declaring war on France in 1798 precisely because it wanted to be able to halt or reverse its informal escalation of conflict in the hope of avoiding an all-out war for which it was ill-prepared and for which it had little domestic support.[144] As Secretary of War McHenry cautioned President Adams, after being tutored by Hamilton:

An express declaration of hostility , . . would . . . subject us to all the chances of evil which can accrue from the vengeance of a nation stimulated by . . . extraordinary success. . . . A mitigated hostility will [therefore] be the most likely to fall in with the general feeling, while it leaves a door open for negotiation, and secures some chances to avoid some of the extremities of a formal war.[145]

Congress may also rationally opt to avoid the domestic and international legal consequences of formal declaration in determining war.[146] Whether in hindsight they were right to do so in the Vietnam War is surely debatable, but it hardly follows that the Declaration Clause forbids them from making the same judgment in another setting such as the Gulf War.

CONCLUSION

From the outset, the President has had implied constitutional authority to repel direct attacks and fight de facto wars commenced by enemies against us. This authority is predicated on actual attack or de facto war and subject to appropriations controls by Congress, provided that they do not impermissibly intrude on the Commander in Chief's "real-time" power of command. It hardly needs saying that there was no attack on us prior to initiating the Gulf War that would have triggered this core defensive war authority.

By custom and statute, the President's authority has been extended to include the use of armed force abroad for rescue, evacuation, and protection of American nationals and their property, and hot pursuit of attackers. Inasmuch as small scale and low risk of general escalation have characterized the practice and been instrumental in securing congressional acquiescence, however, the customary law does not authorize the President to deploy combat forces where there is a risk of sustained hostilities or escalation. It follows that even had Iraq continued to hold American hostages in fall 1990, the President could not have relied on his customary rescue authority alone to launch Operation Desert Storm in order to secure their release.

The argument that the President may also unilaterally order our armed forces to enforce international law in "police actions" rests on an extrapolation from the same historical experience as does the customary rescue authority. If that experience can be construed to support a police action authority, which is debatable, that authority presently embraces at most retail uses of force: small-scale deployments posing little risk of loss or escalation. These, perforce, do not include the massive deployment of lethal force in Operation Desert Storm.

Neither text nor custom presently extends the President's unilateral authority any further. None of the predicates for customary authority is satisfied to support any claim of generic authority of the President to go first. The precedents are not systematic, Congress has never knowingly acquiesced in a claim so sweeping, and such authority would violate the War Clause. It is no answer that Congress can pull the appropriations plug on the President's unilateral deployment of armed force. The Framers did not enact a War Veto clause, and reliance on a congressional veto of war defies the constitutional arithmetic. Furthermore, pulling the plug is politically problematical.

On the other hand, nothing in the Constitutional text or practice requires Congress to declare war formally in order to authorize the use of force. Not only is the argument for formality inconsistent with the Framers' probable understanding of "declare," not to mention with the Marque and Reprisal Clause, but it is inconsistent with our custom from the earliest congressionally authorized war to the present, as well as with the uniform case law. Furthermore, that argument fares no better as a principle of constitutional governance than as a rule of constitutional law. It follows, therefore, that though President Bush did not alone have the authority to order the Gulf War, Congress constitutionally authorized that war by enacting the Authorization for the Use of Military Force Against Iraq Resolution.[147]

In short, John Quincy Adams was only half right.[148] Although some of the war powers of the President and Congress *are* still undetermined, some were defined at the outset, and others have been determined by custom—executive practice with knowing congressional acquiescence.

NOTES

I would like to thank George Washington University National Law Center students Gary Osen, Todd Sinkins, and Daniel Goldfried for their research assistance with this chapter, and my colleagues William C. Banks, Hal Bruff, Stephen Dycus, and Todd Peterson for their comments.

1. "The Congress shall have power to . . . declare War, grant Letters of Marque and Reprisal, and make Rules concerning Captures on Land and Water." U.S. Const. art. I, § 8, cl. 11.

2. 2 *The Records of the Federal Convention of 1787* 318–19 (Max Farrand, ed,. 1911).

3. The number varies depending on how the occasions are defined, the date of the writing, and whether the author bothered to up-date the historical list on which he or she relies. Wormuth and Firmage have traced the peculiar "literary tradition" of the lists, showing that many have uncritically incorporated prior lists dating back to 1912. Francis D. Wormuth & Edwin B. Firmage, *To Chain the Dog of War* 142–45 (2d ed. 1989). The most complete current list is probably Ellen C. Collier, *Instances of Use of United States Armed Forces Abroad, 1798–1989* (Congressional Research Service, 1989).

4. N.Y. Times, Nov. 15, 1990, at A18, col. 1.

5. J. Gregory Sidak, *To Declare War*, 41 Duke L.J. 27 (1991).

6. John Q. Adams, *Eulogy on Madison* 47 (1836).

7. Because the treaty power and the War Powers Resolution are treated elsewhere in this text, I omit them here. *See* Peter Raven-Hansen, *Remarks* in Amer. Soc'y Int'l L. Proceedings of the 85th Annual Meeting 9–10 (1991) (rejecting treaty argument).

8. *See* Farrand, *supra* note 2.

9. *See generally* Chapter 1; Abraham D. Sofaer, *War, Foreign Affairs and Constitutional Power: The Origins* 1–60 (1976); Charles A. Lofgren, *War-Making Under the Constitution: The Original Understanding*, 81 Yale L.J. 672, 691 (1972).

10. *United States v. Smith*, 27 F. Cas. 1192, 1230 (C.C.N.Y. 1806) (No. 16,342). Indeed, so basic is the right of self-defense that it is more accurately termed a truly executive power, available to the ranking officer at the scene of the attack, than a presidential power belonging only to the Chief Executive.

11. U.S. Const. art. I, § 8, cl. 12 ("To raise and support Armies, but no Appropriation of Money to that Use shall be for a longer Term than two Years"); *id.* cl. 13 ("To provide and maintain a Navy").

12. 2 Farrand, *supra* note 2, at 549 (remarks of Mr. Ghorum). *See generally* William Banks & Peter Raven-Hansen, *The Sword and the Purse in American Law* ch. 3 (1994).

13. Former Secretary of State William Rogers, for example, deletes the Marque and Reprisal power altogether from the list of powers relevant to the original understanding, *see* William Rogers, *Congress, the President, and the War Powers*, 59 Calif. L. Rev. 1194, 1195 (1971), as did President Bush's lawyers in *Dellums v. Bush. See* Dept. of Justice, Memorandum of Points and Authorities in Opposition to Plaintiffs' Motion for Preliminary Relief and in Support of Defendant's Motion to Dismiss at 9, *Dellums v. Bush*, 752 F. Supp. 1141 (D.D.C. 1990) (No. 90–2866). His lawyers compounded their error by then asserting that "the Constitution does not elaborate . . . on measures which may be permissible short of . . . declarations, on the branch or branches of government which may make those determinations, and on appropriate actions which may be taken in absence of a declaration of war." Justice Department Memorandum, at 30 n.21. To the contrary, the Marque and Reprisal Clause does just that.

14. Letters were issued during the French and Indian and the Revolutionary Wars, and they critically reinforced the fledgling navy that fought the naval war with France from 1798–1800 and the War of 1812. *See* Jules Lobel, *Covert War and Congressional Authority: Hidden War and Forgotten Power*, 134 U. Pa. L. Rev. 1035, 1044 (1986); Fritz Grob, *The Relativity of War and Peace* 239 (1949).

15. Lobel, *supra* note 14, at 1044–45. *See also* Lofgren, *supra* note 9, at 692–94.

16. Lofgren, *supra* note 9, at 693.

17. *Id.* at 696 (footnote omitted).

18. Lobel, *supra* note 14, at 1046.

19. Letter from Alexander Hamilton to James McHenry (May 17, 1798), *reprinted in* 21 *The Papers of Alexander Hamilton* 461–62 (Harold Syrett ed., 1974). *See generally* Lobel, *supra* note 14, at 1046.

20. For a fuller discussion of customary national security law, from which the following account is partly drawn, *see* Banks & Raven-Hansen, *supra* note 12, ch. 12.

21. *See* Collier, *supra* note 3.

22. Alan Watson, *An Approach to Customary Law*, 1984 U. Ill. L. Rev. 561 ("[T]he nature of any source of law requires theoretical underpinnings regardless of whether these underpinnings are always implicit and never expressed. Accordingly, for custom to be regarded as law . . ., more than simple usage must be and is required, even if the usage is general and has long flourished. The principal issue is that one cannot derive an ought from an is.").

23. *Youngstown Sheet & Tube Co. v. Sawyer*, 343 U.S. 579, 610–11 (1952) (Frankfurter, J., concurring); *see also United States v. Midwest Oil Co.*, 236 U.S. 459, 469–75 (1915).

24. Harold H. Koh, *The National Security Constitution* 70 (1990). *See generally* Michael J. Glennon, *The Use of Custom in Resolving Separation of Powers Disputes*, 64

B.U.L. Rev. 109 (1984). Practice and acquiescence may also evolve as a gloss on a statute. *See, e.g., Haig v. Agee*, 453 U.S. 280, 300 (1981) (inferring statutory authority to restrict the right to travel on national security grounds from congressional acquiescence in executive practice and declared policy); *Zemel v. Rusk*, 381 U.S. 1, 17–18 (1965) (foreign affairs delegation takes "its content from history"). *See generally* Robert J. Gregory, *The Clearly Expressed Intent and the Doctrine of Congressional Acquiescence*, 60 UMKC L. Rev. 27, 30 (1991); William N. Eskridge, Jr., *Interpreting Legislative Inaction*, 87 Mich. L. Rev. 67, 69 (1988); John C. Grabow, *Congressional Silence and the Search for Legislative Intent: A Venture into "Speculative Unrealities,"* 64 B.U.L. Rev. 737 (1985).

25. 453 U.S. 654 (1981).

26. 50 U.S.C. § 1701–06 (1992).

27. 22 U.S.C. § 1732 (1992). *See infra* text accompanying note 99.

28. 453 U.S. at 678–79.

29. *Id.* at 679–80 and n.8. *But see* Lee R. Marks & John G. Grabow, *The President's Foreign Economic Powers After Dames & Moore v. Regan: Legislation By Acquiescence,* 68 Cornell L. Rev. 68, 87 (1982) (disputing length and consistency of prior practice of executive claims settlement).

30. 453 U.S. at 680–82 & n.10.

31. Michael J. Glennon, *Constitutional Diplomacy* 59 (1990). *See also* Edward S. Corwin, *The President's Power*, New Republic, Jan. 29, 1951, at 15, 16 ("[T]he Constitution does not consist primarily of precedents but of principles with which precedents, to be valid, must be squared.").

32. *See* Glennon, *supra* note 31, at 55–58 (relevant factors include consistency, numerosity, duration [period of time over which repeated], density [number of times over period], regularity and normalcy of executive practice); Glennon, *supra* note 24, at 129–34 (consistency is always required to create custom); *cf.* Anthony A. D'Amato, *The Concept of Custom in International Law* 56 (1971) (relevant factors in the making of customary international law include duration, repetition, continuity, and generality).

33. *See* Glennon, *supra* note 31, at 63; Glennon, *supra* note 24, at 134; *cf.* D'Amato, *supra* note 32, at 76–86 (factors in the making of customary international law include knowledge or reason to know and the practical possibility of action).

34. The assumption that mere congressional inaction or silence can constitute acquiescence is under increasing attack. National security disputes especially will often "not involve clear congressional affirmations and will thus require a determination of whether consent can be inferred from silence or no action." Glennon, *supra* note 31, at 62. But it is now commonplace to observe that such a determination is problematical. *See, e.g., Johnson v. Transportation Agency,* 480 U.S. 616, 672 (1987) (Scalia, J., dissenting). *See generally* Gregory, *supra* note 24, at 30–31 ("Acquiescence by silence is presumably the weakest of the acquiescence theories;" acquiescence by rejection "is no more constitutionally significant than mere silence. . . ."); Eskridge, *supra* note 24, at 67, 98–103; Grabow, *supra* note 24, at 749–50; Paul Gewirtz, *The Courts, Congress and Executive Policy–Making: Notes on Three Doctrines*, 40 Law & Contemp. Probs. 46, 79 (1976) (footnotes omitted) (" . . . Congress often acquiesces in the executive's action for reasons having nothing to do with the majority's preferences on the policy issues involved."). If one accepts these critiques, it becomes essential that Congress manifest its acquiescence by more than silence, and perhaps at least by collateral legislation or appropriations.

Even when it has done so, it may not be clear whether Congress is acquiescing just in the policy that a President is executing, or also in the President's authority to execute it. When it agrees with the policy, it is, after all, unlikely to raise a procedural challenge to his authority. This objection is diminished, however, when the President acts repeatedly, because the factual variability of the uses of force makes it more likely that the congressional acquiescence is to the President's assumption of a generic authority to use force of a certain kind than only to the varying policy choices represented by particular uses.

35. It is therefore not a valid objection to the theory of customary national security law that only "legislative usage" can establish constitutional power. Wormuth & Firmage, *supra* note 3, at 106. It is the *combination* of executive practice and knowing legislative acquiescence which makes the law. Nor is it correct that it is only the acquiescence of the first Congresses that counts. *Id.* at 138 n.4. Because these Congresses contained many who were present at the framing of the Constitution, their reactions to executive uses of armed force are entitled to special weight. Thus antiquity goes to the weight, not the admissibility of congressional acquiescence. *See generally* Stephen Dycus, Arthur L. Berney, William C. Banks & Peter Raven–Hansen, *National Security Law* 45–46 (1990).

36. Although discussion of the War Powers Resolution ("WPR") is beyond the scope of this chapter, I should briefly note that it did not call a halt to the development of customary law for two reasons. The WPR is not Congress's last word on the subject, and the 1973 Congress cannot control how the intent of subsequent Congresses may be expressed. *See generally* Banks & Raven-Hansen, *supra* note 12, ch. 16. Second, the WPR has itself been subject to customary evolution by congressional acquiescence in its disregard by the President. As the WPR is now interpreted, Congress must apparently pull "a second trigger" in order to start the sixty-day clock established by the Resolution's sunset provisions. *See* Dycus et al., *supra* note 35, at 131–32.

37. *See Powell v. McCormack*, 395 U.S. 486, 546–47 (1969) ("That an unconstitutional action has been taken before surely does not render that same action any less unconstitutional at a later date."). In *Chadha*, for example, the Supreme Court overturned more than fifty years of legislative practice on the ground that it violated the lawmaking provisions of the Constitution. *Immigration & Naturalization Service v. Chadha*, 462 U.S. 919 (1983). *See generally* Thomas A. Curtis, Note, *Recess Appointments to Article III Courts: The Use of Historical Practice in Constitutional Interpretation*, 84 Colum. L. Rev. 1758, 1783–84 (1984).

38. *See, e.g., Zuber v. Allen*, 396 U.S. 168, 185–86 n.21 (1969) ("The verdict of quiescent years cannot be invoked to baptize a statutory gloss that is otherwise impermissible.").

39. *Inland Waterways Corp. v. Young*, 309 U.S. 517, 524 (1940).

40. Leonard Meeker, *The Legality of United States Participation in Defense of Viet-Nam*, 54 State Dep't Bull. 474, *reprinted in* 75 Yale L.J. 1085, 1100 (1966). *See also* Henry Monaghan, *Presidential War-Making*, 50 B.U.L. Rev. 19, 25–27, 30–31 (Special Issue 1970).

41. *See generally* Wormuth & Firmage, *supra* note 3, at 142–51.

42. Meeker, *supra* note 40, at 1101.

43. *See, e.g.*, Edward Keynes, *Undeclared War* 37 (1982) (more than twenty laws); Wormuth & Firmage, *supra* note 3, at 60 (noting four); Sofaer, *supra* note 9, at 147–54, 159. Without congressional approval, President Adams lifted his own ban on the arming of merchants, but this hardly involved ordering the armed forces abroad. Sofaer, *supra* note 9, at 143. He also ordered a lone U.S. naval vessel to sail off the coast between Virginia and Long Island and to defend itself if attacked on the high seas, which is consistent with his implied power to repel sudden attacks. *See* J. Terry Emerson, *Making War Without a Declaration*, 17 J. Legis. 23, 43 (1990).

44. *Bas v. Tingy*, 4 U.S. (4 Dall.) 37, 43–44 (1800).

45. *Little v. Barreme*, 6 U.S. (2 Cranch) 170 (1804).

46. 236 U.S. 459 (1915).

47. *Youngstown Sheet & Tube Co. v. Sawyer*, 343 U.S. 579, 611 (1952).

48. *Dames & Moore v. Regan*, 453 U.S. 654, 679–80, 684 (1981).

49. James G. Rogers, *World Policing and the Constitution* 79 (1945).

50. Hearings on War Powers Legislation before the Senate Foreign Relations Committee, 93d Cong., 1st Sess. 155–56 (1973).

51. Sofaer, *supra* note 9, at 379.

52. It also omits numerous instances in which the President unilaterally deployed armed forces abroad without hostilities. A Department of Defense study reportedly found 215 instances of minatory deployments between 1946 and 1975 alone. Emerson, *supra* note 43, at 39 (citing Barry M. Blechman & Stephen S. Kaplan, *Force Without War: The Use of Armed Forces as a Political Instrument* 16 [1978]). Leaving the War Powers Resolution to one side, congressional acquiescence in such deployments has established an unmistakable customary authority in the President to order them, which arguably includes the initial deployments to Saudi Arabia in response to Iraq's 1990 invasion of Kuwait. Indeed, James Madison argued in 1789 that "[b]y the constitution, the President has the power of employing troops in the protection of those parts which he thinks require them most." 1 *Annals of Cong.* 724 (Joseph Gates ed., 1789). Of course, the President must still abide by the Appropriation Clause, which may operate to fix a ceiling on the size of such deployments, and he must still report under the War Powers Resolution.

53. Sofaer, *supra* note 9, at 123, 141, 215–16, 320–25. For example, Sofaer traces President Madison's repeated and unsuccessful efforts to get congressional approval for military initiatives in East Florida, culminating in his acceptance of the congressional will. *Id.* at 325.

54. Wormuth & Firmage, *supra* note 3, at 37, 77–87. *See also* W. Taylor Reveley III, *War Powers of the President and Congress: Who Holds the Arrows and the Olive Branch?* 121 (1981).

55. 752 F. Supp. 1141, 1154 (D.D.C. 1990).

56. *See* Clyde Eagleton, *The Form and Function of the Declaration of War*, 32 Am. J. Int'l L. 19, 29, 34 (1938).

57. *See* Robert F. Turner, *The War Powers Resolution: Its Implementation in Theory and Practice* 25 (1983).

58. Stephen L. Carter, *Going to War Over War Powers*, Washington Post, Nov. 18, 1990, at C1; Emerson, *supra* note 43, at 29; Dept. of Justice, *supra* note 13, at 20 ("the ultimate check on such action . . . is with the Congress itself").

59. Banks & Raven-Hansen, *supra* note 12, chs. 8 & 15.

60. *See, e.g.*, William Barr (Attorney General), Panel, *The Appropriations Power and Necessary and Proper Clause*, 68 Wash. U.L.Q. 626, 655 (1990) ("the appropriation clause does not say that the President cannot use other sources of funds").

61. *See* Banks & Raven-Hansen, *supra* note 12, ch. 15.

62. *Mitchell v. Laird*, 488 F.2d 611, 615 (D.C. Cir. 1973). *See also* Note, *Congress, the President, and the Power to Commit Forces to Combat*, 81 Harv. L. Rev. 1771, 1801 (1968) (after hostilities have already begun, "the effective choice remaining to Congress is likely to be severely limited").

63. Dan Morgan, *"Team Player" Breaks Ranks on Support of U.S. Troop Deployments*, Washington Post, Sept. 27, 1990, at A37.

64. Banks & Raven-Hansen, *supra* note 12, ch. 13.

65. *Id.*, ch. 14.

66. *See, e.g.*, Emerson, *supra* note 43, at 60.

67. *See supra* text accompanying note 19.

68. *See* Note, *supra* note 62, at 1784 n.69. Sofaer documents the practice more fully, suggesting that Presidents were not always candid in their reports to Congress. *See* Sofaer, *supra* note 9, *passim*. But what the Presidents told Congress is controlling in the development of customary national security law by *knowing* congressional acquiescence.

69. 27 F. Cas. 1192, 1230–31 (C.C.N.Y. 1806) (No. 16,342).

70. *Id*. at 1230–31.

71. Wormuth & Firmage, *supra* note 3, at 22.

72. *Smith*, 27 F. Cas. at 1230.

73. 25 *Annals of Cong.* 517 (1813).

74. 67 U.S. (2 Black) 635 (1863).

75. *Id*. at 668.

76. 2 James Madison, *Letters and Writings* 600 (1884) (emphasis added).

77. *See* Dycus et al., *supra* note 35, at 288.

78. Note, *supra* note 62, at 1781.

79. *See generally* Banks & Raven-Hansen, *supra* note 12, ch. 14; Keynes, *supra* note 43, at 165 (asserting that President's defensive war power is "plenary," "exclusive" and not subject to legislative restriction).

80. John Norton Moore, *Law and the Indo-China War* 566 (1972). *See* Peter Raven-Hansen, "The Constitutionality of the FAS Proposal: A Critical Summary," in *First Use of Nuclear Weapons: Under the Constitution, Who Decides?* 217–19 (Peter Raven-Hansen ed., 1987).

81. Wormuth & Firmage, *supra* note 3, at 153–54.

82. Edwin Borchard, *The Diplomatic Protection of Citizens Abroad* 29 (1915).

83. Sofaer, *supra* note 9, at 200 and note * (emphasis added).

84. Wormuth & Firmage, *supra* note 3, at 146.

85. *See* Raoul Berger, *Protection of Americans Abroad*, 44 Cinn. L. Rev. 741, 748 (1975) (noting that most of these uses of force "posed no possibility of war because of the vast disparity of power").

86. *See, e.g.*, Sofaer, *supra* note 9, at 119 (noting characterization of Native Americans as "savages," as opposed to "civilized" nations), 371 (noting characterization of pirates as "enemies of human race"); Note, *supra* note 62, at 1788 (noting characterization of pirates and slave-traders as "criminals" and aborigines as "uncivilized"). The peculiar status of Native American tribes in American life and law distinguishes them, but, even so, some uses of force against Native Americans were characterized as deployments against renegades.

87. *Durand v. Hollins*, 8 F. Cas. 111, 112 (C.C.S.D.N.Y. 1860) (No. 4186).

88. Wormuth & Firmage, *supra* note 3, at 39.

89. 135 U.S. 1, 63–66 (1890), citing art II, sec. 3 (President "shall take care that the laws be faithfully executed").

90. Sofaer, *supra* note 9, at 378; Edwin Corwin, *Total War and the Constitution* 146 (1947).

91. At the risk of running afoul of my own critique of rote citations to unexamined history, I here cite only *passim* to Sofaer, *supra* note 9, and Henry B. Cox, *War, Foreign Affairs, and Constitutional Power: 1829–1901* (1984), pleading space limitations in my defense.

92. Sofaer, *supra* note 9, at 378.

93. Act of April 30, 1790, 1 Stat. 112, 113–14; Act of March 3, 1819, 3 Stat. 510–14 (1819). *See* Sofaer, *supra* note 9, at 365–66. The present statute is codified at 33 U.S.C. §§ 381–82 (1988).

94. Wormuth & Firmage, *supra* note 3, 155–56. Monroe advised Congress that the issue of landings for this purpose was for it to decide, but it failed to act on his report and naval landings continued.

95. Act of Sept. 29, 1789, 1 Stat. 95, 96. Sofaer argues that the act impliedly authorized offensive action. Sofaer, *supra* note 9, at 123.

96. Sofaer, *supra* note 9, at 123.

97. *See generally* Wormuth & Firmage, *supra* note 3, at 156–60.

98. *Id.*

99. As amended, 22 U.S.C. § 1732 (1989), *construed in Dames & Moore*, 453 U.S. at 676. *See generally* Abner J. Mikva & Gerald L. Neuman, *The Hostage Crisis and the "Hostage Act*," 49 U. Chi. L. Rev. 292 (1982).

100. Mikva & Neuman, *supra* note 99, at 318–29 (members rejected original bill providing for reprisal because it intruded upon declaration of war power).

101. *See, e.g.*, Natalino Ronzitti, *Rescuing Nationals Abroad Through Military Coercion and Intervention on Grounds of Humanity* 21 (1985); Ann V.W. Thomas & A.J. Thomas, Jr., *The War-Making Powers of the President* 61, 73 (1982). The approval of the United Nations Charter has since made the international legality of rescue operations more doubtful. *See* Ronzitti, *supra*, at 24–68.

102. 453 U.S. at 677.

103. Both restrictions are underscored by the admonition in the 1893 Navy Regulations that force in self-defense or protection of American nationals or their property "can never be exercised with a view to inflicting punishments for acts already committed. It must be used only as a last resort, and then only to the extent which is absolutely necessary to accomplish the end required." *Regulations for the Government of the United States Navy* § 285 (1893). Substantially the same regulations were issued in 1896, 1905, 1920, and 1948. *See* Wormuth & Firmage, *supra* note 3, at 159.

104. The following analysis was adapted from Raven-Hansen, *supra* note 7, at 10–11.

105. Thomas M. Franck & Faiza Patel, *UN Police Action in Lieu of War: "The Old Order Changeth*," 85 Am. J. Int'l L. 63 (1991).

106. 22 U.S.C. § 287d (1988).

107. H. Rep. No. 1383, 79th Cong., 1st Sess., *reprinted in* 1945 U.S. Code Cong. & Admin. News 927, 934; S. Rep. No. 717, 79th Cong., 1st Sess. (1945).

108. Memorandum by John W. Davis, Phillip C. Jessup, & Quincy Wright, *reprinted in* 91 Cong. Rec. 8065, 79th Cong., 1st Sess. (1945). I am indebted to David J. Scheffer for bringing this memorandum to my attention. *See* Scheffer, "War Powers and the U.N. Charter," statement for Hearings on War Powers and the Gulf Crisis before the Senate Judiciary Committee, 102d Cong., 1st Sess. (1991).

109. Davis et al., *supra* note 108, at 8066.

110. *Id.*

111. *Id.*

112. *See, e.g.*, U.S. armed intervention to protect Kurdish refugees in Iraq during 1991.

113. Davis et al., *supra* note 108, at 8066.

114. *See* Eugene V. Rostow, *Great Cases Make Bad Law: The War Powers Act*, 50 Tex. L. Rev. 833, 850 n.28 (1972) (defensive war power to respond with force to any foreign action "directed against the security of the United States"); Craig Mathews, *The Constitutional Power of the President to Conclude International Agreements*, 64 Yale L.J. 345, 365 (1955) (President may take military action "under his independent powers whenever the interests of the United States so require"); Reveley, *supra* note 54, at 144–45 (citing claims to this effect). Recall that the treaty power is treated elsewhere in this collection. *See* chapter 4; *see also supra* note 7.

115. Emerson, *supra* note 43, at 30 n.51.

116. Carter, *supra* note 58, at C4.

117. Articles of Confederation art. VI, cl. 5.

118. Raoul Berger, *War-Making by the President*, 121 U. Pa. L. Rev. 29, 43 (1972).

119. *The Federalist No. 41*, at 263 (J. Madison) (C. Rossiter ed., 1961).

120. 2 *Debates in the Several State Conventions on the Adoption of the Federal Constitution* 528 (Jonathan Elliot ed., 2d ed. 1836) (emphasis added). *See also id.* at 513.

121. Note, *supra* note 62, at 1783.

122. *See supra* quote accompanying note 70.

123. Leonard G. Ratner, *The Coordinated Warmaking Power—Legislative, Executive and Judicial Roles*, 44 S. Cal. L. Rev. 461, 469 (1971).

124. Emerson, *supra* note 43, at 59–60 (asserting that "the President can unilaterally initiate self-defense actions" to protect these security interests).

125. Sidak, *supra* note 5, at 33.

126. Lofgren, *supra* note 9, at 680, 684–85; Sofaer, *supra* note 9, at 56. *See also* Wormuth & Firmage, *supra* note 3, at 20.

127. For a fuller development of arguments against this claim, *see* Banks & Raven-Hansen, *supra* note 12, ch. 13.

128. 4 U.S. (4 Dall.) 37 (1800).

129. *Id.* at 40–41 (emphasis added).

130. *Id.* at 41.

131. *Id.* at 43.

132. *Id.* at 45–46 (emphasis added).

133. *Talbot v. Seeman*, 5 U.S. (1 Cranch) 1, 28 (1801) (emphasis added).

134. 443 F.2d 1039, 1042 (2d Cir.) (footnotes omitted), *cert. denied*, 404 U.S. 869 (1971).

135. *Massachusetts v. Laird*, 451 F.2d 26, 33 (1st Cir. 1971).

136. Sidak, *supra* note 5, at 34, 90, 99.

137. *See, e.g.*, Harold H. Koh, *The Coase Theorem and the War Power: A Response*, 41 Duke L.J. 122, 128 (1991).

138. *Compare* Sidak, *supra* note 5, at 102.

139. *Id.* at 80. Ironically, Sidak adopts the conclusion that only the "declaration of imperfect war against France in the Quasi-War of 1798–1800 . . . explained the nature of the warlike provocation . . .," *id.*, even though the Quasi-War was authorized by a series of ordinary statutes and was never declared.

140. H.J. Res. 77, Pub. L. No. 102–1 (Jan. 14, 1991).

141. Ratner, *supra* note 123, at 465.

142. Sidak, *supra* note 5, at 95, 100–101, 103.

143. Carl von Clausewitz, *On War* 87 (Howard & Paret eds., 1976).

144. *See Bas v. Tingy*, 4 U.S. (4 Dall.) 37, 45 (1800) (Chase, J.) (noting that "the popular feeling may not have been ripe for a solemn declaration of war").

145. *The Life and Correspondence of James McHenry* 291–95 (B. Steiner ed., 1907). *See generally* Sofaer, *supra* note 9, 139–47.

146. *Orlando v. Laird*, 443 F.2d 1039, 1043 (2d Cir.), *cert. denied*, 404 U.S. 869 (1971). *See also Mitchell v. Laird*, 488 F.2d 611, 615 (D.C. Cir. 1973); Thomas & Thomas, *supra* note 101, at 87 (footnote omitted); Charles Bennett, et al., *The President's Powers as Commander-in-Chief Versus Congress' War Power and Appropriations Power*, 43 U. Miami L. Rev. 17, 31–32 (1988) (declaration "heightens conflict, challenges the other side, deters compromise, complicates relations with allies, and may even benefit the enemy by

dignifying the very behavior that we are opposing") (remarks of Geoffrey P. Miller); Eagleton, *supra* note 56, at 24.

147. Pub. L. No. 102–1, 105 Stat. 3 (1991).

148. *See supra* quote accompanying note 6.

3   Statutory Constraints: The War Powers Resolution[1]

Ellen C. Collier

The nineteen year history of the War Powers Resolution[2] has provided a varied experience that has left the statute as controversial as ever. The issues raised by this experience have become increasingly serious. Early problems concerned whether Presidents were complying with the consultation and reporting requirements of the resolution. Later the effectiveness and appropriateness of the War Powers Resolution became an issue. Finally, in the lead up to the war against Iraq, it became clear that the issue was not the War Powers Resolution but the meaning of the war powers under the Constitution itself.

It is not possible to say flatly either that Presidents have complied with the War Powers Resolution or that they have not. Since passage of the War Powers Resolution Presidents have complied to the extent of submitting approximately twenty-five reports to Congress under the resolution. But the reports, except for the one on the *Mayaguez* seizure, have not cited section 4(a)(1), indicating that forces have been introduced into hostilities, which would trigger the 60-day time limit. Even in the *Mayaguez* crisis, President Ford waited until the action was over before reporting, so the question of a time limit was moot. It has become clear that Presidents who wish to take military action independently of Congress are unlikely to cite section 4(a)(1) and thus trigger the 60-day time limit.

Presidents failed to report at all a number of deployments of U.S. Armed Forces into potential hostilities or other situations in which the War Powers Resolution required reports. Most of these deployments were short-lived and uncontroversial, however, and Congress closely monitored the other, longer lasting situations. Compliance with the consultation requirement was the first issue raised in experience with the War Powers Resolution and has been a persistent issue since. Presidents contend they have complied with the War Powers Resolution by calling in congressional leaders to brief them before commencing an operation. Because such meetings were held after the President made the decision and gave orders to launch an operation, Members of Congress have not considered this adequate consultation. Moreover, although these were gestures of consultation that might not have occurred in the absence of the War Powers Resolution, they have not brought congressional advice into the decision-making process.

Some Members of Congress believe the Resolution has served well as a restraint on the use of armed forces by Presidents on some occasions, provided a mode of communication, increased congressional leverage, and given Congress a vehicle for asserting its war powers that it can employ if it wishes. In their view it presents a valuable option for presidential and congressional action, an option that should be kept open.

Others have proposed amendments to the Resolution because they believe it has not been effective in assuring a congressional voice in committing U.S. troops to potential conflicts abroad. Numerous flaws in the Resolution have been found, and some of these might be corrected by amendments. But proponents of the Resolution doubt that it can be opened to amendment without subjecting it to the possibility of being weakened beyond repair, as any amendment would require presentment to the President.

Still other Members of Congress have contended that the President needs more flexibility in the conduct of foreign policy and that the time limitation in the War Powers Resolution is unconstitutional and impractical. Some have suggested it be repealed. While the same Members might not favor repeal if the Presidency changed hands, it can be fairly certain that most Presidents would readily sign such a measure.

One area in which work is needed concerns United Nations actions. Enforcement actions which may bind the United States under international law remain one of the biggest loopholes in the congressional war power. In the case of military action sought by others, the United States can veto Security Council decisions, but control of the veto is wholly in the hands of the President. In the case of military action proposed by the President, Operation Desert Storm showed that Congress cannot count on the United Nations to perform the task of saying no. Finally, Congress needs to make clear to the public that although U.N. Security Council resolutions may provide international authority, they do not presently provide domestic authority for the use of U.S. force. Future Congresses will have to wrestle with whether to approve military agreements with the Security Council that could enable the President to supply troops without further congressional action. Or they might seek to clarify the relationship of U.N. actions to congressional war powers or the War Powers Resolution in some other way.

At this point the future of the statute is unpredictable, dependent on the actions of future Presidents and Congresses. A future President could take a new tack and use the War Powers Resolution as a vehicle for congressional sharing in difficult decisions. Or a future President could again undertake military action by fait accompli, and complain that the War Powers Resolution was an undue restraint. A new Congress could use the War Powers Resolution to contain or support a President's unilateral action; or a new Congress could amend the law or repeal it. The question Members must ask themselves is whether Congress and the Nation are better off with or without the War Powers Resolution.

This chapter examines the experience gained with the War Powers Resolution since 1973, and various amendments that have been proposed.

BACKGROUND ON THE WAR POWERS RESOLUTION

The War Powers Resolution responded to a steady accretion of power by the President after the Second World War. Members of Congress expressed concern about presidential use of armed forces without congressional authorization during the Korean War; Republican Senator Robert Taft protested that President Truman had committed American troops to Korea without consulting Congress or getting its authorization.

During the Vietnam War, when the United States found itself involved for many years in an undeclared and unpopular war, Congress searched for a way to reassert its authority to determine when the United States should become involved in a war or a commitment that might lead to war. With this in mind, in 1969 the Senate adopted the National Commitments Resolution stating its sense that a national commitment by the United States resulted only from "affirmative action taken by the executive and legislative branches of the United States Government by means of a treaty, statute, or concurrent resolution of both Houses of Congress specifically providing for such commitment."[3]

In 1970, after the invasion of Cambodia by U.S. forces as part of the Vietnam conflict, both Houses of Congress began considering broad war powers legislation. The Senate and House developed different approaches to the objective of circumscribing the President's authority to send armed forces abroad into potential hostilities without a declaration of war or other congressional authorization, while providing enough flexibility to permit him to respond to attack or emergencies.

The Senate passed a measure that attempted to delineate the powers of the President to use armed forces in an emergency situation. It enumerated four situations in which U.S. forces could be introduced into hostilities or potential hostilities without a declaration of war. These were (1) to repel an attack on the United States or to forestall the direct threat of such an attack; (2) to repel an armed attack against U.S. Armed Forces outside the United States, and to forestall the direct threat of such an attack; (3) to rescue American citizens, and (4) pursuant to specific statutory authorization. The bill established a 30 day time limit on the use of force in these emergency situations, triggered by the date the President acted, although this could be extended by the President for the safety of the forces or by legislation.[4] The House bill did not enumerate the authorities of the President, but established a 120 day time limit on military actions not authorized by a declaration of war or statute, triggered by receipt of a required report of the President.[5]

Some Members feared that the Senate version would either restrict the President too much, because all possible emergency needs could not be enumerated, or that it would provide too much leeway by authorizing action to forestall an attack or protect Americans while evacuating them. Other Members feared that the House version would give the President a 120 day free period for any mischief. Conferees compromised on the current language which established a 60 to 90 day time limit.[6]

In addition, section 2(c) stated the policy that the powers of the President as Commander in Chief to introduce U.S. armed forces into situations of hostilities or imminent hostilities

are exercised only pursuant to—(1) a declaration of war, (2) specific statutory authorization, or (3) a national emergency created by attack upon the United States, its territories or possessions, or its armed forces.

This was a scaled-down version of the Senate's enumeration of Presidential powers, omitting the forestalling of an attack or the rescue of American citizens, and was not linked to the operative parts of the resolution.

The Senate and House agreed to the conference report on October 10 and 12, 1973, respectively. President Nixon vetoed the conference bill on October 24, and the House and Senate overrode the veto on November 7, 1973, enacting it into law.[7]

Congress saw the War Powers Resolution as buttressing, clarifying, and implementing, but not changing the Constitution's division of war powers between Congress and the President. Congress considered war powers appropriate for legislation. Section 2(b) of the War Powers Resolution points out that "[u]nder Article I, section 8, of the Constitution it is specifically provided that Congress shall have the power to make all laws necessary and proper for carrying into execution, not only its own powers but also all other powers vested by the Constitution in the Government of the United States. . . ." Section 8(d) states that nothing in the Resolution is intended to alter the constitutional authority of either the Congress or the President. It also specifies that nothing is to be construed as granting any authority to introduce troops that would not exist in the absence of the Resolution. The House report said that this provision was to help insure the constitutionality of the Resolution by making it clear that nothing in it could be interpreted as changing the powers delegated by the Constitution.

President Nixon vetoed the bill on two major grounds. He argued that the legislative veto provision, permitting Congress to direct the withdrawal of troops by concurrent resolution, was unconstitutional. He also argued that the provision requiring withdrawal of troops after 60–90 days unless Congress authorized the use was unconstitutional because it checked presidential powers without affirmative congressional action. In his veto message, President Nixon noted that the Resolution would impose restrictions upon the authority of the President which would be dangerous to the safety of the Nation and "attempt to take away, by a mere legislative act, authorities which the President has properly exercised under the Constitution for almost 200 years."[8] Rather, Nixon and other Presidents have contended that the Executive branch has much broader authority to use force, including for such purposes as to rescue American citizens abroad, rescue foreign nationals where such action facilitates the rescue of U.S. citizens, protect U.S. embassies and legations, suppress civil insurrection, implement the terms of an armistice or cease-fire involving the United States, and carry out the terms of security commitments contained in treaties.[9]

Legislative Veto

On June 23, 1983, the Supreme Court supported the first of the Nixon arguments when, in *INS v. Chadha*, it ruled unconstitutional the legislative veto provision in section 244(c)(2) of the Immigration and Nationality Act.[10] Although the case involved the use of a one-House legislative veto, the decision cast doubt on the validity of any legislative veto device that was not presented to the President for signature. The Court held that to accomplish what the House attempted to do in the *Chadha* case "requires action in conformity with the express procedures of the Constitution's prescription for legislative action: passage by a majority of both Houses and presentment to the President." Similarly, on July 6, 1983, the Supreme Court summarily affirmed the decision of the D.C. Court of Appeals striking down a provision of the Federal Trade Commission Improvements Act of 1980 that provided for a disapproval by concurrent (two-House) resolution.[11]

Since section 5(c) of the War Powers Resolution requires forces to be removed by the President if Congress so directs by a concurrent resolution, it is constitutionally suspect under the reasoning applied by the Court.[12] A concurrent resolution must be adopted by both chambers, but it does not require presentment to the President. Some legal analysts contend, nevertheless, that the War Powers Resolution is in a unique category which differs from statutes containing a legislative veto over delegated authorities.[13] Perhaps more important, some observers contend that if a majority of both Houses ever voted to withdraw U.S. forces, the President would be unlikely to continue the action for long, and Congress could withhold appropriations to finance further action.

The War Powers Resolution contains a separability clause in Section 9, stating that if any provision or its application is found invalid, the remainder of the Resolution is not to be affected. Therefore most analysts take the view that the remainder of the statute would not be affected even if section 5(c) were found unconstitutional. On July 20, 1983, Deputy Attorney General Edward Schmults told the House Foreign Affairs Committee that "the Supreme Court's decision does not affect any of the procedural mechanisms contained in the War Powers Resolution other than that procedure specified in section 5(c), which purported to authorize Congress effectively to recall our troops from abroad by a resolution not presented to the President for his approval or disapproval."[14]

Congress has not tried to use the legislative veto provision in the War Powers Resolution, but it has taken action to fill the gap left by the possible invalidity of the concurrent resolution mechanism for the withdrawal of troops. On October 20, 1983, the Senate in action on a State Department authorization bill voted to amend the War Powers Resolution by substituting a joint resolution for the concurrent resolution in section 5(c), and providing that it would be handled under the expedited procedures in section 7. A joint resolution requires presentment to the President.

House and Senate conferees on the bill agreed not to amend the War Powers Resolution itself, but to adopt a free standing measure relating to the withdrawal of troops. The measure, which became law, provided that any joint resolution or bill to require the removal of U.S. armed forces engaged in hostilities outside the United States without a declaration of war or specific statutory authorization would be considered in accordance with the expedited procedures of section 601(b) of the International Security and Arms Export Control Act of 1976,[15] except that it would be amendable and debate on a veto would be limited to 20 hours.[16] The priority procedures embraced by this provision applied in the Senate only. Handling of such a joint resolution by the House was left to that Chamber's discretion.

Automatic Withdrawal Provision

The automatic withdrawal provision has become perhaps the most controversial provision of the War Powers Resolution. Section 5(b) requires the President to withdraw U.S. forces from hostilities within 60–90 days after a report is submitted or required to be submitted under section 4(a)(1). The triggering of the time limit has been a major factor for the reluctance of Presidents to report under section 4(a)(1) and of Congress to state that such a report was required in a specific instance.

Drafters of the War Powers Resolution included a time limit to provide some teeth in the event a President assumed a power to act from provisions of resolutions, treaties, or the Constitution which did not constitute an explicit authorization. The Senate report on its version called the time limit "the heart and core" of the bill that "rests squarely and securely on the words, meaning and intent of the Constitution and thus represents, in an historic sense, a restoration of the constitutional balance which has been distorted by practice in our history and, climatically, in recent decades."[17] The House report emphasized that the Resolution did not grant the President any new authority or any freedom of action during the time limits that he did not already have.

Administration officials have objected that the provision would require the withdrawal of U.S. forces simply because of congressional inaction during an arbitrary period. Since the resolution recognizes that the President has independent authority to use the armed forces in certain circumstances, they state "on what basis can Congress seek to terminate such independent authority by the mere passage of time?"[18] In addition, they argue, the imposition of a deadline interferes with successful action, signals a divided nation and lack of resolve, gives the enemy a basis for hoping that the President will be forced by domestic opponents to stop an action, and increases risk to U.S. forces in the field.

In one sense, experience has not brought any major confrontations on the time limit. Most of the relevant uses of armed forces since the War Powers Resolution was passed have been of short duration. Combat forces were withdrawn from Grenada and Panama within 60 days. Marines were withdrawn from Lebanon before the expiration of the eighteen months authorized in the Multinational Force in Lebanon Resolution. The Authorization for Use of Military Force against Iraq Resolution contained no time limit. In another sense the time limit has been at the heart of confrontations on invoking the War Powers Resolution. The imposition of a time was a major reason some Members objected to invoking the War Powers Resolution in various situations. Many Members seem to agree with the President that a time limit on the use of forces places the United States at a disadvantage in a military operation.

Presidential Compliance

Since the passage of the War Powers Resolution, each President has complied with it to some extent. Presidents have submitted approximately two dozen reports under the War Powers Resolution, but only one, that concerning the *Mayaguez* incident, cited section 4(a)(1) of the Resolution triggering the time limit.[19] Moreover, because as a general matter the Executive branch resists the specific requirements of the statute, the reports have been made "consistent with" rather than "pursuant to" the War Powers Resolution. This has had the effect of placing on Congress the burden of determining that forces have been introduced into hostilities or imminent hostilities, that a report under section 4(a)(1) has been or should have been submitted, and that the time limitations of the resolution would apply.

In several cases Presidents have also in their view fulfilled the consultation requirement by briefing congressional leaders before public announcement of an operation. But there have been other instances that were not reported at all. The frequency with which Presidents have introduced forces into hostilities or potential hostilities has risen, and during the last decade the kind of military operation undertaken by Presidents on their own authority moved beyond small operations to rescue citizens to invasions and bombings.

Instances Reported

President Ford submitted four reports under the War Powers Resolution. On April 4, 12, and 30, 1975, he reported the use of forces to help evacuate refugees and U.S. nationals from Cambodia and Vietnam. On May 15, 1975, President Ford reported that he had ordered U.S. military forces to rescue the crew of and retake the ship *Mayaguez* that had been seized by Cambodian naval patrol boats on May 12, that the ship had been retaken, and that the withdrawal of the forces had been undertaken.

President Carter submitted one report. On April 26, 1980, he reported the use of six aircraft and eight helicopters in the April 24th unsuccessful attempt to rescue the American hostages in Iran.

President Reagan submitted fourteen reports. One of these, on March 19, 1982, concerned the deployment of military personnel and equipment to the Multinational Force and Observers in the Sinai, which Congress had authorized in the Multinational Force and Observers Participation Resolution, Pub. L. No. 97–132, signed December 29, 1981. In another isolated case, on August 8, 1983, President Reagan reported the deployment of two AWACS electronic surveillance planes and eight F-15 fighter planes and ground logistical support forces to Sudan to assist Chad and other friendly governments helping Chad against Libyan and rebel forces.

Three of President Reagan's reports concerned Lebanon. On August 24, 1982, he reported the dispatch of 800 Marines to serve in the multinational force to assist in the withdrawal of members of the Palestine Liberation Organization force from Lebanon. On September 29, 1982, President Reagan reported the deployment of 1,200 Marines to serve in a temporary multinational force to facilitate the restoration of Lebanese government sovereignty. On August 30, 1983, after the Marines participating in the Multinational Force in Lebanon were fired upon and two were killed, President Reagan submitted a report "consistent with section 4 of the War Powers Resolution."

On October 25, 1983, President Reagan reported that U.S. Army and Marine personnel had begun landing in Grenada to join collective security forces of the Organization of Eastern Caribbean States in assisting in the restoration of law and order in Grenada and to facilitate the protection and evacuation of U.S. citizens.

Two reports dealt with Libya. On March 26, 1986, President Reagan reported that, on March 24th and 25th, U.S. forces conducting freedom of navigation exercises in the Gulf of Sidra had been attacked by Libyan missiles and in response, the United States fired missiles at Libyan vessels and at Sirte, the missile site. On April 16, 1986, he reported that on April 14th U.S. air and naval forces had conducted bombing strikes on terrorist facilities and military installations in Libya.

The other six reports concerned the buildup in the Persian Gulf. On September 23, 1987, President Reagan reported that two U.S. helicopters had fired on an Iranian landing craft observed laying mines in the Gulf. On October 10, 1987, he reported that three U.S. helicopters were fired upon by small Iranian naval vessels and the helicopters returned fire and sank one of the vessels. On October 20, 1987, he reported U.S. destruction of the Iranian Rashadat armed platform used to support attacks and mine-laying operations. On April 19, 1988, President Reagan reported that in response to the U.S.S. *Samuel B. Roberts* striking a mine, U.S. Armed Forces attacked and "neutralized" two Iranian oil platforms and, after further Iranian attacks, damaged or sank Iranian vessels. A report of July 4, 1988, stated that the U.S.S. *Vincennes* and U.S.S. *Elmer Montgomery* had fired upon approaching Iranian small craft, sinking two. Firing in self-defense at what it believed to be a hostile Iranian military aircraft, the *Vincennes* had shot down an Iranian civilian airliner, and the President expressed deep regret. Finally, on July 14, 1988, President Reagan reported that two U.S. helicopters, responding to a distress call from a Japanese-owned Panamanian tanker, were fired at by two small Iranian boats and returned the fire.

President Bush submitted seven reports. On December 2, 1989, President Bush submitted a report describing assistance of combat air patrols to help the Aquino government in the Philippines restore order and to protect American lives. On December 21, 1989, President Bush reported "consistent with the War Powers Resolution" that he had ordered U.S. military forces to Panama to protect the lives of American citizens and bring General Noriega to justice. On August 6, 1990, President Bush reported to Congress that following discussions with congressional leaders, a reinforced rifle company had been sent to provide additional security to the U.S. Embassy in Monrovia and helicopter teams had evacuated U.S. citizens from Liberia. The report did not mention the War Powers Resolution or cite any authority.

Three reports related to the Iraqi invasion of Kuwait. On August 9, 1990, President Bush reported that he had ordered the forward deployment of substantial elements of the U.S. Armed Forces into the Persian Gulf region to help defend Saudi Arabia after the invasion of Kuwait by Iraq. On November 16, 1990 he reported, without mention of the War Powers Resolution but referring to the August 9 letter, the continued buildup to ensure "an adequate offensive military option." On January 18, 1991, President Bush reported to Congress that on January 16th he had directed U.S. Armed Forces to commence combat operations against Iraqi forces and military targets in Iraq and Kuwait. On January 12th Congress had passed the Authorization for Use of Military Force against Iraq Resolution (Pub. L. No. 102-1), which stated it was the specific statutory authorization required by the War Powers Resolution.

Finally, on December 10, 1992, President Bush reported the introduction of forces into Somalia for humanitarian purposes. He said it was not intended that the forces become involved in hostilities, but they were equipped to take measures necessary to achieve their objectives and defend themselves.

Instances Not Reported

Presidents have also failed to report the introduction of forces into numerous situations which might be considered subject to the reporting requirements or which were similar to earlier situations that had been reported. During President Ford's tenure there were three such incidents: the evacuation of Americans from Cyprus in July 1974, from Lebanon in June 1976, and the augmentation of troops in Korea in August 1976 after a tree-cutting incident in the demilitarized zone. During President Carter's tenure the May 1978 evacuations from Zaire raised questions because they were not reported.

During President Reagan's terms ten situations were not reported: the augmentation of military advisers in El Salvador in February 1981; the shooting down of two Libyan jets over the Gulf of Sidra in August 1981 and over the Mediterranean in January 1989; the dispatch of AWACs to Egypt in March 1983; a series of military exercises in Honduras from 1983 to 1989; the shooting down of two Iranian fighter planes in the Persian Gulf by Saudi Arabian jet fighter planes assisted by U.S. surveillance and refueling planes in June 1984; the interception of an Egyptian airliner carrying hijackers of the Italian cruise ship *Achille Lauro* in October 1985; Bolivian anti-drug assistance in July 1986; the build-up of the fleet in the Persian Gulf area in connection with the escorting of Kuwait oil tankers in 1987; and increases of military personnel in Panama in March 1988.

Under President Bush four situations were not reported. These were the augmentation of forces in Panama in May 1989; the September 1989 dispatch of military assistance to Colombia, Bolivia, and Peru in the Andean Initiative in the war on drugs; and evacuations of American nationals from Zaire in September 1991 and from Sierra Leone in May 1992.

MAJOR CASES AND ISSUES

Following is further discussion of the major cases reported, or not reported, under the War Powers Resolution and the issues they raised concerning it.

Vietnam Evacuations and *Mayaguez*: Problems with Consultation

As the United States ended its participation in the Vietnam War, on three occasions in April 1975 President Ford used U.S. forces to help evacuate American citizens and foreign nationals. In addition, in May 1975 President Ford ordered the retaking of a U.S. merchant vessel, the S.S. *Mayaguez* which had been seized by Cambodian naval patrol vessels. He reported all four actions to Congress citing the War Powers Resolution. The report on the *Mayaguez* recapture was the only War Powers report to date to specifically cite section 4(a)(1), but the question of the time limit was moot because the action was over by the time the report was filed.

A major problem revealed by these first four cases was legislative-executive differences on the meaning of consultation. The Ford Administration held that it had met the consultation requirement because the President had directed that congressional leaders be notified prior to the actual commencement of the introduction of armed forces. Members of Congress contended that adequate consultation required the President to seek congressional opinion, and take it into account, prior to making a decision to commit armed forces.[20]

It also became apparent in these early incidents that the consultation and reporting requirements in the War Powers Resolution were not parallel. Whereas reporting was required for a variety of situations, consultation was required only for the introduction of forces into hostilities or imminent hostilities, the situation that triggered the time limit. State Department Legal Adviser Monroe Leigh said that for the Danang sealift consultation was not technically required because the administration was confident that the evacuation forces would not be involved in hostilities.[21]

Iran Hostage Rescue Attempt: Consultation and Secrecy

After the unsuccessful attempt to rescue the Iranian hostages on April 24, 1980, President Carter submitted a report to Congress to meet the requirements of the War Powers Resolution—but he did not consult in advance. The Administration took the position that consultation was not required because the mission was a rescue attempt, not an act of force or aggression against Iran. In addition, the Administration contended that consultation was not possible or required because the mission depended upon total surprise.

Some Members of Congress complained about the lack of consultation, especially because legislative-executive meetings had been going on since the Iranian crisis had begun the previous year. Just before the rescue attempt the Senate Foreign Relations Committee had sent a letter to Secretary of State Cyrus Vance requesting formal consultations under the War Powers Resolution. Moreover, shortly before the rescue was attempted, the President had outlined plans for a rescue attempt to Senate Majority Leader Robert Byrd but did not say it was about to begin. In Senate Foreign Relations Committee hearings on the incident, Chairman Frank Church stressed three points to consider for the future. First, consultation required giving Congress an opportunity to participate in the decision-making process, not just informing Congress that an operation was underway. Second, the judgment could not be made unilaterally, but should be made by the President and Congress. Third, the Iranian hearings showed lack of agreement on the question of who in Congress should be consulted.[22]

El Salvador: Military Advisers and Potential Hostilities

One of the first cases to generate substantial controversy because it was never reported under the War Powers Resolution was the dispatch of U.S. military advisers to El Salvador. At the end of February 1981, the Department of State announced the dispatch of 20 additional military advisers to El Salvador to aid its government against guerilla warfare. There were already 19 military advisers in El Salvador sent by the Carter Administration, but their number and mission were in keeping with other ongoing military aid missions and therefore did not provoke discussion of the War Powers Resolution.[23] The Reagan Administration said the insurgents were organized and armed by Soviet bloc countries, particularly Cuba. By March 14th the Administration had authorized a total of 54 advisers, including experts in intelligence, combat training, helicopter maintenance, communications, and counterinsurgency.

Yet President Reagan did not report the situation under the War Powers Resolution. A State Department memorandum said a report was not required because the U.S. personnel were not being introduced into hostilities or a situation of imminent hostilities, but that if a change in circumstances occurred that raised the prospect of imminent hostilities, the Resolution would be complied with. A justification for not reporting under section 4(a)(2) was that the military personnel being introduced were not equipped for combat.[24] They would, it was maintained, carry only personal sidearms which they were authorized to use only in their own defense, and would not accompany Salvadoran forces in combat or on operational patrols.

Several Members of Congress introduced legislative proposals relating to the War Powers Resolution. Some proposals required a specific authorization prior to the introduction of U.S. forces into hostilities or combat in El Salvador.[25] Other proposals declared that the commitment of U.S. Armed Forces in El Salvador necessitated compliance with section 4(a) of the War Powers Resolution, requiring the President to submit a report.[26] Neither approach was adopted in legislation, but the Senate Foreign Relations Committee reported that the President had "a clear obligation under the War Powers Resolution to consult with Congress prior to any future decision to commit combat forces to El Salvador."[27] The House rejected an amendment to the Defense Authorization bill (H.R. 2969) to limit the number of active duty military advisers in El Salvador to 55, unless the President reported them under section 4(a)(1) of the War Powers Resolution,[28] but the Administration continued to observe the limit anyway.

On May 1, 1981, eleven Members of Congress challenged the President's action in *Crockett v. Reagan* by filing suit on grounds that he had violated the Constitution and the War Powers Resolution by sending the advisers to El Salvador. Eventually there were 29 co-plaintiffs, but by June 18, 1981, an equal number of Members (13 Senators and 16 Representatives) filed a motion to intervene on the other side, contending that a number of legislative measures were then pending before Congress and that Congress had ample opportunity to vote to end military assistance to El Salvador if it wished.

On October 4, 1982, U.S. District Court Judge Joyce Hens Green dismissed the suit. She ruled that Congress, not the court, must resolve the question of whether the U.S. forces in El Salvador were involved in a hostile or potentially hostile situation.[29] While there might be situations in which a court could conclude that U.S. forces were involved in hostilities, she ruled, the "subtleties of fact-finding in this situation should be left to the political branches." She noted that Congress had taken no action to show it believed the President's decision was subject to the War Powers Resolution. On November 18, 1983, the Court of Appeals for the District of Columbia Circuit affirmed the dismissal, and on June 8, 1984, the Supreme Court declined to review that decision.[30]

Honduras: Military Exercises for Purposes Beyond Training

Military exercises in Honduras in 1983 and subsequent years raised the question of when military exercises should be reported under the War Powers Resolution. Section 4(a)(2) requires the reporting of introduction of troops equipped for combat but exempts deployments which relate solely to training.

On July 27, 1983, President Reagan announced two "joint training exercises" planned for Central America and the Caribbean. One was a series of ground exercises in Honduras with the forces of Honduras and U.S. Army and Marine combat troops; the second was a series of ocean exercises with the U.S. fleet. The first contingent of U.S. troops for the maneuvers landed in Honduras on August 8, 1983, and the series continued for several years, involving thousands of ground troops plus warships and fighter planes. In addition, airstrips, radar sites, and other military facilities were constructed for the maneuvers.

The President did not report the exercises under the War Powers Resolution. He characterized the maneuvers as routine and said the United States had been regularly conducting joint exercises with Latin American countries since 1965. Some Members of Congress, on the other hand, contended that the exercises were part of a policy to support the rebels or "contras" fighting the Sandinista Government of Nicaragua and increased the possibility of U.S. military involvement in hostilities in Central America.

Several Members of Congress called for reporting the actions under the War Powers Resolution, but some sought other vehicles for maintaining congressional control.[31] In 1982 the Boland Amendment to the Defense Appropriations Act had already prohibited use of funds to overthrow the Government of Nicaragua or provoke a military exchange between Nicaragua or Honduras.[32] Variations of this amendment followed in subsequent years. After press reports in 1985 that the option of invading Nicaragua was being discussed, the Defense Authorization Act for Fiscal Year 1986 stated the sense of Congress that U.S. armed forces should not be introduced into or over Nicaragua for combat.[33] In 1986, after U.S. helicopters ferried Honduran troops to the Nicaraguan border area, Congress prohibited U.S. personnel from participating in assistance on land areas of Honduras and Costa Rica within 120 miles of the Nicaraguan border, or from entering Nicaragua to provide military advice or support to paramilitary groups operating in that country.[34] After the Iran-Contra affair, U.S. involvement receded and then died with peace agreements in the region and the 1990 electoral defeat of the Sandinista regime in Nicaragua.

Lebanon: Congress Invokes the War Powers Resolution

The War Powers Resolution faced a major test when Marines sent to participate in a multinational force in Lebanon in 1982 became the targets of hostile fire in August 1983. During this period President Reagan filed three reports under the War Powers Resolution, but he did not report under section 4(a)(1) that the forces were being introduced into hostilities or imminent hostilities, which would have triggered the 60–90 day time limit.

Nonetheless, on September 29, 1983, Congress passed the Multinational Force in Lebanon Resolution determining that the requirements of section 4(a)(1) of the War Powers Resolution became operative on August 29, 1983.[35] In the same resolution, Congress authorized the continued participation of the Marines in the multinational force for 18 months. The resolution was a compromise between Congress and the President. Congress obtained the President's signature on legislation invoking the War Powers Resolution for the first time, but the price for this concession was a congressional authorization for the U.S. troops to remain in Lebanon for 18 months.

The events leading to the compromise began on July 6, 1982, when President Reagan announced he had agreed to contribute a small contingent of U.S. troops to a multinational force for temporary peacekeeping in Lebanon. After overseeing the departure of the Palestine Liberation Organization force, the Marines in the first multinational force left Lebanon on September 10, 1982. The second dispatch of Marines to Lebanon began on September 20, 1982. President Reagan announced that the United States, France, and Italy had agreed to form a new multinational force to return to Lebanon for a limited period of time to help maintain order until the lawful authorities in Lebanon could discharge those duties.

On September 29, 1982, President Reagan submitted a report that 1,200 Marines had begun to arrive in Beirut. As a result of incidents in which Marines were killed or wounded, there was again controversy in Congress on whether the President's report should have been filed under section 4(a)(1). In mid-1983 Congress passed the Lebanon Emergency Assistance Act of 1983 requiring statutory authorization for any substantial expansion in the number or role of U.S. Armed Forces in Lebanon.[36]

President Reagan reported on the Lebanon situation for the third time on August 30, 1983, still not citing section 4(a)(1), after fighting broke out between various factions in Lebanon and two Marines were killed. The level of fighting heightened, and on September 1st, President Reagan ordered a naval task force including 2,000 Marines, fighter planes, and artillery to the shores of Lebanon. On September 12th, President Reagan authorized the Marines in Beirut to call in air strikes against forces shelling their position.

As the Marine casualties increased and the action enlarged, there were more calls in Congress for invocation of the War Powers Resolution. On September 20th, congressional leaders and President Reagan agreed on a compromise resolution invoking section 4(a)(1) and authorizing the Marines to remain for 18 months. The resolution became the first legislation to be handled under the expedited procedures of the War Powers Resolution. On September 28, the House passed H.J. Res. 364 by a vote of 270 to 161. After three days of debate, on September 29th, the Senate passed S.J. Res. 159 by a vote of 54 to 46. The House accepted the Senate bill by a vote of 253 to 156. As enacted, the resolution enumerated four occurrences that would terminate the authorization before eighteen months.

Shortly afterward, on October 23, 1983, 241 U.S. Marines in Lebanon were killed by a suicide truck bombing, bringing new questions in Congress and U.S. public opinion about U.S. participation. On February 7, 1984, President Reagan announced that the Marines would be "redeployed" and on March 30, 1984, reported to Congress that U.S. participation in the multinational force in Lebanon had ended.

Grenada: Incomplete Action on War Powers Resolution

On October 25, 1983, President Reagan reported to Congress "consistent with" the War Powers Resolution that he had ordered a landing of approximately 1,900 U.S. Army and Marine Corps personnel in Grenada. He said that the action was in response to a request from the Organization of Eastern Caribbean States which had formed a collective security force to restore order in Grenada, where anarchic conditions and serious violations of life had occurred, and to protect the lives of U.S. citizens. President Reagan met with several congressional leaders at 8 p.m. on October 24.[37] This was after the directive ordering the landing had been signed at 6 p.m., but before the actual invasion that began the next morning at 5:30 a.m.

Many Members of Congress contended that the President should have cited section 4(a)(1) of the War Powers Resolution, which would have triggered the 60–90 day time limitation. On November 1, 1983, the House supported this interpretation when it adopted, by a vote of 403–23, H.J. Res. 402 declaring that the requirements of section 4(a)(1) had become operative on October 25. H.J. Res. 402 was put on the Senate calendar but the Senate took no further action on it. The Senate had adopted a similar measure on October 28 by a vote of 64 to 20, but on

November 17th the provision was deleted in the conference report on the debt limit bill to which it was attached.[38]

On November 17th, White House spokesman Larry Speakes said the Administration had indicated that there was no need for action as the combat troops would be out within the 60–90 day time period. Speaker Thomas O'Neill took the position that, whether or not Congress passed specific legislation, the War Powers Resolution had become operative on October 25th. By December 15, 1983, all U.S. combat troops had been removed from Grenada.

Libya: Response to International Terrorism

The use of U.S. forces against Libya in 1986 focused attention on the application of the War Powers Resolution in actions against international terrorism. Tensions between the United States and Libya under the leadership of Colonel Muammar Qadhafi had been mounting for several years, particularly after terrorist incidents at the Rome and Vienna airports on December 27, 1985. On January 7, 1986, President Reagan said that the Rome and Vienna incidents were the latest in a series of brutal terrorist acts committed with Qadhafi's backing that constituted armed aggression against the United States.

The war powers issue was first raised on March 24, 1986, when Libyan forces fired missiles at U.S. aircraft operating in the Gulf of Sidra. In response, the United States fired missiles at Libyan vessels and at Sirte, the Libyan missile site involved. The U.S. presence in the Gulf of Sidra, an area claimed by Libya, was justified as an exercise to maintain freedom of the seas, but it was widely considered a show of force in response to terrorist activities.

Subsequently, on April 5, 1986, a terrorist bombing of a discotheque in West Berlin killed an American soldier. On April 14th President Reagan announced that Libya had been responsible, and U.S. Air Force planes conducted bombing strikes on headquarters, terrorist facilities, and military installations in Libya in response. President Reagan had invited approximately a dozen congressional leaders to the White House at about 4 p.m. on April 14th and discussed the situation until 6 p.m. He indicated that he had ordered the bombing raid and that the aircraft, which took off from the United Kingdom, were on their way to Libya and would reach their targets about 7 p.m.

The President reported both cases to Congress, although the report on the bombing did not cite section 4(a)(1), and the Gulf of Sidra report did not mention the War Powers Resolution at all. Since the actions were short lived, there was no problem of seeking to have the forces withdrawn, but several Members introduced bills to amend the War Powers Resolution. One bill called for improving consultation by establishing a special consultative group in Congress.[39] Others called for strengthening the President's hand in combatting terrorism by authorizing the President, notwithstanding any other provision of law, to use all measures deemed necessary to protect U.S. persons against terrorist threats.[40]

The Persian Gulf: When Are Hostilities Imminent?

The War Powers Resolution became an issue in activities in the Persian Gulf after an Iraqi aircraft fired a missile on the U.S.S. *Stark* on May 17, 1987, killing 37 U.S. sailors. The attack broached the question of whether the Iran-Iraq War had made the Persian Gulf an area of hostilities or imminent hostilities for U.S. forces. Shortly afterwards, the U.S. adoption of a policy of reflagging and providing a naval escort of Kuwaiti oil tankers through the Persian Gulf raised full force the question of whether U.S. policy risked getting the United States involved in war without congressional authorization. During 1987 U.S. Naval forces operating in the Gulf increased to 11 major warships, 6 minesweepers, and over a dozen small patrol boats, and a battleship-led formation was sent to the Northern Arabian Sea and Indian Ocean to augment an aircraft carrier battle group already there.

For several months the President did not report any of the incidents under the War Powers Resolution, although on May 20, 1987, after the *Stark* incident, Secretary of State Shultz submitted a report similar to previous war powers reports but not mentioning the Resolution. No reports were submitted after the U.S.S. *Bridgeton* struck a mine on July 24, 1987, the U.S.-chartered *Texaco-Caribbean* struck a mine on August 10, and a U.S. F-14 fighter plane fired two missiles at an Iranian aircraft perceived as threatening.

Later, however, after various military incidents on September 23, 1987, and growing congressional concern, the President began submitting reports "consistent with" the War Powers Resolution and on July 13, 1988, submitted the sixth report relating to the Persian Gulf.[41] None of the reports were submitted under section 4(a)(1) or acknowledged that U.S. forces had been introduced into hostilities or imminent hostilities. The Reagan Administration contended that the military incidents in the Persian Gulf, or isolated incidents involving defensive reactions, did not add up to hostilities or imminent hostilities as envisaged in the War Powers Resolution.

Some Members of Congress contended that if the President did not report under section 4(a)(1), Congress itself should declare that such a report should have been submitted, as it had in the Multinational Force in Lebanon Resolution. Several resolutions to this effect were introduced, some authorizing the forces to remain, but none were passed.[42] The decisive votes on the subject took place in the Senate. On September 18, 1987, the Senate voted 50–41 to table an amendment to the Defense Authorization bill (S. 1174) to apply the provisions of the War Powers Resolution. The Senate also sustained points of order against consideration of S.J. Res. 217 invoking the War Powers Resolution on December 4, 1987, and S.J. Res. 305 on June 6, 1988. Instead, the Senate opted to use legislation to assure a congressional role in the Persian Gulf policy without invoking the War Powers Resolution.

As in the case of El Salvador, some Members took the War Powers issue to court. On August 7, 1987, Representative Lowry and 110 other Members of Congress filed suit in the U.S. District Court for the District of Columbia, asking the court to declare that a report was required under section 4(a)(1). On December 18, 1987, the court dismissed the suit, holding it was a nonjusticiable political question, and that the plaintiffs' dispute was "primarily with fellow legislators."[43]

Compliance with the consultation requirement was also an issue. The Administration developed its plan for reflagging and offered it to Kuwait on March 7, 1987, prior to discussing the plan with Members of Congress. A June 15, 1987 report to Congress by the Secretary of Defense on the reflagging policy stated: "As soon as Kuwait indicated its acceptance of our offer, we began consultations with Congress which are still ongoing."[44] This was too late for congressional views to be weighed in on the initial decision, after which it became more difficult to alter the policy. Subsequently, however, considerable consultation took place and the President met with various congressional leaders prior to some actions, such as the April 1988 retaliatory actions against an Iranian oil platform involved in mine-laying.

As a result of the Persian Gulf situation, in the summer of 1988 both the House Foreign Affairs Committee and the Senate Foreign Relations Committee, which established a Special Subcommittee on War Powers, undertook extensive assessments of the War Powers Resolution. Interest in the issue waned after a cease-fire between Iran and Iraq began on August 20, 1988, and the United States reduced its forces in the Persian Gulf area.

Invasion of Panama: Little Talk of the War Powers Resolution

On December 20, 1989, President Bush ordered 14,000 U.S. military troops to Panama, in addition to 13,000 already present, for combat. On December 21st he reported to Congress under the War Powers Resolution but without citing section 4(a)(1). His stated objectives were to protect the 35,000 American citizens in Panama, restore the democratic process, preserve the integrity of the Panama Canal treaties, and apprehend General Manuel Noriega, who had been accused of massive electoral fraud in the Panamanian elections and indicted on drug trafficking charges by two U.S. federal courts. The operation proceeded swiftly and General Noriega surrendered to U.S. military authorities on January 3, 1990. President Bush said the objectives had been met, and U.S. forces were gradually withdrawn. By February 13th all combat forces had been withdrawn, leaving the strength just under the 13,597 troops stationed in Panama prior to the invasion.

The President did not consult with congressional leaders before his decision, although he did notify them a few hours in advance of the invasion. In October 1989, before it adjourned, Congress had called for the President to intensify unilateral, bilateral, and multilateral measures and consult with other nations on ways to coordinate efforts to remove General Noriega from power.[45] The Senate had adopted an amendment supporting the President's utilization of appropriate diplomatic, economic, and military options "to restore constitutional government to Panama and to remove General Noriega from his illegal control of the Republic of Panama," but had defeated an amendment authorizing the President to use U.S. military force to secure the removal of General Noriega "notwithstanding any other provision of law."[46]

The Panama action did not raise much discussion in Congress about the War Powers Resolution. This was in part because Congress was out of session. The first session of the 101st Congress had ended on November 22, 1989, and the second session did not begin until January 23, 1990, when the operation was essentially over and it appeared likely the additional combat forces would be out of Panama within 60 days of their deployment. Moreover, the President's action in Panama was very popular in American public opinion and supported by most Members of Congress. After it was over, on February 7, 1990, the House passed H. Con. Res. 262, which stated that the President had acted "decisively and appropriately in ordering United States forces to intervene in Panama."

Iraq: U.N. Auspices and a Real War

On August 2, 1990, Iraqi troops under the direction of President Saddam Hussein invaded Kuwait and moved on toward the border with Saudi Arabia. Efforts to repel the invasion led to the largest war in which the United States has been involved since the passage of the War Powers Resolution. Throughout the effort to repel the Iraqi invasion, President Bush worked in tandem with the United Nations, organizing and obtaining international support and authorization for action against Iraq.

A new issue raised, but not fully addressed, became the President's authority to commit U.S. forces to support a U.N. Security Council resolution without specific congressional authorization. The issue had not arisen during the Cold War, when the agreement among the five permanent members required for such action did not exist, except in the case of the Korean War, which was prior to the passage of the War Powers Resolution.[47]

A week after the invasion, on August 9th, President Bush reported to Congress, "consistent with the War Powers Resolution," that he had deployed U.S. armed forces to the region prepared to take action with others to deter Iraqi aggression. He did not cite section 4(a)(1) and specifically stated, "I do not believe involvement in hostilities is imminent."

The President did not consult with congressional leaders prior to the deployment, but both houses of Congress had already adopted legislation supporting efforts to end the Iraqi occupation of Kuwait, particularly economic sanctions and multilateral efforts. On August 2nd, shortly before its August recess, the Senate had adopted by a vote of 97–0 a resolution (S. Res. 318) urging the President "to act immediately, using unilateral and multilateral measures, to seek the full and unconditional withdrawal of all Iraqi forces from Kuwaiti territory" and to work for collective international sanctions against Iraq including, if economic sanctions prove inadequate, "additional multilateral actions, under Article 42 of the United Nations Charter, involving air, sea, and land forces as may be needed. . . ." Senate Foreign Relations Committee Chairman Pell stressed, however, that the measure did not authorize unilateral U.S. military actions. Also on August 2nd, the House had passed H.R. 5431 condemning the Iraqi invasion and calling for an economic embargo against Iraq.

The United Nations imposed economic sanctions against Iraq on August 7th, and the United States and United Kingdom organized an international naval interdiction effort. Later, on August 25th, the U.N. Security Council authorized "such measures as may be necessary" to halt shipping and verify cargoes that might be going to Iraq.

Both Houses of Congress adopted measures supporting the deployment but neither measure was enacted. On October 1, 1990, the House passed H.J. Res. 658 supporting the deployment by the President and citing the War Powers Resolution without stating that Section 4(a)(1) had become operative. The resolution quoted the President's statement that involvement in hostilities was not imminent. Representative Fascell stated that H.J. Res. 658 was not to be interpreted as a Gulf of Tonkin resolution that granted the President open-ended authority, and that it made clear that "a congressional decision on the issue of war or peace would have to be made through joint consultation." The Senate did not act on H.J. Res. 658.

On October 2, 1990, the Senate adopted by a vote of 96–3 S. Con. Res. 147. It stated that "Congress supports continued action by the President in accordance with the decisions of the United Nations Security Council and in accordance with United States constitutional and statutory processes, including the authorization and appropriation of funds by the Congress, to deter Iraqi aggression and to protect American lives and vital interest in the region." As in the House, Senate leaders emphasized that the resolution was not to be interpreted as an open-ended resolution similar to the Gulf of Tonkin resolution. The House did not act on S. Con. Res. 147. Congress also supported the action by appropriating funds for Operation Desert Shield in 1990.[48]

Some Members introduced legislation to establish a special consultation group, but the Administration objected to a formally established group. On October 23, 1990, Senate Majority Leader Mitchell announced that he and Speaker Foley had designated Members of the joint bipartisan leadership and committees of jurisdiction to make themselves available as a group for consultation on developments in the Persian Gulf.

On November 8, 1990, after the 101st Congress had adjourned, President Bush ordered an estimated additional 150,000 troops to the Gulf. He incurred considerable criticism because he had not informed the consultation group of the buildup although he had met with them on October 30th. After meeting with the group on November 14th, President Bush sent a second report to Congress two days later describing the continuing and increasing deployment of forces to the region. He did not cite the War Powers Resolution, but stated that the action was a continuation of the deployment described in his August 9th letter, and further that his opinion that hostilities were not imminent had not changed.

As the prospect of a war without congressional authorization increased, on November 20, 1990, Representative Dellums and 53 other Democratic Members of Congress sought a judicial order enjoining the President from offensive military operations in connection with Operation Desert Shield unless he obtained an authorization from Congress pursuant to the Constitution; the lawsuit did not mention the War Powers Resolution. On November 26th, 11 prominent law professors filed a brief in favor of the action, arguing that the Constitution clearly vested Congress with the authority to declare war, and that Federal judges should not use the political questions doctrine to avoid ruling on the issue; the American Civil Liberties Union also filed a brief in favor of the plaintiffs. On December 13th Judge Harold Greene of the Federal District Court in Washington denied the injunction, holding that the controversy was not ripe for judicial resolution because a majority of Congress had not sought relief and the executive branch had not shown sufficient commitment to a definitive course of action.[49] The Court nonetheless stated that the Constitution prohibits the president from initiating the war without congressional authorization.

On November 29, 1990, the U.N. Security Council passed Resolution 678, which stated that unless Iraq complied with the U.N. resolutions by Jan. 15, 1991, member states were authorized to use "all necessary means" to implement the Council's resolutions and restore peace and security in the area. As the U.N. Security Council deadline for Iraqi withdrawal from Kuwait neared, President Bush indicated that if the Iraqi forces did not withdraw, he was prepared to use force to implement the U.N. Security Council resolutions. Administration officials contended that the President did not need any additional congressional authorization for this purpose.[50]

After the 102nd Congress convened on January 4th, House and Senate leaders announced they would debate U.S. policy beginning January 10th. A week before the January 15th deadline, on January 8th, 1991, President Bush requested a congressional resolution supporting the use of all necessary means to implement U.N. Security Council Resolution 678. The House, by a vote of 250 to 183, and the Senate, by a vote of 52 to 47, passed the "Authorization for Use of Military Force Against Iraq Resolution."[51] H.J. Res. 77 stated that it was intended to constitute specific statutory authorization within the meaning of Section 5(b) of the War Powers Resolution. On January 18th President Bush reported to Congress "consistent with the War Powers Resolution" that he had directed U.S. forces to commence combat operations on January 16th.

After the war began, Members of Congress strongly supported the President in his conduct of the war as Commander in Chief. On March 19, 1991, President Bush reported to Congress that the military operations had been successful, Kuwait had been liberated, and combat operations had been suspended on February 28, 1991. House Foreign Affairs Committee Chairman Dante Fascell took the position that "the War Powers Resolution is alive and well." He cited as reasons: the President had submitted a report; the debate and legislative actions taken by Congress reaffirmed Congress's proper constitutional war powers authorities; H.J. Res. 77, now Pub. L. No. 102-1, provided specific statutory authorization for the use of force, and therefore U.S. forces could continue for beyond 60 days without additional congressional authorization. Representative Fascell added, "[T]he strength and wisdom of the War Powers Resolution is that it establishes procedures and a process by which Congress can authorize the use of force in specific settings for limited purposes short of a total state of war."[52]

Nevertheless, legislative-executive tension over war powers and the War Powers Resolution promised to continue. In signing H.J. Res. 77, the authorization for the use of force against Iraq, President Bush said, "[A]s I made clear to congressional leaders at the outset, my request for congressional support did not, and my signing this resolution does not, constitute any change in the longstanding positions of the executive branch on either the President's constitutional authority to use the Armed Forces to defend vital U.S. interests or the constitutionality of the War Powers Resolution."

PROPOSED AMENDMENTS

After nineteen years of experience, controversy continues over the effectiveness and appropriateness of the War Powers Resolution as a system for maintaining a congressional role in the use of armed forces in conflict.

One view is that the War Powers Resolution is basically sound and does not need amendment.[53] In this view the legislation has brought about better communication between the two branches in times of crisis, although better consultation under the Resolution would improve the process. It has given Congress a vehicle by which it can act when a majority of Members wish to do so. In some cases the Resolution has served as a restraint on the use of armed forces by the President because of the awareness that certain actions might invoke its provisions. For example, the threat of invoking the War Powers Resolution appeared helpful in getting U.S. forces out of Grenada and in keeping the number of military advisers in El Salvador limited to 55. Although not invoked in the buildup of forces against Iraq, the War Powers Resolution heightened congressional awareness of its war powers and helped prod Congress to take a stand on the issue of authorizing the war.

A contrary view is that the War Powers Resolution has not been effective in accomplishing its objectives and needs to be strengthened or reshaped. In this view, Presidents have continued to introduce U.S. armed forces into hostilities without consulting Congress and without congressional authorization. Presidents have been able to nominally comply with the reporting requirements without triggering the teeth of the resolution. And the provision permitting Congress to withdraw troops by concurrent resolution is under a cloud because of the *Chadha* decision.

The third conceptual position is that the War Powers Resolution is an inappropriate instrument that restricts the President's effectiveness in foreign policy and should be repealed.[54] In this view, the basic premise of the War Powers Resolution is wrong because in it, Congress attempts excessive control of the deployment of U.S. military forces, encroaching on the responsibility of the President.[55] Opponents of the Resolution contend that the President needs more flexibility in the conduct of foreign policy and that the time limitation in the War Powers Resolution is unconstitutional and impractical. Some holding this view contend that Congress has always had the power, through appropriations and general lawmaking, to inquire into, support, limit, or prohibit specific uses of U.S. armed forces if there is majority support. The War Powers Resolution does not fundamentally change this equation, it is argued, but it complicates action and diverts attention from key policy questions.[56]

Various types of amendments to the War Powers Resolution have been proposed. These include returning to the version originally passed by the Senate, establishing a congressional consultation group, adding a cutoff of funds, and providing for judicial review.

Return to Senate Version: Enumerating Exceptions for Emergency Use

In 1977, Senator Eagleton proposed that the War Powers Resolution return to the original language of the version passed by the Senate, and this proposal has been made several times since. This would require prior congressional authorization for the introduction of forces into conflict abroad without a declaration of war except for the enumerated situations—(1) to respond to or forestall an armed attack against the United States; (2) to protect its armed forces outside the United States; or (3) to protect U.S. citizens while evacuating them. The amendment would eliminate the construction that the President has 60 to 90 days in which he can act militarily without authorization. Opponents fear the exceptions to forestall attacks or rescue American citizens abroad would serve as a blanket authorization and might be abused, yet that it might not provide flexibility in other circumstances.

Refine Reporting Requirement

Some observers have proposed changing the reporting requirement so that the 60-day time limit is triggered automatically when forces are introduced into situations of imminent hostilities, whether or not the President cites section 4(a)(1) or acknowledges that the situations constitute imminent hostilities.[57] Others suggest that the meaning of hostilities or imminent hostilities be further defined.

Change Time Limitation

Another approach is to change the time limit. Some would shorten the time period that the President could maintain forces in hostile situations abroad without congressional authorization from 60 to 30 days, or eliminate it altogether. Proponents contend the current War Powers Resolution gives the President 60 to 90 free days to do as he chooses. The original Senate version provided that the use of armed forces in hostilities or imminent hostilities in any of the emergency situations could not be sustained beyond 30 days without specific congressional authorization, extendable by the President upon certification of necessity for safe disengagement. Others would lengthen the time limit, perhaps to 120 days as the original House version proposed, to give the President more flexibility.

Replace Automatic Withdrawal Requirement

The War Powers Resolution has an automatic requirement for withdrawal of troops 60 days after the President submits a section 4(a)(1) report. Some Members of Congress favor replacing this provision with expedited procedures for a joint resolution to authorize the action or require disengagement. One of the main executive branch objections to the War Powers Resolution has been that the withdrawal requirement could be triggered by congressional inaction, and that adversaries can simply wait out the 60 days. This amendment would also deal with the legislative veto provision which is under a cloud because of the *Chadha* decision, by providing for withdrawal by a joint resolution. On the other hand, a joint resolution requiring disengagement could be vetoed by the President and thus would likely require a two-thirds majority vote for enactment.

Cutoff of Funds

Some proposals call for prohibiting the obligation or expenditure of funds for any use of U.S. armed forces in violation of the War Powers Resolution or laws passed under it except for the purpose of removing troops.[58] Congress could use the power of the purse to enforce this provision by refusing to appropriate further funds to continue the military action. On the other hand, some contend, Congress would remain reluctant not to appropriate funds to support U.S. armed forces abroad.

Consultation Group

While congressional leaders have been informed of some actions, they have complained that Presidents have notified them after the key decisions were made rather than seeking their advice prior to the decisions. Several proposed amendments have focused on improving consultation under the resolution, particularly by establishing a specific consultation group in Congress for this purpose. For example, Senators Byrd, Nunn, Warner, and Mitchell proposed that the President regularly consult with an initial group of six Members—the majority and minority leaders of both Chambers plus the Speaker of the House and President pro tempore of the Senate. Upon a request from a majority of this core group, the President is to consult with a permanent consultative group of 18 Members consisting of the leadership and the chairmen and ranking minority members of the Committees on Foreign Relations, Armed Services, and Intelligence. The permanent consultative group would also be able to determine that the President should have reported an introduction of forces and to introduce a joint resolution of authorization or withdrawal that would receive expedited procedures.[59] Other Members favor a consultation group, but consider that legislation is not required for designation of such a group by Congress.[60]

Another proposal would attempt to improve consultation by broadening the instances in which the President is required to consult. This proposal would cover all situations in which a President is required to report, rather than only circumstances that invoke the time limitation, as is now the case.[61]

Judicial Review

Proposals have been made that any member of Congress may bring an action in the United States District Court for the District of Columbia that the President or the U.S. Armed Forces have not complied with the Resolution.[62] The intent of this legislation is to give standing to Members to assert the interest of the House or Senate. Whether it would impel courts to exercise jurisdiction is uncertain.[63] Another proposal is to state that presidential noncompliance creates an impasse within the meaning of the ripeness doctrine, and that the political question doctrine may not be used as a grounds for dismissal.[64]

U.N. Actions

The Persian Gulf War raised the issue of the power of the President to commit U.S. forces to support a U.N. Security Council resolution or a peacekeeping or enforcement action without specific authorization from Congress. The United States has a veto in the Security Council so it cannot be bound to a resolution without its consent, but whether or not to cast a veto is determined by the executive branch. Thus the United States may be called upon to send forces in support of U.N. Security Council action without participation by Congress.

The War Powers Resolution does not exclude U.N. actions from the requirements of the Resolution, and it makes no provision concerning actions under U.N. auspices. With the end of the Cold War and the growing possibility of international actions, many observers believe this gap in the War Powers Resolution should be closed.

The matter might be handled without amendment of the War Powers Resolution. Section 6 of the U.N. Participation Act authorizes the President to negotiate special agreements with the Security Council, "which shall be subject to the approval of the Congress by appropriate Act or joint resolution, providing for the numbers and types of armed forces . . . [and] facilities . . . to be made available to the Security Council."[65] After the agreements are concluded, further authorization by Congress is not required for the President to make the forces available to the Security Council. As of yet no such agreements have been concluded. Section 7 of the U.N. Participation Act authorizes the detail of up to 1,000 personnel to serve in any noncombatant capacity for U.N. peaceful settlement actions.

Change of Name

Section 1 of the legislation established the title, "The War Powers Resolution," but the law is frequently referred to as the "War Powers Act," the title of the measure passed by the Senate. Although the latter is not technically correct, it emphasizes that a joint resolution, which is presented to the President for signature and complies with constitutional requirements for lawmaking, is a law.

Another approach would construct a new Hostilities Act[66] or Use of Force Act[67] in place of the War Powers Resolution. Possible objections to the name War Powers Resolution are reluctance to escalate international tension by implying a situation is war and the frequency of hostilities and conflicts that are not called war.

Whatever its name, a statute attempting to clarify or facilitate the congressional power to declare war and control a President's fait accompli in using military forces will in all likelihood be vetoed by the President. Any amendment strengthening the War Powers Resolution or a successor law will therefore probably require a two-thirds majority in Congress for enactment.

NOTES

1. The views expressed in this chapter are those of the author and do not necessarily represent the views of the Congressional Research Service or the Library of Congress.

2. 50 U.S.C. §§ 1541–48.

3. S. Res. 85, 91st Cong., 1st Sess., adopted June 25, 1969.

4. S. 440, 93d Cong., 1st Sess., passed Senate on July 20, 1973.

5. H.J. Res. 542, 93d Cong., 1st Sess., passed House on July 18, 1973.

6. Section 5(b), 50 U.S.C. § 1544(b), requires the President to terminate the use of force within 60 days if Congress has not specifically authorized the action, but allows for an additional 30 days for purposes of withdrawal.

7. Pub. L. No. 93–148, codified at 50 U.S.C. §§ 1541–48. For full description of the legislative history of the War Powers Resolution, see John H. Sullivan, The War Powers Resolution, A Special Study of the House Committee on Foreign Affairs, 97th Cong., 2d Sess. (1982).

8. Message of President Nixon vetoing House Joint Resolution 542, A Joint Resolution Concerning the War Powers of Congress and the President, H. Doc. No. 93–171, Oct. 24, 1973.

9. Hearings on War Powers: A Test of Compliance relative to the Danang Sealift, the Evacuation of Phnom Penh, the Evacuation of Saigon, and the Mayaguez Incident, before the House Committee on International Relations, 94th Cong., 1st Sess., at 69 (May 7 & June 4, 1975) (hereafter 1975 War Powers Hearings).

10. 462 U.S. 919 (1983).

11. *Process Gas Consumers Group v. Consumer Energy Council*, 463 U.S. 1216 (1983), *aff'g*, 673 F.2d 425 (D.C. Cir. 1982).

12. Raymond J. Celada, "Effect of the Legislative Veto Decision on the Two-House Disapproval Mechanism to Terminate U.S. Involvement in Hostilities Pursuant to Unilateral Presidential Action," C.R.S. Report, Aug. 24, 1983.

13. Hearings on the U.S. Supreme Court Decision Concerning the Legislative Veto before the House Committee on Foreign Affairs, 98th Cong., 1st Sess., at 155–57 (July 19, 20, and 21, 1983) (statement of Prof. Eugene Gressman).

14. *Id.* at 52.

15. Pub. L. No. 94–329, signed June 30, 1976, 90 Stat. 729, § 601 (this section was not classified to the code).

16. 50 U.S.C. § 1546a.

17. The Senate bill had a time limit of 30 days. *See* Report to accompany S. 440, S. Rep. 93–220, 93d Cong., 1st Sess., at 28 (1973).

18. Hearings on the War Power After 200 Years: Congress and the President at a Constitutional Impasse, before the Special Subcommittee on War Powers of the Senate Committee on Foreign Relations, 100th Cong., 2d Sess., at 1059 (July 13–Sept. 29, 1988) (S. Hearing 100–1012) (statement of Abraham D. Sofaer) ["War Power After 200 Years"].

19. Two of the reports did not mention the War Powers Resolution but met the basic requirement of reporting specified deployments or uses of forces. For the text of the reports up until 1988, see The War Powers Resolution, Relevant Documents, Correspondence, Reports, Subcommittee on Arms Control, International Security, and Science, House Committee on Foreign Affairs, 100th Cong., 2d Sess. (May 1988).

20. 1975 War Powers Hearings, *supra* note 9, at 3.

21. *Id.* at 3–9.

22. Hearings on the Situation in Iran before the Senate Committee on Foreign Relations, 96th Cong., 2nd Sess., at iii (May 8, 1980).

23. For further discussion, see Larry K. Storrs, *Congress and El Salvador*, in *Congress and Foreign Policy 1981*, at 116 (House Foreign Affairs Committee, 1982).

24. Cong. Rec., Mar. 5, 1981, at E901 (daily ed.).

25. On March 8, 1982, Senator Robert Byrd introduced the War Powers Resolution Amendment of 1982 (S. 2179) specifically providing that U.S. armed forces shall not be introduced into El Salvador for combat unless (1) the Congress has declared war or specifically authorized such use; or (2) such introduction was necessary to meet a clear and present danger of attack on the United States or to provide immediate evacuation of U.S. citizens. Similar bills were introduced in the House—e.g., H. R. 1619 and H.R. 1777 in the 98th Congress.

26. H. Con. Res. 87, 97th Cong.

27. S. Rep. 97–470, 97th Cong., 2d Sess. (June 9, 1982).

28. Cong. Rec., July 26, 1983, at H5623 (daily ed.).

29. *Crockett v. Reagan*, 558 F. Supp. 893 (D.D.C. 1982).

30. *Crockett v. Reagan*, 720 F.2d 1355 (D.C. Cir. 1983), *cert. denied*, 467 U.S. 1251 (1984).

31. For example, on July 27, 1983, Senator Gary Hart introduced S. 1692, the "War Powers in Central America Act," which would have permitted an increase in military involvement in Central America only after a joint resolution of Congress or a written request by the President stating that an increase was necessary to protect the lives of American citizens or respond to the danger of an attack on the United States.

32. The initial statutory restriction was contained in the Continuing Appropriations Resolution for 1983, Pub. L. No. 97–377. This was followed by a $24 million ceiling on intelligence agency support in fiscal year 1984.

33. Pub. L. No. 99–145, § 1451, approved Nov. 8, 1985. A similar provision was contained in the defense authorization for FY-1989, Pub. L. No. 100–180, § 1405, approved Dec. 4, 1987.

34. Continuing Appropriations Resolution, Pub. L. No. 99–591, approved Oct. 30, 1986. Continued in Pub. L. No. 100–202, approved Dec. 22, 1987.

35. Pub. L. No. 98–119, approved Oct. 12, 1983.

36. Pub. L. No. 98–43, approved June 27, 1983.

37. *U.S. Declares Goal is to Protect Americans and Restore Order*, Wash. Post, Oct. 26, 1983, at A7.

38. H. Rep. 98–566 on H.J. Res. 308 (Senate amendment number 3), Cong. Rec., Nov. 17, 1983, at H10189 (daily ed.).

39. S.J. Res. 340, introduced May 8, 1986. The bill was not acted upon, but the proposal was later incorporated in other proposed amendments.

40. S. 2335 and H.R. 4611, Anti-Terrorism Act of 1986, introduced April 17, 1986, but not acted upon.

41. For the reports, see list above under section on reporting requirements.

42. Bills to this effect in the House included H.J. Res. 387, introduced Oct. 22, 1987, which also authorized the continued presence of U.S. forces in the Gulf.

43. *Lowry v. Reagan*, 676 F. Supp. 333 (D.D.C. 1987). *See also* Raymond J. Celada, War Powers Resolution: The Controversial Act's Search for a Successful Litigation Posture, C.R.S. Report No. 88–64 A (Jan. 14, 1988).

44. Secretary of Defense Caspar W. Weinberger, A Report to the Congress on Security Arrangements in the Persian Gulf, at 14 (June 15, 1987).

45. Pub. L. No. 101–162, signed November 21, 1989.

46. Amendments to National Drug Control Strategy bill, S. 1711, Cong. Rec., Oct. 5, 1989, at S12657–94 (daily ed.).

47. In that case, the Soviet Union had absented itself from the Council temporarily, and the Security Council had requested members to supply the Republic of Korea with sufficient military assistance to repel the invasion of North Korea. President Truman ordered U.S. air, naval, and ground forces to Korea to repel the attack without any authorization from Congress. Senator Robert Taft complained on January 5, 1951, that "[T]he President simply usurped authority in violation of the laws and the Constitution, when he sent troops to Korea to carry out the resolution of the United Nations in an undeclared war." 97 Cong. Rec. at 57.

48. On September 30, 1990, Congress provided a supplemental appropriation of $1.9 billion for Operation Desert Shield for FY 1990. Pub. L. No. 101–403. In the Defense Authorization Act for FY 1991, Congress authorized imminent danger pay and other special measures for military personnel involved in the action. Pub. L. No. 101–510. In the Defense Appropriation Act for FY 1991, Congress appropriated $1 billion for transfer from the Defense Cooperation Account in support of Operation Desert Shield. Pub. L. No. 101–511.

49. *Dellums v. Bush*, 752 F. Supp. 1141 (D.D.C. 1990). In a separate case, Sergeant Michael Ray Ange also sought a preliminary injunction claiming that the President's order deploying him to the Persian Gulf exceeded the President's authority under the War Powers Clause of the Constitution and the War Powers Resolution. On December 13 U.S. District Judge Royce Lamberth dismissed the suit, holding that the Constitution leaves resolution of war powers disputes to the political branches, not the judicial branch. *Ange v. Bush*, 752 F. Supp. 509 (D.D.C. 1990).

50. Hearings on the Crisis in the Persian Gulf Region: U.S. Policy Options and Implications before the Senate Committee on Armed Services, 101st Cong., 2d Sess., at 701–02 (Sept. 11–Dec. 3, 1990) (S. Hearing 101–1071) (statement by Secretary of Defense Richard Cheney).

51. The House passed H.J. Res. 77. The Senate passed S.J. Res. 2 and then considered H.J. Res. 77 as passed. Pub. L. No. 102-1, signed Jan. 14, 1991. On January 12th, the House also adopted, by a vote of 302 to 131, H. Con. Res. 32 expressing the sense of Congress that Congress must approve any offensive military actions against Iraq.

52. Committee on Foreign Affairs, Press Release of Jan. 22, 1991, *reprinted in* Cong. Rec., Mar. 12, 1991, at E890 (daily ed.) (remarks of Rep. Dante Fascell).

53. Testimony of Rep. Dante B. Fascell, Hearings on the War Power After 200 Years, *supra* note 18, at 11–15.

54. Examples of bills to repeal the War Powers Resolution include S. 2030, introduced by Senator Barry Goldwater on October 31, 1983, and H.R. 2525, introduced by Rep. Robert Dornan on May 27, 1987.

55. Cong. Rec., July 12, 1983, at S9670 (daily ed.) (statement by Senator Barry Goldwater).

56. *See* statements of Abraham Sofaer, John Tower, Robert Turner, and others in Hearings on the War Power After 200 Years, *supra* note 18.

57. Michael J. Glennon, *The Gulf War and the Constitution*, 70 Foreign Affairs 100 (Spring 1991).

58. S.J. Res. 323, introduced by Senators Byrd, Warner, and Nunn, May 19, 1988. On September 29, 1983, Senators Cranston, Eagleton, and Stennis introduced an amendment to this effect that had been proposed in the Senate Foreign Relations Committee on July 1, 1977, reprinted in Hearings on the War Powers Resolution before the Senate Committee on Foreign Relations, 95th Cong., 1st Sess. 338 (July 13, 14 & 15, 1977).

59. S.J. Res. 323, introduced May 19, 1988.

60. *See* Hearings on the War Power After 200 Years, *supra* note 18 (testimony of Rep. Dante Fascell).

61. "Strengthening Executive-Legislative Consultation on Foreign Policy," House Foreign Affairs Committee Print, at 67 (Oct. 1983).

62. H.J. Res 462, introduced by Rep. De Fazio, Feb. 18, 1988.

63. Raymond J. Celada, The War Powers Resolution (WPR): Some Implications of S.J. Res. 323, "War Powers Resolution Amendments of 1988," C.R.S. Rep. No. 88–464 A, at 10.

64. Glennon, *supra* note 57, at 100.

65. 22 U.S.C. § 287d.

66. H.R. 3912, introduced by Rep. Lungren, Feb. 4, 1988.

67. Senator Joseph R. Biden, Jr. and John B. Ritch III, *The War Power at a Constitutional Impasse: A 'Joint Decision' Solution*, 77 Geo. L. J. 367 (1988).

4   Treaty Constraints: The United Nations Charter and War Powers

Jane E. Stromseth

The division of war powers between Congress and the President has never been free of ambiguity or tension. The Constitution gives Congress the power to declare war, to raise and support armies, to provide and maintain a navy, and to make rules for the regulation of the armed forces. The President, on the other hand, is the Commander in Chief of U.S. armed forces. Most scholars agree that the framers sought to strike a balance: the President alone could not commence "war," but he could use force to "repel sudden attacks" on the United States or its armed forces.[1] Disagreement rages, however, over what the sparse words of the Constitution should mean today, when wars are hardly ever "declared" in advance, U.S. forces are stationed on foreign soil on a semi-permanent basis, and the country's security interests are intertwined with those of other states in an increasingly interdependent international system.

Any adequate contemporary theory of the division of war powers between Congress and the President must take account of the growing role of the United Nations Security Council in responding to threats to international peace and security. In 1945, the drafters of the U.N. Charter responded to the devastation of World War II by seeking to limit the unilateral use of force as a method for resolving international disputes, and by creating a mechanism to prevent war and resolve disputes peacefully. If threats to the peace or acts of aggression did occur, however, the U.N. Security Council could recommend or decide to take action, including imposing economic and diplomatic sanctions. If necessary, it could authorize collective military enforcement action to restore international peace and security.[2]

To make U.N. enforcement action possible, the members of the United Nations pledged in Article 43 of the Charter "to make available to the Security Council, on its call and in accordance with a special agreement or agreements, armed forces . . . necessary for the purpose of maintaining international peace and security."[3] These special agreements would be negotiated "as soon as possible" and would be subject to ratification by member states "in accordance with their respective constitutional processes."[4] Once these agreements were concluded, the Security Council could make use of the earmarked national contingents as the need arose, assisted by a U.N. Military Staff Committee comprised of the Chiefs of Staff of the five permanent Security Council members.[5]

The tensions of the Cold War soon eclipsed efforts to negotiate any special agreements, leaving the Security Council dependent on the willingness of member states to provide troops on an ad hoc basis. Moreover, with the notable exception of Korea, superpower disagreement essentially barred the United Nations from authorizing collective military action[6] in response to acts of aggression—until the Persian Gulf War following Iraq's invasion of Kuwait in August 1990. Instead, during the Cold War, the United Nations developed a more limited capacity for responding to conflict, namely, deployment of lightly-armed "peacekeeping" forces with the consent of the parties to perform tasks such as monitoring ceasefires and observing the demobilization of opposing forces.[7]

Although the U.N. Charter's vision of collective security has been only imperfectly realized in the decades since 1945, the role of the U.N. Security Council seems bound to grow in the future. From the Gulf War to Bosnia and Herzegovina to internal conflicts in Somalia and elsewhere, the international community is turning increasingly to the United Nations to authorize collective responses, including the use of force if necessary. As expectations rise concerning the U.N.'s role in conflict resolution, U.N. Secretary-General Boutros Boutros-Ghali and many others have proposed reforms designed to ensure that the United Nations has the military resources and operational capacity to meet these expectations. The Secretary-General has proposed, for example, that member states finally enter into Article 43 special agreements providing forces "on call" for military enforcement actions authorized by the Security Council. He has also asked governments to earmark troops for "peace enforcement" missions—such as actively enforcing a ceasefire with military force as needed—which go beyond traditional peacekeeping.[8] Numerous other individuals, including political leaders, former U.N. officials, and scholars have proposed building a more formal U.N. military capability, including a rapid deployment force under Security Council control to respond to emerging conflicts around the world.[9]

The question of how to reconcile the demands of U.N. participation with the constitutionally imposed balance of war powers has yet to be resolved. In the face of mounting expectations and proposals for a greater U.N. military role, it is time to rethink the proper balance of war powers between Congress and the President under the U.S. Constitution in cases in which the U.N. Security Council has authorized the use of military force. Does Congress's constitutional power to declare war apply in such cases, or does U.N. authorization provide the President with sufficient legal authority to commit U.S. forces to armed conflict without the prior consent of Congress? Does it make a difference, in constitutional terms, whether the conflict is large or small, whether the forces are placed under a U.N. command or under U.S. command, or whether the troops are deployed as peacekeepers or as "peace enforcers"?

The United States' ability to help the Security Council respond effectively to threats to peace and security will be undermined if the domestic terms and conditions for the use of American forces in U.N.-authorized military actions are not resolved. At the heart of the matter is the scope of the President's constitutional authority to commit U.S. military forces to hostilities, either in the U.N. context or more generally. Few scholars or politicians question the President's authority to take emergency military action to defend against an attack or imminent attack on the United States or to protect U.S. military forces and citizens abroad. Beyond these generally agreed examples of "repelling sudden attack," however, there are tremendous differences of view over the scope of the President's authority to send U.S. forces to combat.[10] Naturally, these differences lead to different conclusions regarding the effect of Security Council authorization of the use of force on the President's authority.

The issue of the proper division of war powers between Congress and the President in the U.N. context has arisen directly in three historical periods: in 1945 when the Senate reviewed the U.N. Charter and gave its consent to the treaty's ratification; in the early 1950s during the conflict in Korea; and in the recent Persian Gulf War. Three distinct conceptions or models of the respective war powers of Congress and the President have emerged from this historical experience.[11] These three approaches—which may be called the *contract* model, the *police power* model, and the *political accommodation* model, respectively, offer quite different answers to the war powers questions that will arise in the years ahead with respect to U.N.-authorized military actions. After describing the emergence of each model historically, this chapter explores the implications of each approach for the future and ultimately argues in favor of building on the contract model first articulated in 1945.

THE UNITED NATIONS AND CONSTITUTIONAL WAR POWERS

The 1945 Debates and the U.N. Participation Act

When the Senate gave its advice and consent to ratification of the U.N. Charter in 1945,[12] Senators understood that the Charter would give far-reaching powers to the Security Council. Under Article 39, the Security Council would have the authority to determine whether a threat to the peace, breach of the peace, or act of aggression existed, and to recommend or decide what action to take in response, including collective military enforcement action under Article 42 to restore international peace and security. These provisions raised war powers concerns that were not lost on members of Congress.

Several Senators argued that the war powers of Congress were being delegated unconstitutionally to the Security Council or to the U.S. Representative on the Security Council, who would vote at the direction of the President.[13] For these Senators, the argument that U.N.-approved military actions would be defensive actions to repel or prevent attack—and thus within the President's constitutional authority—was not dispositive, because U.S. troops could be used to defend not only Americans but citizens of other states as well "wherever and whenever the [Security] Council determines that there is an aggression."[14] Recognizing the difficulty of reaching agreement on the scope of the President's "police" power under the U.N. Charter, Senator Millikin urged his colleagues to establish a practical definition of the division of war powers between Congress and the President through an Article 43 agreement.[15]

Under this *contract* or *special agreement* approach, which was ultimately codified in the U.N. Participation Act of 1945, a limited number of U.S. forces would be made available to the Security Council through a special agreement concluded pursuant to Article 43 of the Charter. That agreement would delineate the number and type of armed forces placed "on call" to the Security Council as well as their degree of readiness and general location. Under the U.N. Participation Act, Congress would have to approve any special agreement through a joint resolution or act; the President could not conclude such an agreement on his own.[16] Once Congress approved the agreement, the President could use those designated forces in military enforcement actions approved by the U.N. Security Council.[17] If the President wanted to provide the Security Council with additional forces *beyond* those set forth in the agreement, however, he would need to return to Congress for authorization.

By drawing this line, the 79th Congress sought to strike a war powers balance, giving the Security Council and the President the ability to respond promptly to threats to the peace in small-scale actions, but preserving Congress's constitutional power to declare war in cases involving a large-scale mobilization of U.S. forces, where the risk of war and great physical sacrifice was real. An overwhelming majority in Congress concluded that this limited delegation of U.S. forces to the Security Council was constitutionally acceptable both because Congress had to approve any special agreement in the first place, and because these forces would be used only in U.N.-authorized "police actions" of limited scope designed to preserve the peace, in contrast to full-scale mobilization of U.S. forces in "war." As it turned out, however, Article 43 agreements were early casualties of the Cold War, and this "contractual" war powers model has yet to be implemented.

The Korean War

A second war powers approach—a *police power* model—emerged during the Korean War, when President Truman claimed the authority to send U.S. forces to combat as part of a U.N.-approved military action without the prior consent of Congress. Shortly after North Korean forces attacked the Republic of Korea in June 1950, the U.N. Security Council met in an emergency session. On June 25th, the Council adopted a resolution proposed by the United States, which denounced the attack and called for an immediate ceasefire and withdrawal of North Korean forces to the 38th parallel.[18] The Security Council also called upon all U.N. members to "render every assistance to the United Nations in the execution of this resolution."[19] Although the Security Council did not authorize member states to use force to "repel the armed attack" until June 27th,[20] after President Truman had already ordered U.S. air and naval forces to combat in support of the Republic of Korea, Truman defended his actions as a response to the U.N.'s call for assistance.[21] Moreover, he argued, "if this challenge had not been met squarely, the effectiveness of the United Nations would have been all but ended."[22]

Members of Congress of both parties rallied in support of Truman's decisions, despite the fact that U.S. air, naval, and ground troops were deployed to Korea without prior authorization from Congress. Most members supported the substance of Truman's decisions and believed the President needed to act promptly in the Korean emergency. The U.N. Security Council resolutions calling for assistance from U.N. member states were also an important factor in congressional support for Truman's actions.

When a few Senators challenged the President's authority to send U.S. troops into combat without the prior approval of Congress,[23] Truman and his Administration advanced several arguments in favor of a police power model of presidential authority in the U.N. context. First, Truman contended that the President has customary or traditional power as Commander in Chief to take military action not only to defend the United States, its forces and citizens, but also to protect "the broad interests of American foreign policy"—including preserving the U.N.'s effectiveness as an institution and responding to threats to the Charter as they arise.[24] Second, Truman argued, because the U.N. Charter is a treaty which the President has the duty to faithfully execute, he has the authority to send U.S. troops to combat—without the consent of Congress—once the Security Council has voted in favor of such action.[25] A third argument made by Truman in support of a police power model was that any U.N.-authorized use of force—by definition—is an international "police action," *not* a war, and thus Congress's power to declare war does not apply. In short, under this model, the President has unilateral authority to send U.S. forces to combat in U.N. "police actions," regardless of their size or riskiness.

The Persian Gulf War

The police power model was also invoked by the Bush Administration following Iraq's 1990 invasion of Kuwait. At U.S. urging, the Security Council decided on November 29, 1990 to authorize the use of force to expel Iraqi forces from Kuwait unless Saddam Hussein removed them by January 15, 1991.[26] As that deadline approached, Bush Administration officials argued, like President Truman before them, that prior congressional approval was not required to send U.S. forces to combat because the Security Council had authorized the collective use of force.[27] President Bush ultimately decided to seek the support of Congress before taking military action against Iraq, which Congress provided on January 12, 1991, but he persisted in the view that he did not need "permission from some old goat in the United States Congress to kick Saddam Hussein out of Kuwait."[28]

To the majority of Congress, however, the *Constitution* itself—and not just prudent politics—required congressional approval before nearly half a million

American troops were sent into combat against Iraq. As one Senator put it, such action would "plainly be war,"[29] which required the consent of Congress. In the end, Congress authorized the use of force against Iraq,[30] but did not endorse any open-ended claims of presidential power to engage in U.N. "police actions." Indeed, most members of Congress soundly rejected the police power arguments which had garnered congressional support in the early days of the Korean War, namely, that the President has constitutional authority to commit U.S. forces to combat by virtue of Security Council authorization or, more broadly, to protect the U.S. foreign policy interests embodied in the U.N. Charter. Congress in 1991 insisted that *it* was the body with the constitutional authority to decide whether U.S. forces should be sent to combat against Iraq.[31]

The fact that Congress finally asserted itself and the President ultimately sought its support before taking military action against Iraq suggests a third war powers model—one of *political accommodation*. Under this approach, the President needs congressional approval before committing substantial American forces to combat as part of a military action authorized by the U.N. Security Council. Such a commitment implicates Congress's constitutional power to declare war because of the degree of physical sacrifice and the risk of loss involved. In contrast, participation in smaller and less risky U.N. actions would fall, under this model, within the President's own inherent or customary authority to take defensive action on a limited scale.[32] The support in Congress for President Bush's decision to send troops to Somalia, and the minimal concern initially expressed over his failure to seek the approval of Congress in advance, provides another example of the political accommodation approach.[33]

THREE MODELS OF THE DIVISION OF CONSTITUTIONAL WAR POWERS WITH RESPECT TO U.N. ACTIONS

The three war powers models discussed above differ significantly in their view of the proper division of war powers between Congress and the President with respect to U.N.-authorized military actions. The "police power" model articulated during the Korean War and the Gulf War is premised on an expansive conception of the President's constitutional war powers and views congressional authorization as essentially irrelevant in U.N. "police actions." The "political accommodation" and "contract" models, in contrast, are premised on the view that the war powers of Congress remain relevant in the U.N. context, particularly in any large-scale action that places substantial numbers of American forces at risk. The remaining question is which model provides the soundest foundation for the future.

In addressing this question, it is important to distinguish between different types of U.N.-authorized military operations and the forces likely to conduct them in the future, because their implications for the constitutional division of war powers may differ. At one end of the spectrum are large-scale enforcement actions authorized by the Security Council under Chapter VII of the U.N. Charter to restore international peace and security. Such large-scale actions can be undertaken in a variety of ways. The U.N.-authorized military actions in Korea and the Persian Gulf were carried out by a coalition of national forces acting at the behest of the Security Council and under the overall command of an American general.[34] Ad hoc coalitions of national forces may continue to act on behalf of the Security Council in the future under "delegated mandates"[35] as in the Gulf, which leave considerable discretion over military objectives and tactics in the hands of the state commanding the troops. It also may be possible (and desirable) to create delegated mandates that are more specific about political goals and provide for greater collective political control by the Security Council.[36]

Now that Cold War tensions have dissipated, however, U.N. Secretary-General Boutros-Ghali has urged member states to give the Security Council a more permanent capacity for collective military action by negotiating Article 43 agreements, thereby placing designated national forces, assistance, and facilities "on call" for use by the Security Council.[37] So far, the response from the United States and Great Britain has been cautious, in large part because of concerns about the role that the Military Staff Committee created by the U.N. Charter might play in commanding such forces.[38]

At the other end of the spectrum are classic U.N. "peacekeeping" operations, in which unarmed observers or lightly armed forces are supplied with the consent of the parties to undertake tasks such as monitoring a ceasefire, safeguarding local stability so that elections can be held, and monitoring human rights practices. Peacekeeping forces have traditionally been under the political control of the Security Council and under the overall command of the Secretary-General, with forces supplied by member states on a voluntary basis. While some states already hold peacekeeping forces ready for U.N. action, the Secretary-General has urged member states to confirm through an exchange of letters with the U.N. Secretariat "stand-by arrangements . . . concerning the kind and number of skilled personnel they will be prepared to offer the United Nations as the needs of new operations arise."[39]

American participation in peacekeeping operations has been minimal up to this point, but this may change now that Cold War tensions no longer serve as an effective bar to such participation.[40] Based upon factors such as size and type of mission, force capacity and risk, it is likely that the war powers issue will be easier to resolve with respect to peacekeeping operations than with respect to Chapter VII enforcement. Indeed, under section 7 of the U.N. Participation Act, the President currently is authorized to detail up to 1,000 armed forces personnel to U.N. operations aimed at the peaceful settlement of disputes to serve as "observers, guards, or in any noncombatant capacity," so long as the operation does not involve "the employment of armed forces contemplated by Chapter VII" of the U.N. Charter.[41]

In a world ridden with ethnic and secessionist conflicts and civil war, however, the United Nations will increasingly be called upon to engage in actions that fall somewhere between consensual peacekeeping and large-scale military enforcement action. In situations where there is no peace to be kept, and where only some of the parties desire a U.N. presence, the United Nations may authorize "peace enforcement" actions, such as actively restoring and maintaining a ceasefire (not just monitoring one) or assisting in the delivery of humanitarian relief in hostile territory.[42] Such forces would need to be armed more heavily than traditional peacekeepers and would be deployed in situations where armed conflict is likely to occur. The Security Council's resolution of August 1992 authorizing member states to take "all measures necessary" to facilitate delivery of "humanitarian assistance" wherever it is needed in Bosnia and Herzegovina—although not fully implemented—is an example of one of the more difficult "peace enforcement" missions the United Nations may undertake in the future.[43] Another example is the U.N.-approved military operation in Somalia, in which forces predominantly from the United States were authorized to use "all necessary means" to establish "a secure environment for humanitarian relief operations."[44] Adopted under Chapter VII, these resolutions stop well short of authorizing major military enforcement action but clearly go beyond traditional peacekeeping.

The need for forces trained and equipped to engage in such "peace enforcement" missions seems increasingly clear, even as questions concerning the precise nature and command of such forces remain open. The Security Council resolution concerning humanitarian relief in Bosnia, as well as a subsequent resolution authorizing enforcement of the economic embargo against Serbia, both called on states to take action "nationally or through regional agencies or arrangements"—effectively operating under a "delegated mandate" approach.[45] The Somalia resolution authorized the Secretary-General and the concerned member states "to make the necessary arrangements for the unified command and control of the forces involved," reflecting the offer of troops from the United States which was conditioned on American command.[46]

Such ad hoc arrangements provide valuable flexibility in responding to unfolding crises, but they also pose difficulties. They delegate considerable political and military control to individual states at a time when a growing number of states are expressing opposition to repeated reliance on single-nation command arrangements of the sort used in the Persian Gulf.[47] The Somalia resolution attempted to meet such concerns in a number of ways. It called for the establishment of "appropriate mechanisms for coordination" between the United Nations and the allied forces, invited the Secretary-General to establish a U.N. peacekeeping liaison staff at the headquarters of the unified command, and requested regular reporting to the Security Council on the progress of the mission "to enable the Council to make the necessary decision for a prompt transition to continued peacekeeping operations."[48]

Another difficulty in continuing to rely on ad hoc arrangements is that troops may not always be available on a prompt enough basis. After all, starvation in Somalia continued for months before the United States offered to provide forces to ensure the delivery of relief supplies. Thus, some commentators favor creating a more formal U.N. capacity for "peace enforcement" actions in the future, such as a rapid-deployment force of earmarked national troops which would train together on a regular basis and could be deployed promptly by the Security Council as the need arose.[49] Whether such forces would be created through Article 43 agreements or through some other mechanism has yet to be resolved.[50]

In short, the U.N. Security Council is likely to authorize a wide variety of military operations in the future, ranging from consensual peacekeeping to small-scale peace enforcement to large-scale military action. The constitutional balance of war powers between Congress and the President may differ depending on the nature, size, and risk of the U.N. military action. The value of the three war powers models thus will depend, at least in part, on their responsiveness to these factors.

The Police Power Model

The police power model of war powers does not adequately take into account the varying characteristics of future U.N.-authorized military responses to international crises. The model is based upon an expansive conception of presidential power reinforced by the commitments embodied in the U.N. Charter. With no special agreements in place to set limits on the forces at the President's disposal, the police power model posits broad authority for the President to deploy U.S. forces in *any* U.N.-authorized use of force, regardless of its size or character.

Three distinct claims underlie the police power conception, each of which was advanced directly by the Truman Administration and implicitly, if not explicitly, by the Bush Administration or its supporters.[51] First, under this model, the President's customary or "traditional" power as Commander in Chief to take military action abroad is not limited to defensive actions to protect the United States and its citizens, but includes the authority to use military force without congressional consent to protect "the broad interests of American foreign policy."[52] Those broad interests include preserving the effectiveness of the United Nations as an institution, and responding to threats to the U.N. Charter as they arise.

Grounding an expansive notion of presidential power in the global commitments and responsibilities undertaken by the United States in the U.N. Charter may have been acceptable to most members of Congress during the early days of the Korean crisis—the first major military emergency of the Cold War. But in a non-emergency context, such as sending substantial troops to Europe as part of the North Atlantic Treaty Organization, Congress was not willing to let the President alone determine what was in "the broad interests of American foreign policy."[53] Similarly, as the Persian Gulf crisis unfolded, many members of Congress differed with the President over how best to respond to the threat that Iraq's invasion of Kuwait posed to the U.N. Charter and to U.S. political and economic interests.

To claim that the President has unilateral authority as Commander in Chief to send U.S. forces to combat whenever he thinks it is in the interests of the United States or the United Nations to do so, regardless of the size or riskiness of the operation, is essentially to read Congress's power to declare war out of the Constitution. Such an expansive conception of executive war power has virtually no limits. It relegates Congress to the role of bystander in questions of war and peace, rather than a partner in determining the nature and scope of U.S. participation in international institutions such as the United Nations which have the authority to use military force. In a world no longer dominated by Cold War tensions, it is hard to see any political, let alone constitutional, basis for such a vision.

A second, related claim advanced by proponents of the police power model is that the U.N. Charter—a treaty ratified by the United States—is the "law of the land," which the President has the constitutional duty to "faithfully execute."[54] As the Truman Administration put it: "The power to send troops abroad is certainly one of the powers which the President may exercise in carrying out such a treaty as . . . the United Nations Charter."[55]

Faithfully executing the U.N. Charter, however, does not necessarily require the use of force. In neither Korea nor the Persian Gulf did the Security Council require member states to use force—it simply authorized them to do so. Thus, in neither case was there a treaty obligation to commit American soldiers to combat.[56] More fundamentally, the Constitution stands supreme to any treaty. The war powers granted to Congress as a whole by the U.S. Constitution cannot be preempted by a treaty approved by the Senate alone,[57] nor did the U.N. Charter attempt to do this. Instead, the Charter explicitly provided that any forces committed to the Security Council through the anticipated special agreements would be subject to the "constitutional processes" of member states.[58] Moreover, the Senate gave its advice and consent to the Charter on the explicit understanding that Congress would approve any special agreements, and that the President would return to Congress for any additional forces required in a U.N.-authorized military enforcement action.[59]

The absence of special agreements does not mean the President can "execute" the U.N. Charter in any way he sees fit. On the contrary, under the U.N. Participation Act, the President can claim no authorization from the Congress to use forces in the absence of a special agreement.[60] The President thus must either come to Congress for specific authorization in an individual case or act within his own inherent constitutional authority to repel sudden attacks. Furthermore, the scope of that authority should be interpreted narrowly in the U.N. context given Congress's clear intent in the U.N.P.A. to participate in any decision to commit forces to the U.N. Security Council. In sum, the President cannot "execute" the U.N. Charter without reference to the war powers of Congress.

The third claim of police power proponents begins with a sound insight and then takes it too far. The sound insight is that there is an important difference between the unilateral decision of a state to go to "war," on the one hand, and the collective authorization of force by the Security Council to protect international peace and security, on the other. The difference between these two situations as a matter of international law is clear. Proponents go too far, however, in claiming that any U.N.-authorized "police action" regardless of its size—by definition—does not constitute "war" under the U.S. Constitution, and thus is not subject to Congress's constitutional power to "declare war."[61]

Some of these proponents argue that the Security Council is a deliberative body that can provide the same sort of check on resort to force that the framers of the Constitution sought in Congress.[62] There are several problems with this analysis, however. First, the President alone controls the U.S. vote on the Security Council and, as the Korean and Gulf War experiences make clear, the United States wields sufficient power that the President largely has been able to shape the Security Council's response to accord with his own views on whether to use force. In both

Korea and the Gulf, the Security Council hardly constituted a significant check—much less a democratic one—on the President's decision regarding whether and how to use force.

Second, the framers of the Constitution did not vest the power to declare war in one body: they vested it in two, the Senate and the House, both to restrain any rush to war and to enhance democratic participation.[63] This democratic concern underlying the constitutional division of war powers remains important in the U.N. context because American troops—by virtue of U.S. military preeminence—are likely to do much of the fighting and dying on behalf of the United Nations. Moreover, if there is time for the Security Council to deliberate about authorizing the use of force, there will usually be time for Congress to do so as well.

To be sure, Congress may decide, as the U.N. Participation Act envisions, to cede limited military forces to the control of the President and the Security Council. As in the Gulf War, however, Congress is unlikely to relinquish its power to decide in cases involving the substantial commitment of American troops in a U.N. "police action" that nevertheless "plainly is war." In short, the "this isn't war" argument would simply eliminate by definitional fiat the constitutional role of Congress as the voice of the American people, even in cases like Korea and the Persian Gulf involving combat by American soldiers on a major scale.[64]

The Political Accommodation Model

An alternative model of the division of war powers with respect to U.N.-authorized military action is the political accommodation model, which emerged during the Gulf crisis. This model focuses on the size and risk of particular U.N.-authorized actions in determining where the line between the President's "police" powers and Congress's war powers should be drawn. In the absence of an attack on the United States or its people, this approach requires congressional approval before U.S. forces are committed to combat in substantial numbers because the risk of great physical sacrifice—of war—is real.[65] In contrast, the President on his own authority could order U.S. participation in small-scale actions authorized by the Security Council that involve minimal risk of escalation,[66] including peacekeeping operations undertaken with the consent of the parties. Determinations of risk under this model are made on a case by case basis, with Congress and the President engaging in their usual struggle over their respective war powers.[67]

The political accommodation approach has advantages over the police power model. It is more consistent with the vision of shared war powers embodied in the Constitution. Under the accommodation model, U.N. authorization is no substitute for deliberation by Congress when a substantial number of American soldiers are sent into combat and asked to put their lives at risk. At the same time, the political accommodation approach aims to give the President and the Security Council the ability to respond promptly to small-scale threats to the peace while preserving for Congress the power to approve major commitments of U.S. forces. This model has the virtue of flexibility; it leaves to Congress and the President the task of reaching an accommodation in each case based on the size and risk of the mission.

The political accommodation war powers model has two drawbacks, however, one political and one conceptual. As the Gulf War experience illustrates, the political accommodation approach depends on the willingness of Congress to share in the burden and responsibility of making hard decisions about whether to use military force in the face of conflicting pressures and uncertain outcomes.[68] It also depends on the *ability* of Congress to assert its constitutional role in specific cases, which may be difficult when the President makes unilateral decisions that come close to preordaining the outcome. It is never easy to make responsible choices about authorizing military force; it is even harder when troops have already been deployed, the stakes have been raised, and the credibility of the United States as a participating member of the United Nations has been placed on the line. Unless Congress is vigilant at an early stage in a conflict, events may overtake its ability to exercise a meaningful decision on the ultimate question of committing U.S. troops to combat. In the end, if Congress is reluctant to express itself, it will be left to the predilection of the President to decide whether to seek congressional approval and, even then, Congress may find itself presented with a virtual fait accompli.

As a conceptual matter, assessments of risk and distinctions between large- and small-scale commitments of U.S. forces are generally in the eye of the beholder. The Persian Gulf conflict was an easy case—it plainly was "war" by almost anyone's definition—but future U.N.-authorized actions may be more ambiguous in size and risk, especially in volatile civil war situations where conflict can escalate beyond original expectations. While consensual peacekeeping activities will surely continue, even more demanding "peace enforcement" operations are likely in the future. The hazard of this model is that when the risk of armed conflict is present but uncertain and the consent of all the parties is not obtainable, the political accommodation approach may not provide clear enough guidance on the respective authority of the President and the Congress to decide on the commitment of U.S. forces.

A Modern Contract Model

The contract model mitigates the drawbacks of the political accommodation model by establishing statutory numerical and purpose-based limits on U.S. participation in U.N.-authorized military actions, rather than relying simply on the ongoing struggle between Congress and the President to determine the war powers balance in each case as it arises. The contract approach takes as its starting point the central role of Congress in making U.S. troops available to the United Nations, based on Congress's constitutional power to raise and support military forces and its power to declare war. Just as in 1945 the 79th Congress expected that it would determine how many troops would be placed "on call" for use by the Security Council, a modern contract model aims to ensure that Congress plays a constructive and significant role in determining the scope and nature of U.S. commitments to the United Nations *in advance* of conflict, rather than simply responding to presidential decisions in individual crises. In short, Congress is not just the "on/off switch" in particular cases; it would also help define in a more general and prospective way the contours of American participation in U.N. military operations.

Under the contract model, authorization of the use of force by the U.N. Security Council does not replace the need for democratic deliberation by the U.S. Congress. The President retains the authority to defend the United States and its citizens from "sudden attack." But when the risk of war and great physical sacrifice is real, Congress should be involved in the decision to send American troops into combat,[69] even on behalf of the United Nations. On this view, congressional authorization would be required not only to establish the basic parameters of any "permanent" U.S. troop commitments to the United Nations, but also to send any substantial number of American soldiers into combat or other hostile situations that pose the risk of war. Recognizing that terms such as "substantial" and "risk of war" are subjective, the contract model attempts, as Senator Millikin urged in 1945, to draw some practical lines indicating where the President's power to conduct "policing operations" ends and the war powers of Congress begin.[70]

A modern contract approach would build on the U.N. Participation Act, including its provision authorizing the President to negotiate a "special agreement" with the Security Council pursuant to Article 43 of the U.N. Charter, delineating the troops "on call" for its use in actions to safeguard international peace and security. The United States could probably contribute most to the United Nations in the near future by earmarking and training forces to participate in Chapter VII "peace enforcement" missions, such as securing the delivery of relief supplies in hostile territory or actively enforcing a ceasefire—missions that fall short of large-scale enforcement action but go well beyond consensual peacekeeping.[71] If the President ultimately negotiates a "special agreement" for such purposes, it would be submitted to Congress for approval by joint resolution or act, as required by the U.N.P.A.[72] Once Congress approves an agreement, the President could make the designated forces available for enforcement action authorized by the Security Council.

In reviewing any proposed agreement, Congress could, and should, insist on certain safeguards. First, the number of troops provided to the Security Council should be limited. Although Congress could ultimately raise the number in light of subsequent experience, it could initially approve as few as three or four brigades (about 2,000 troops each).[73] Forces in this range would enable the United States to participate immediately in small "peace enforcement" actions, but a more substantial commitment of American forces would require specific authorization by Congress in individual cases. Without an agreed statutory limit, Presidents may be more likely to operate on a police power model and commit U.S. forces to U.N. actions without seeking prior authorization from Congress, at least in cases where the forces are under U.S. command as part of a delegated U.N. mandate.[74]

Second, in order to promote well-informed discussion of the merits of participating in specific U.N. actions, the U.N.P.A. should be amended to establish regular and more effective channels for consultation between the President and Congress. One approach would be to form a special bipartisan select committee on U.N.-authorized military operations in each House of Congress, perhaps on the model of the House and Senate Intelligence Committees.[75] The U.N.P.A. currently requires the President to report to Congress at least once a year on U.N. activities, and to make "special current reports on decisions of the Security Council to take enforcement measures."[76] The statute could be amended to require ongoing reports on a regular basis—every two months, for instance—on all U.N.-authorized military activities (both peace enforcement and peacekeeping) in which the United States is participating. These reports could be reviewed by the select committees in each House and provide a basis for follow-up hearings. The U.N.P.A. could also be amended to require the President to consult with the committees before U.S. special agreement forces are actually sent into combat.[77]

The contract approach aims to establish clear numerical and purpose-based parameters on the commitment of U.S. troops to U.N.-authorized actions. With respect to consensual peacekeeping operations, the 1949 amendments to the U.N.P.A. provide a useful starting point but need to be refined.[78] Those provisions, contained in section 7 of the U.N.P.A., authorize the President to detail up to 1,000 U.S. armed forces personnel to U.N. activities directed at peaceful settlement of disputes and "not involving the employment of armed forces contemplated by Chapter VII of the United Nations Charter" to serve as guards, observers, or "in any noncombatant capacity."[79] Under this section, U.S. troops should be able to participate in consensual peacekeeping operations under the traditional rules of nonuse of force except in self-defense. In light of the evolution of peacekeeping operations since 1949, however, an explicit reference to "consensual peacekeeping operations" should be added to the statute as an example of an authorized activity; this will clarify the President's statutory authority. In terms of numbers, the U.N.P.A.'s current 1,000–person limit is too low to permit the United States to become a significant participant in U.N. peacekeeping operations. Earmarking and training on the order of three to six battalions (about 700 troops each) for peacekeeping functions would allow the United States to make a more substantial contribution.[80]

The War Powers Resolution[81] must be taken into account in implementing the contract approach. To avoid any uncertainty, the joint resolution or act of Congress approving an Article 43 special agreement should state expressly that it, together with the U.N.P.A., provides authorization to the President from Congress to use the earmarked forces—authorization that the War Powers Resolution requires within 60 days when U.S. forces are introduced into hostilities or situations where hostilities are imminent.[82] Peace enforcement operations under Chapter VII of the Charter, which lack the consent of all the parties and involve deployment of U.S. troops into hostile terrain, are likely to raise a risk of imminent hostilities in most cases, and thus generally will require the authorization of Congress. The section of the U.N.P.A. providing for U.S. participation in peacekeeping would also provide statutory authorization from Congress, although it is not clear the War Powers Resolution would require such authorization in cases of consensual peacekeeping, which generally will not involve U.S. troops in hostilities or situations where hostilities are imminent.[83]

The contract approach aims to create a framework around which expectations could coalesce. By preauthorizing a limited number of forces for both peace enforcement and peacekeeping, Congress would assure the President and the Security Council of an intermediate military option that could be used promptly without the need for specific congressional approval in each case. Such an approach has both domestic and international benefits. Domestically, by establishing a practical war powers balance, the contract approach reduces the risk that U.S. participation in U.N. actions will generate divisive war powers disputes between Congress and the President. By establishing in advance an agreed framework, it may help forge a stronger domestic consensus in favor of participation in U.N. actions, even in hard cases. Internationally, the ready availability of special agreement forces will strengthen the U.N.'s capacity to respond promptly to humanitarian emergencies, civil disorders, and small-scale cross-border conflicts. The existence of such forces may also help deter the outbreak or escalation of some conflicts.

As with the police power and political accommodation models, the contract approach is not problem-free. Advocates of presidential power may argue that it would limit the President's ability to respond flexibly to crises as they arise, constraining his freedom to fashion ad hoc approaches outside of the Article 43 framework. Certainly, the existence of a contract framework would undercut the validity of unilateral police power claims by the President with respect to U.N.-authorized actions. But it would not preclude the President from arguing the need to use troops other than Article 43 forces in specific cases.[84]

Advocates of congressional power, in contrast, may view the contract approach as delegating too much authority to the President, preferring instead specific approval by Congress of any commitment of U.S. forces to a nonconsensual U.N. military operation.[85] There admittedly is always a risk that deploying a small number of preauthorized troops would make it difficult for Congress to turn down a later request to approve more forces, even if it has doubts about the wisdom of the operation.[86] Nevertheless, the contract model—more than the police power or political accommodation approaches—would give Congress the chance to shape the nature of U.S. participation in future U.N. military actions in advance of conflict instead of being forced simply to respond to executive-initiated decisions in the middle of a crisis.

CONCLUSION

This chapter has examined three different models of the division of war powers between Congress and the President and has explored their implications for the kinds of military actions likely to be authorized by the U.N. Security Council in the future. As the foregoing analysis suggests, the police power model is too expansive and unbounded a view of executive power. The political accommodation model accords better with the shared war powers set forth in the Constitution, but it depends critically on the willingness of the President and the Congress to resolve war powers differences cooperatively on a case by case basis—which may not be possible if the President is determined to act unilaterally or if Congress is unwilling to act. The contract model is a principled effort to strike a practical war powers balance before a crisis even occurs, and to give the United Nations the capacity to take prompt action on a limited scale.

In addressing the constitutional war powers issues raised by U.N.-authorized military actions, the President and Congress should keep in mind the differences between the three war powers models as they work to strengthen the U.N.'s ability to respond to the many diverse threats to international peace and security. In the immediate future, the political accommodation approach may prevail, as it ultimately did during the Gulf War. In the longer term, however, the contract approach deserves greater attention than it has received thus far, if only because the types of conflicts for which it is applicable will be so numerous.

Despite its advantages, however, the contract model will not resolve all the war powers questions that will arise in the U.N. context. Member states entering into Article 43 agreements are likely to attach too many conditions and limitations upon them for Article 43 forces to be of much value in large-scale conflicts requiring a substantial force deployment. In future cases of major cross-border aggression, the Security Council may rely again on a delegated mandate approach, in which U.S. troops participate not under Article 43 agreements but as part of an ad hoc coalition of national forces assembled for a specific large-scale response.[87]

In such cases, it will largely be up to the Congress and the President—in their usual war powers tug of war—to determine whether a political accommodation will be reached or whether the police power model will reign by default. Even in these cases, however, the existence of a contract framework (and the numerical limits it establishes) would undercut the legitimacy of police power claims that the President has unilateral authority once the Security Council has authorized an action. The contract approach may thus contribute to a greater and more effective congressional role in assessing the merits of U.S. participation in specific U.N. military operations, especially when substantial numbers of American troops are involved.

NOTES

1. 2 *The Records of the Federal Convention of 1787* 318–19 (Max Farrand ed., 1911). For a discussion of the history of the Constitution's War Clause, see Chapters 1 and 2.

2. U.N. Charter, Art. 39 & Art. 42. At the same time, Article 51 affirms that "[n]othing in the present Charter shall impair the inherent right of individual or collective self-defense if an armed attack occurs against a Member of the United Nations, until the Security Council has taken the measures necessary to maintain international peace and security."

3. U.N. Charter, Art. 43, para. 1.

4. *Id.* para. 3.

5. U.N. Charter, Art. 47. The five permanent Security Council members are the United States, China, France, Great Britain, and Russia (which replaced the former Soviet Union).

6. The Security Council did impose sanctions under Chapter VII in several cases, however. In 1965, the Council called upon states to apply sanctions against Southern Rhodesia, SC Res. 217 (1965), and in 1966 it authorized Britain to take limited forcible steps to enforce those sanctions, SC Res. 221 (1966). Comprehensive mandatory economic sanctions were imposed in 1968, SC Res. 253 (1968). The Security Council also imposed an arms embargo against South Africa in 1977, SC Res. 418 (1977).

7. *See* John Mackinlay & Jarat Chopra, *Second Generation Multinational Operations*, Wash. Q. (Summer 1992), at 113; William Durch & Barry Blechman, *Keeping the Peace: The United Nations in the Emerging World Order* (1992).

8. *See* Report of the Secretary-General, An Agenda for Peace: Preventive diplomacy, peacemaking, and peace-keeping, A/47/277, S/24111, at 12–13 (June 17, 1992).

9. *See, e.g.,* Senator David Boren, *The World Needs an Army on Call*, N.Y. Times, Aug. 26, 1992, at A21; Richard Gardner, *Collective Security and the 'New World Order': What Role for the United Nations?*, in *After the Storm: Lessons from the Gulf War* 31–47 (J. Nye and R. Smith eds., 1992); Brian Urquhart, *Who Can Stop Civil Wars?*, N.Y. Times, Dec. 29, 1991, at A9.

10. See Joseph Biden & John Ritch, *The War Power at a Constitutional Impasse: A 'Joint Decision' Solution*, 77 Geo. L.J. 367, 370–72 (1988) for a comparison of "monarchist" views with a "joint decision" approach.

11. For a fuller analysis of this historical experience, see Jane Stromseth, *Rethinking War Powers: Congress, the President, and the United Nations*, 81 Geo. L.J. 597 (1993).

12. The vote was 89 to 2, 91 Cong. Rec. 8190 (July 28, 1945).

13. *See, e.g.,* 91 Cong. Rec. 7988 (1945) (Senator Wheeler); 91 Cong. Rec. 7156 (Senator Bushfield).

14. *See, e.g.,* 91 Cong. Rec. 10966 (1945) (Senator Wheeler).

15. 91 Cong. Rec. 8033 (1945).

16. United Nations Participation Act (U.N.P.A.), Pub. L. No. 79–264, 59 Stat. 621, § 6 (1945) (codified at 22 U.S.C. § 287d (1988)); *see also* Senate Foreign Relations Committee, S. Rep. No. 717, 79th Cong., 1st Sess., at 8 (1945) ("all were agreed on the basic proposition that the military agreements could not be entered into solely by executive action").

17. U.N.P.A., § 6, 22 U.S.C. § 287d.

18. U.N. Document S/1501 (1950).

19. *Id.*

20. U.N. Document S/1511 (1950).

21. *Foreign Relations of the United States*, 1950, Vol. VII, Korea, at 202 (1976). Some scholars have argued that the Korean action was an act of collective self-defense under Article 51 of the Charter rather than a U.N. enforcement action under Chapter VII because it did not involve a "decision" by the Security Council under Articles 39 and 42 but merely a recommendation. *See, e.g.,* Eugene V. Rostow, *Until What? Enforcement Action or Collective Self-Defense*, 85 Am. J. Int'l L. 506, 508 (1991). Professor Bowett argues persuasively, however, that the "better view is to regard the Korean action as enforcement action authorized by recommendations under Article 39." D.W. Bowett, *United Nations Forces* 34 (1964). Even if all the technical requirements of Article 42 were not met, the participating countries "regarded their action as essentially United Nations action under the authority of the Security Council." *Id.*; *see also id.* at 45–47.

22. Special Message to the Congress Reporting on the Situation in Korea, July 19, 1950, Papers of Harry S. Truman, 1950, at 528.

23. *See* 96 Cong. Rec. 9322 (1950) (Senator Taft); 96 Cong. Rec. 9538 (1950) (Senator Wherry).

24. *Authority of the President to Repel the Attack in Korea*, State Dep't Bull., at 174, 176–77 (July 31, 1950).

25. *Powers of the President to Send the Armed Forces Outside the United States*, Prepared for the Use of the Joint Committee Made Up of the Committee on Foreign Relations and the Committee on Armed Services of the Senate, 82d Cong., 1st Sess., at 2, 11–12, 20–21, 25, 27 (Feb. 28, 1951).

26. SC Res. 678 (1990).

27. *See, e.g.,* Testimony of Secretary of Defense Richard Cheney, in Hearings on the Crisis in the Persian Gulf Region: U.S. Policy Options and Implications before the Senate Committee on Armed Services, 101st Cong., 2nd Sess., at 701–03, 730–31 (Dec. 3, 1990).

28. Remarks of President George Bush to the Texas State Republican Convention in Dallas, Texas, 28 Weekly Comp. Pres. Doc. 1119, 1120–21 (1992).

29. 137 Cong. Rec., Jan. 10, 1991, at S101 (daily ed.) (Senator Mitchell).

30. Pub. L. No. 102–1, 105 Stat. 3 (1991) ("Authorization for Use of Military Force Against Iraq Resolution").

31. The House of Representatives, for example, adopted the Bennett-Durbin resolution by a vote of 302 to 131, affirming that any offensive military action against Iraq required prior and explicit congressional approval. 137 Cong. Rec., Jan. 12, 1991, at H405 (daily edition). For the full text of the resolution, see *id.* at H390 and the Introduction to this book.

32. *See* Peter Raven-Hansen, *Remarks* in Am. Soc'y Int'l L. Proceedings of the 85th Annual Meeting 11, 13 (1991). Raven-Hansen invokes "customary constitutional law" to argue that some "historical uses of force by the President were defensive responses to immediate attack on the United States or its people, falling within the President's implied constitutional power to repel sudden attacks." *Id.* at 11. Other historical uses of force "did not require prior congressional approval because they posed no significant risk of loss or war for the United States given their scale." *Id.* Raven-Hansen goes on to distinguish between smaller or "retail" "police actions," on the one hand, and larger or "wholesale" actions on the other, and, invoking custom, argues that "the retail-wholesale distinction suggests that there will be many cases in which the President does have inherent or customary constitutional power to deploy forces in police actions without prior congressional authorization." *Id.* at 13. In cases involving a substantial risk of loss, however, prior congressional authorization would be required. *Id.* at 11. *See also* Chapter 2.

33. In December 1992, few members of Congress thought the President's decision to send U.S. troops to Somalia to help deliver relief supplies raised a risk of imminent hostilities or war. Congressional leaders did express concern, however, about defining the objectives of the operation clearly and about the length of time U.S. forces would stay in Somalia. They also expressed a desire for ongoing consultation while the mission was underway. *See* Walter Pincus, *Lawmaker: 'Define the Mission,'* Washington Post, Dec. 4, 1992, at A20. A few members of Congress argued that Congress should take a stand on the mission. *See A Few in Congress Advising Caution, or Vote, on Somalia,* N.Y. Times, Dec. 7, 1992, at A13. In light of the uncertain risks and duration of the Somalia operation, there was wisdom in that view. Indeed, the Senate subsequently voted to authorize the deployment pursuant to the War Powers Resolution within the 60 day time limit. S.J. Res. 45, 103d Cong., 1st Sess., 139 Cong. Rec., Feb. 4, 1993, at S1368 (daily ed.). The House passed a similar version on May 25. 139 Cong. Rec. at H2744-65 (daily ed.).

34. Scholars continue to debate whether the Korean action is best viewed as a U.N. enforcement action or an exercise of collective self-defense. *See supra* note 21. The collective military action in the Persian Gulf began and ended in accordance with Security Council resolutions. *See* SC Res. 678 (1990) & SC Res. 687 (1991). Resolution 678 was adopted under Chapter VII of the U.N. Charter, but made no mention of Article 42. Professor Schachter argues that the joint military action in the Gulf is best viewed as an exercise of collective self-defense under Article 51, but he recognizes that Resolution 678 "may be read as consistent with both Article 51 and Article 42." Oscar Schachter, *United Nations Law in the Gulf Conflict,* 85 Am. J. Int'l L. 452, 462 (1991). For a full discussion, *see id.* at 457–63.

The forces in Korea operated under a U.N. flag, while the forces in the Persian Gulf operated under a U.N. "umbrella." In both cases, however, an American general was in command and the United States contributed the preponderance of the armed forces.

35. I am grateful to William Durch for introducing me to this term.

36. *See* Mackinlay and Chopra, *supra* note 7, at 127–28. The Security Council attempted to do this in the case of Somalia. *See* SC Res. 794, paras. 12, 13, 15, 18 (1992).

37. An Agenda for Peace, *supra* note 8, at 13.

38. *See, e.g.,* John Goshko and Barton Gellman, *Idea of a Potent U.N. Army Receives a Mixed Response*, Washington Post, Oct. 29, 1992, at A22; Paul Lewis, *France's UN Plan at Odds with US*, N.Y. Times, Feb. 2, 1992, at 7. Prior to the Secretary-General's proposal, Secretary of State James A. Baker III expressed reluctance to place U.S. forces under the operational command of the Military Staff Committee in testimony before Congress during the Gulf War. *See* Hearings on U.S. Policy in the Persian Gulf before the Senate Foreign Relations Committee, 101st Cong., 2d Sess., at 157 (Dec. 5, 1990).

The language of Chapter VII is flexible, however, regarding the precise role of the Military Staff Committee. Article 42 makes no mention of the Committee. Article 47 provides that the Military Staff Committee "shall be responsible under the Security Council for the strategic direction of any armed forces placed at the disposal of the Security Council," but it also says that "[q]uestions relating to the command of such forces shall be worked out subsequently." The Military Staff Committee could, for instance, be given a coordinating role in the training of Article 43 forces and could help translate the Security Council's broad political goals into "strategic objectives," with operational command issues left flexible and resolved in concrete cases, as in Korea and the Persian Gulf. Other members of the Security Council may insist on a greater role for the Military Staff Committee, however; and numerous other obstacles remain before a network of special agreements will be concluded.

39. An Agenda for Peace, *supra* note 8, at 15.

40. United States involvement still may not be desirable in cases where it would be perceived as a partisan rather than a neutral party, however.

41. 22 U.S.C. § 287d-1.

42. Other tasks might include helping to maintain law and order and guaranteeing rights of passage. *See* Mackinlay and Chopra, *supra* note 7, at 117.

43. SC Res. 770 (1992). *See also* Paul Lewis, *UN Council Votes for Use of Force for Bosnia Relief*, N.Y. Times, Aug. 14, 1992, at A1; Trevor Rowe, *UN Approves Use of Military Force for Bosnia Aid, Seeks War Crime Data*, Washington Post, Aug. 14, 1992, at A1.

44. SC Res. 794, para. 10 (1992). The resolution also called upon member states "nationally or through regional agencies or arrangements" to use "such measures as may be necessary" to ensure the "strict implementation" of a prior resolution calling for an embargo on all delivery of weapons and military equipment to Somalia. *Id.* para. 16 (referring to para. 5 of SC Res. 733 [1992]).

45. *See* SC Res. 770 para. 2 (1992); SC Res. 787, para. 12 (1992).

46. SC Res. 794, para. 12. *See also* S/24868, Letter of Nov. 29, 1992 from the Secretary-General to the Security Council, particularly the discussion of the fourth option.

47. *See* Mackinlay and Chopra, *supra* note 7, at 124–26.

48. SC Res. 794 (1992), paras. 13, 15, 18.

49. *See, e.g.,* Gardner, *supra* note 9, at 31–47; Alan K. Henrikson, *How Can the Vision of a 'New World Order' be Realized*, 16 Fletcher F. World Aff. 63, 74–77 (1992); David J. Scheffer, *Use of Force after the Cold War: Panama, Iraq and the New World Order*, in *Right v. Might* 156 (2d ed. 1991).

50. Senator Boren has proposed creating such forces through Article 43 agreements. *See* Boren, *supra* note 9. The Secretary-General has proposed a somewhat different arrangement: he favors "peace enforcement units" consisting of volunteer troops which train within their national forces but are made available to the Security Council by member states. He urges that these forces be placed under the command of the Secretary-General as are peacekeeping forces. Recognizing that "peace enforcement" is neither traditional peacekeeping nor large-scale military enforcement action, the Secretary-General cautioned that "[s]uch peace enforcement units should not be confused with the forces that may eventually be constituted under Article 43 to deal with acts of aggression or with the military personnel which Governments may agree to keep on stand-by for possible contribution to peace-keeping operations." An Agenda for Peace, *supra* note 8, at 13.

51. For a perceptive discussion and critique of "custom," "treaty," and "police action" arguments advanced during the Gulf War, see Raven-Hansen, *supra* note 32 and Chapter 2.

52. *Authority of the President to Repel the Attack in Korea, supra* note 24, at 174.

53. *Id.*; *see* Stromseth, *supra* note 11, at 635–38 (describing 1951 congressional debate over deploying troops to Europe).

54. U.S. Constitution, Art. II, § 3; Art. VI, cl. 2.

55. *Powers of the President to Send the Armed Forces Outside the United States, supra* note 25, at 20.

56. Moreover, as Professor Henkin stated in his testimony before the Senate Judiciary Committee in January 1991: "[I]t is far from obvious that the Charter gives the Security Council authority to order states to take military action, as distinguished from authorizing them to do so, or recommending that they do so. In any event, whatever the power of the Security Council in theory, in fact, it has not purported to order states to use force." Hearing on the Constitutional Roles of Congress and the President in Declaring and Waging War before the Senate Judiciary Committee, 102d Cong., 1st Sess., at 88 (1991) [hereinafter "Constitutional War Powers Hearings"]. *See also* Schachter, *supra* note 34, at 464 (arguing that Article 43 of the Charter "makes clear that member states cannot be legally bound to provide armed forces unless they have agreed to do so"). More recently, Professor Henkin has argued that "the President has constitutional authority to send U.S. forces into war pursuant to a *decision* of the Security Council, but not pursuant to its *recommendation* or *authorization*, unless Congress authorizes it." Notes from the President, Newsletter of the American Society of International Law, Nov.–Dec. 1992, at 1–2 (emphasis in original). However, Henkin argues that, even in the case of a Security Council decision, "the President may not act if Congress has forbidden it." *Id.* at 2.

During the Gulf War, the Security Council "decided" to impose economic sanctions. *See* SC Res. 661 (1990). The member states of the United Nations are obliged to carry out Security Council decisions under Articles 25 and 48 of the U.N. Charter. When it came to enforcing the sanctions against Iraq, however, the Security Council did not "decide" to take military action, but instead "call[ed] upon" member states with maritime forces in the region to help enforce the sanctions. *See* SC Res. 665, para. 1 (1990). Similarly, the Security Council "authorized," but did not require, the use of "all necessary means" to expel Iraq from Kuwait. *See* SC Res. 678, para. 2 (1990). Likewise, in the Korean War, the Security Council "recommended" that member states help "repel the armed attack." *See* U.N. Doc. S/1511 (1950).

57. *See* Michael J. Glennon, *Constitutional Diplomacy* 192–205 (1990); Note, *Congress, the President, and the Power to Commit Forces to Combat*, 81 Harv. L. Rev. 1771, 1798–1800 (1968); Raven-Hansen, *supra* note 32, at 10; S. Exec. Rep. No. 12, 95th Cong., 2d Sess., at 66 (1978) ("A treaty may not declare war because the unique legislative history

of the declaration-of-war clause . . . clearly indicates that the power was intended to reside jointly in the House of Representatives and the Senate").

58. U.N. Charter, Art. 43.

59. In addition, under section 8 of the War Powers Resolution, authority to introduce U.S. forces into hostilities "shall not be inferred . . . from any treaty" unless the treaty is implemented by legislation which specifically authorizes introducing U.S. forces into hostilities. 50 U.S.C. § 1547(2).

60. Professor Henkin argued during the Gulf crisis that the U.N. Participation Act "can be read as prohibiting the President from using armed forces" in the absence of congressionally-approved special agreements. Constitutional War Powers Hearings, *supra* note 56, at 89. Senator Taft made a similar argument in June 1950 during the Korean crisis: "there is no authority to use armed forces in support of the United Nations in the absence of some previous action by Congress dealing with the subject and outlining the general circumstances and the amount of the forces that can be used." 96 Cong. Rec. 9323 (1950).

61. *See* Thomas Franck & Faiza Patel, *UN Police Action in Lieu of War: 'The Old Order Changeth,'* 85 Am. J. Int'l L. 63, 64, 67–69 (1991); Franck, *Declare War? Congress Can't*, N.Y. Times, Dec. 11, 1990, at A27. Although the Senate Foreign Relations Committee wrote in its 1945 report on the U.N. Charter that U.N.-authorized "enforcement" action was not war and the declaration clause thus was inapplicable, the Senate debate over the U.N. Charter as well as the U.N. Participation Act reflect a clear consensus that Congress had to approve any special agreement in the first place *and* that any large-scale commitment of forces would be more akin to "war" and would require specific congressional approval. *See* Stromseth, *supra* note 11, at 604–12, 614–18. *See also* David Scheffer, *War Powers and the U.N. Charter*, Constitutional War Powers Hearings, *supra* note 56, at 5–27; Michael J. Glennon, *The Constitution and Chapter VII of the United Nations Charter*, 85 Am. J. Int'l L. 74 (1991).

62. Franck & Patel, *supra* note 61, at 74.

63. 2 *Debates in the Several State Conventions on the Adoption of the Federal Constitution* 528 (Jonathan Elliot ed., 1866) (remarks of James Wilson to the Pennsylvania ratifying convention).

64. Even if a U.N.-authorized military action is viewed as an exercise of collective self-defense, *see* Rostow, *supra* note 21, the authorization of Congress may still be constitutionally required. This would depend on the specific circumstances and on the scope of the President's authority to "repel sudden attacks," particularly attacks not launched against the United States or its forces directly. Almost all of the collective security treaties to which the United States is a party provide that collective self-defense commitments will be carried out in accordance with "constitutional processes"; and executive branch officials have regularly assured the Senate that treaty commitments would not preempt Congress's power to declare war. *See* Glennon, *supra* note 57, at 209–20. For a helpful discussion of the President's constitutional authority to take defensive action, see Chapter 2, text accompanying note 117 ("There is utterly no support in the history of the framing and ratification of the War Clause for any claim that the framers intended the implied repel-sudden-attack power of the President to include attacks on other nations.").

65. Compare *Congress, the President, and the Power to Commit Forces to Combat*, *supra* note 57, at 1775 (arguing that one of the rationales underlying the "war-declaring clause" is to give the people a say in decisions involving "a risk of great economic and physical sacrifice," which suggests the need for congressional approval "prior to engaging in 'major' hostilities above a certain level of intensity"). *See also* Louis Henkin, *Constitutionalism, Democracy, and Foreign Affairs* 33 (1990) ("The President may deploy forces for foreign policy purposes, but he may not, without congressional authorization, engage

them in hostilities that amount to war, or put them where they court war."); *id.* at 40 ("A line between foreign affairs and war is not easily drawn. . . . But it is a line drawn by the framers and redrawn by our history. . . ."). Even if Presidents dispute that congressional authorization is constitutionally required, they may still seek such authorization for prudential reasons. *See* Chapter 10 by Gary M. Stern and Morton H. Halperin, at text following note 38 (arguing that the President "should therefore cut through the entire constitutional debate about war powers by simply asserting that, as a matter of prudence and policy, force will not be used except in a true emergency to repel an attack, without the passage of a congressional resolution"); *see also* Morton H. Halperin, *The Way to Pick a Fight*, Washington Post, Jan. 10, 1993, at C4.

66. *See* Raven-Hansen, *supra* note 32, at 13 (distinguishing between "retail" and "wholesale" police actions, with only the latter requiring prior congressional authorization). The fact that only a few members of Congress raised war powers concerns about President Bush's decision to send less than 28,000 troops to Somalia without prior congressional approval reflects the political accommodation model in action. *See supra* note 33 and accompanying text.

67. Gary Born argues that a constant struggle over shared war powers is exactly what the framers wanted. *See* Constitutional War Powers Hearings, *supra* note 56, at 456 ("The Framers deliberately chose not to attempt to allocate those powers with any rigid legal formula. Rather, when threats to the Nation arise, the Framers intended that Congress and the President would work through the democratic process to decide whether military forces should be used.").

68. For a perceptive discussion of the political pressures in favor of congressional inaction, see Todd Peterson, *The Law and Politics of Shared National Security Power (Book Review)*, 59 G.W.U.L. Rev. 747, 769–72 (1991).

69. *See* Louis Henkin, *supra* note 65, at 39–40; *Congress, the President, and the Power to Commit Forces to Combat*, *supra* note 57, at 1775.

70. 91 Cong. Rec. 8033 (1945).

71. These forces could also be used for "preventive deployments" in cases where a state requests and the Security Council authorizes deployment of a U.N. force to deter an attack before it takes place.

72. 22 U.S.C. § 287d. When U.N.-authorized forces are sent into hostile or contested territory to impose peace, not just "keep" it, the risk of war will generally be present, and Congress thus should have a voice in determining U.S. participation.

73. A brigade generally consists of three battalions, plus support units. States usually contribute battalion-sized units for peacekeeping operations. Some "peace enforcement" operations may require larger military forces, however.

74. If U.S. forces are placed under a non-American U.N. commander, for instance in peacekeeping or possibly under Article 43, the President may be more reluctant to commit substantial numbers of U.S. forces and the operation may thus be self-limiting.

75. Alternatively, a special joint committee drawn from the Foreign Affairs and Armed Services Committees of both Houses could be formed.

76. 22 U.S.C. § 287b.

77. Alternatively, if the select committee idea does not get off the ground, the U.N.P.A. could be amended to require consultation between the President and a designated group of congressional leaders before U.S. special agreement forces are sent into combat. This group could include the majority and minority leaders of both Houses and the Chairperson and ranking minority member of the Armed Services, Foreign Relations, and Intelligence Committees of both Houses. Compare the Byrd-Nunn-Warner-Mitchell proposal to amend the War Powers Resolution, S.J. Res. 323, 100th Cong., 2d Sess. (May 19, 1988), discussed

in Harold Koh, *The National Security Constitution* 189–93 (1990). Consultation with an informal bipartisan leadership group was carried on during the Gulf War and was advocated by some members of Congress with respect to the Somalia operation. *See* Pincus, *supra* note 33.

78. Because American participation in consensual "peacekeeping" operations is unlikely to involve the United States in war or significant hostilities, the authorization provided by Congress in the 1949 Amendments to the U.N.P.A. may not be constitutionally required. At the same time, any standing commitment to provide armed forces to the United Nations would implicate Congress's power to raise and support armies and is certainly contingent on appropriations by Congress. Even if not constitutionally compelled, a contract approach in the peacekeeping context may help build a political consensus in favor of greater U.S. involvement in peacekeeping as well as provide some assurances to the United Nations of a serious U.S. commitment in this area.

79. 22 U.S.C. § 287d-1.

80. In a speech to the U.N. General Assembly in September 1992, President Bush indicated that U.S. troops would train for peacekeeping missions in the future, but he made no formal commitments with respect to U.S. participation in U.N. peacekeeping operations. Thomas Friedman, *Bush, in Address to U.N., Urges More Vigor in Keeping the Peace*, N.Y. Times, Sept. 22, 1992, at A1, A14.

81. Pub. L. No. 93–148, 87 Stat. 555 (1973) (codified at 50 U.S.C. §§ 1541–1548 [1982]).

82. Sections 4(a)(1) & 5(b), 50 U.S.C. §§ 1543(a)(1) & 1544(b). If the U.N.P.A. is amended to include the reporting and consultation requirements proposed above, the War Powers Resolution should also be amended to reflect the fact that the U.N.P.A.'s procedures apply when U.S. special agreement forces are used in U.N.-authorized military actions.

83. 50 U.S.C. § 1544(b). In explosive civil war situations, however, even operations that begin with the consent of the parties may sometimes break down and involve U.N. forces in hostilities. This happened, for example, during the U.N. operation in the Congo in the 1960s. *See generally* Georges Abi-Saab, *The United Nations Operation in the Congo, 1960–1964* (1978).

84. The Article 43 approach, for example, does not impair the ability of the United States to exercise its right of self-defense under Article 51 of the U.N. Charter.

85. Despite the limits built into a special agreement, concerns might still be raised about the constitutionality of an arrangement under which Congress preauthorizes the use of force without specifying the particular conflict or the specific party against whom the troops would be used. Such concerns could be addressed in several ways. Congressional approval for individual operations could be provided on a fast-track basis once the Security Council has authorized a military action. Alternatively, Congress could condition use of U.S. special agreement forces on its approval of specific U.N. operations in annual appropriations legislation.

Senator Biden, who has taken a leadership role on this issue, has advocated fairly broad predelegation to the President in U.N.-authorized actions. *See* Biden, *supra* note 10, at 397–98 (urging amendment of War Powers Resolution to provide, inter alia, that "the President, through powers vested by the Constitution and by this law, is authorized to use force abroad . . . to participate in multilateral actions undertaken under urgent circumstances and pursuant to the approval of the United Nations Security Council"). In October 1990, before the President's November troop build-up in the Persian Gulf, Biden introduced a resolution to provide statutory authorization for the President "to participate in collective security actions in the event that the United Nations directs the use of military force to counter threats to regional security posed by the Iraqi regime." 136 Cong. Rec., Oct. 2, 1990, at S14,334 (daily ed.). In July 1992, Biden introduced S.J. Res. 325 urging the President to negotiate an Article 43 special agreement with the Security Council and affirming the preauthorization provisions of the U.N.P.A. 138 Cong. Rec., July 2, 1992, at S9853 (daily ed.).

86. As one Senator argued in 1945, Congress was mistaken if it thought that by limiting the troops available to the President for U.N. actions and reserving its authority over the remainder Congress could "retain its constitutional responsibility to declare or to not declare war." This was "fantastic nonsense," Senator Johnson contended, "One does not go 1 foot down Niagara Falls and then make up his mind about the wisdom of going the rest of the way. If he even goes prowling around close to the Falls he will be sucked in. War is exactly like that. There is no halfway measure." 91 Cong. Rec. 11085 (1945).

87. There will be strong domestic pressure in such situations for the United States to assume command of the entire operation if its combined land, air, and naval forces are disproportionately represented in the forces to be employed in combat. At the same time, one cannot rule out the development of modified command structures in which a U.S. force commander would have a multinational (and possibly U.N. appointed) general staff and receive guidance from the Security Council via the Military Staff Committee and the Secretary-General. This would be especially true if U.S. forces were a smaller component of the total.

5 International Law Constraints

Jules Lobel

Most commentary on the President's constitutional power to utilize military force abroad omits any discussion of international law. The constitutional limitations on such Executive power are viewed as stemming from Congress's article I, § 8 war powers, not from any proscriptions based upon international law. Even some scholars who generally recognize that international law is part of our law view the President's constitutional powers as Commander in Chief and "sole organ of foreign affairs" as providing the Executive with the constitutional authority to use force in violation of international law.[1]

This chapter will argue that the President's foreign affairs power is constitutionally limited by international law norms. These limitations apply in two general areas. The first is the President's conduct of a war. The President's choice of weaponry within a war ought to be constitutionally circumscribed by international norms. To the extent that international law prohibits the first use of nuclear weapons or the use of biological or chemical weapons, or intentionally bombing civilians, the President's constitutional power as Commander in Chief to conduct a war is accordingly limited. Second, the President's asserted constitutional power to use limited military force against foreign nations—assassinating foreign leaders, bombing other nations to achieve certain foreign policy goals, invading another country to bring its leader back to the United States for trial, initiating covert paramilitary warfare—is also circumscribed by international law. While I have elsewhere argued that Congress's article I, § 8 war powers prevents such unilateral presidential use of force,[2] an additional constitutional limitation deriving from international law also exists. In sum, international law and constitutional law are not two separate spheres; rather the interplay between the two bodies of law must inform our definition of and limitations on Executive power.

The end of the Cold War creates both a better opportunity for and a greater importance to recognizing the interplay between international norms and constitutional distributions of power. Many of the arguments opposing international law restrictions on presidential power are now outmoded relics of a different era. To the extent a 21st century America eschews unilateralism in favor of internationalism, the incorporation of international law norms into our constitutional framework would seem both appropriate and wise.

That incorporation should take two forms. First, certain basic norms of international law prohibiting aggression, war crimes, genocide, slavery, or other human rights violations ought to be constitutionally binding on Congress and the President.[3] Second, at a minimum the President cannot constitutionally violate international law norms in the absence of explicit congressional authorization. This chapter addresses only the constitutional limitations imposed on the President acting without express congressional authorization.

SEPARATION OF POWERS AND INTERNATIONAL LAW

Our system of constitutional separation of powers recognizes that certain important foreign policy decisions, affecting the vital interests of the nation, ought not be made by one person. The framers spoke of war as "among the greatest of national calamities,"[4] and therefore legislative approval was required to ensure that we will "not hurry . . . into war,"[5] and that our constitutional system encourage "clogging rather than facilitating war."[6] Thomas Jefferson noted that even lesser hostilities such as a "reprisal" against another country was also "a very serious thing" and therefore within congressional and not the Executive's power.[7] As Alexander Hamilton explained in the *Federalist*, certain actions such as entering into treaties are "so delicate and momentous," that entrusting them "to the sole disposal" of the President is inappropriate.[8]

Decisions to conduct or launch hostilities in violation of customary international law or our treaty obligations are "delicate and momentous" due to their potential for creating serious international tensions and repercussions. These decisions must thus be distinguished from routine foreign policy determinations or even the multitude of decisions a Commander in Chief ordinarily makes in conducting warfare. Hamilton argued that the Executive had a constitutional duty to execute international law, "to avoid giving a cause of war to foreign powers."[9] As Professor Glennon has pointed out, violations of international law may lead to serious costs: diplomatic isolation, loss of prestige, countermeasures, economic sanctions, or damages.[10] The international outcry provoked by the recent Supreme Court decision permitting the Executive to kidnap Mexican citizens and bring them to trial in the United States[11] illustrates why actions in violation of international norms, if permissible at all, ought to be subject to the restraint of collective decision making.

That international law has been viewed since our republic's founding as a part of the supreme law of the land[12] also suggests that the Executive's use of force is limited by that body of law. For the Executive is under a constitutional duty to faithfully execute the law of the land.[13] At minimum, the incorporation of international law into federal law indicates that decisions to breach international law are potentially serious and ought not be left to the discretion of one branch or one individual.

Finally, the rule firmly entrenched in our jurisprudence that "an act of Congress ought never to be construed to violate the law of nations, if any other construction remains,"[14] supports applying separation of powers restraints to Executive use of force in violation of international law. That doctrine reflects a presumption that Congress intends to maintain the rules of international law in force absent express, intentional derogation. It follows that congressional silence should mean that Congress wants the President to follow international law. Thus, presidential violations of international law are contrary to the implied will of Congress, and under Justice Jackson's widely accepted Youngstown formulation, constitute executive "power at its lowest ebb."[15] As Professor Quincy Wright wrote in discussing the Vietnam War, "the executive in conducting war or engaging in lesser military activity must act on the presumption that the United States intends to observe international law unless Congress makes explicit authorizations to the contrary."[16]

In sum, the values of world order and justice reflected in international law are related to the concern for checks on arbitrary governmental conduct that underlies separation of powers. This relationship dictates that where United States policy violates existing treaties or customary norms of international society, such action requires the greater scrutiny provided by joint decision making of Congress and the President.

HISTORICAL PERSPECTIVE

Substantial evidence indicates that the framers viewed customary international law as constitutionally limiting the President's discretion in conducting foreign policy. In their famous debate over President Washington's Proclamation of Neutrality of 1793, both Madison and Hamilton recognized that the President had a constitutional duty to enforce international law. Hamilton utilized the President's duty to execute the law of nations to support Washington's authority to issue the Proclamation: "the Executive is charged with the execution of all laws, the laws of Nations as well as the Municipal law, which recognizes and adopts those laws. It is consequently bound, by faithfully executing the laws of neutrality, when that is the state of the Nation, to avoid giving a cause of war to foreign Powers."[17] Madison sought a narrower view for Executive authority which would not, in his opinion, impinge on congressional war powers.

That the executive is bound faithfully to execute the laws of neutrality, whilst those laws continue unaltered by the competent authority, is true; but not for the reason here given, to wit, to avoid giving cause of war to foreign powers. It is bound to the faithful execution of these as of all other laws, internal and external, by the nature of its trust and the sanction of its oath.[18]

While Hamilton and Madison may have used the law of nations for different purposes, they agreed that the President was obligated to faithfully execute the laws of nations.

Madison returned to this theme five years later in his dispute with the Adams Administration conduct of the quasi-war with France. The Adams Administration had prohibited the arming of ships in United States ports as a violation of neutrality, but as tensions mounted between France and the United States, the Executive revoked its prohibition, thereby granting "an indirect license to arm." Congress had not yet acted. Madison complained that the Executive had no power to grant such an indirect license: "The first instructions were not otherwise legal than as they were in pursuance of the law of nations, and consequently in execution of the law of the land. The revocation of the instructions is a virtual change of the law, and consequently a usurpation by the executive of a legislative power."[19] During the ensuing debate over relations with France, various Congressmen noted, without contradiction, that the President could use the nation's armed forces only in a "manner authorized by the law of nations."[20]

The Supreme Court's opinion in *Brown v. United States* further supports international law limits on the Executive's Commander in Chief and other foreign affairs powers.[21] The question before the Court in *Brown* was whether the President could confiscate enemy property in the United States after war had been declared, even though Congress had not authorized such confiscation. The Executive argued that the declaration of war itself gave the President the right to seize and condemn enemy property. Chief Justice Marshall canvassed international law and held that the scope of the President's constitutional war powers should be construed consistently with the law of nations to require congressional authorization prior to executive seizure of alien property.[22] For Marshall, "in expounding that constitution [of the United States], a construction ought not lightly to be admitted which would give to a declaration of war an effect in this country it does not possess elsewhere."[23]

The government, in arguing for greater war powers, recognized that congressional approval was probably necessary for the Executive to take actions that violated international law. The Executive (and the dissent's) argument was that the President could seize all property which, according to the modern law of nations, is subject to confiscation, "although it might require an act of the legislature to justify the condemnation of that property which, according to modern usage, ought not to be confiscated."[24] Since modern usage generally permitted confiscation of the property in question, the Executive had acted constitutionally.

Marshall responded to this argument by noting that this modern "usage is a guide which the sovereign follows or abandons at his will. . . . [A]nd although it cannot be disregarded by him without obloquy, yet it may be disregarded."[25] Marshall's statement has sometimes been taken to mean that customary international law could be abandoned at will by the President.[26]

However, the context of his remarks makes clear that Marshall meant no such thing. The modern usage that he referred to was the permissive rule that allowed sovereigns to take enemy property upon a war's commencement, although as a policy matter this was generally discouraged. Application of this permissive rule therefore was, to Marshall, not an "immutable rule of law," but "a question rather of policy than of law."[27] Like other questions of policy, Marshall thought the question of whether to confiscate enemy property was a legislative determination.[28] The case would have been different had there been an international law rule mandating confiscation of enemy property upon the outbreak of war, for then the

Executive's duty to enforce the law might have applied. Marshall's point was not that customary international law could be abandoned at will, but rather that this was a discretionary rule that the legislative and not Executive branch could decide to disregard.

Justice Story dissented. He agreed that the international law rule was permissive, but to him that meant that the Executive had the constitutional authority to seize enemy property. The Executive's constitutional power to carry on war could only be limited by statute or the law of nations. Since Congress had not limited the President, "he has a discretion vested in him, as to the manner and extent; but he cannot lawfully transcend the rules of warfare established among civilized nations. He cannot lawfully exercise powers or authorize proceedings which the civilized world repudiates and disclaims."[29] Marshall's opinion did not dispute Story on the point, but merely went further, holding that the President had no constitutional authority to seize enemy property located here, irrespective of whether such confiscation was permitted by international law.

Attorney General William Wirt agreed with Justice Story in an 1822 opinion concluding that the obligation of the President as executive officer to enforce the laws of the country extended to the "general laws of nations."[30] Attorney General James Speed also agreed in 1865, stating that the laws of war,

[l]ike the other laws of nations[,] . . . are of binding force upon the departments and citizens of the Government, though not defined by any law of Congress. . . . Under the Constitution of the United States no license can be given by any department of the Government to take human life in war, except according to the law and usages of war.[31]

As late as 1870, even the question of whether Congress and the Executive acting jointly could violate the laws of war was unsettled: certainly the Constitution was not read to tolerate unilateral violation by the President of the laws of war. In *Miller v. United States*,[32] an 1870 case arising out of the Civil War, the majority of justices expressly refused to decide whether Congress could constitutionally violate the laws of war, holding that no such violation had occurred.[33] Two dissenting justices, however, were forced to reach the question the majority avoided, since they found that the challenged statute violated the law of nations. Justices Field and Clifford argued that

The power to prosecute war granted by the Constitution . . . is a power to prosecute war according to the law of nations, and not in violation of that law. . . . There is a limit to the means of destruction which government, in the prosecution of war, may use, . . . imposed by the law of nations, and is no less binding upon Congress than if the limitation were written in the Constitution. [Citation to Halleck's International Law.] The plain reason of this is, that the rules and limitations prescribed by that law were in the contemplation of the parties who framed and the people who adopted the Constitution.[34]

The 20th century has brought a change in U.S. governmental attitudes toward limiting the President's discretion based on international law. In *The Paquete Habana*, the Supreme Court struck down action taken by naval officers in violation of international law.[35] While Justice Gray's opinion noted that international law was a part of our law, it qualified that statement by stating that international law was binding "where there is no treaty, and no controlling executive or legislative act or judicial decision."[36]

More recently, the Eleventh Circuit in *Garcia-Mir v. Meese*, relied on Justice Gray's dictum in *The Paquete Habana* to hold that the Attorney General's indefinite incarceration of Cuban refugees was a controlling executive act which trumped any customary international law limitations for purposes of domestic law.[37] And the Justice Department's Office of Legal Counsel, relying on Gray's dictum, has issued an opinion stating that "under our constitutional system, the executive and legislative branches, acting within the scope of their respective authority, may take or direct actions which depart from customary international law."[38] With respect to our domestic system, "such actions constitute 'controlling executive or legislative acts' that supplant legal norms otherwise furnished by customary international law."[39]

Thus, the Bush Administration claimed the inherent constitutional authority to use force to kidnap foreign citizens and bring them to trial in the United States. While not explicitly ruling on the constitutionality of such actions, the Supreme Court held in 1992 that such kidnappings, even if violative of customary international law, could not be remedied in domestic courts.[40] The Court's opinion implicitly upheld the President's power to take such action in violation of customary international law.

The recent trend has been to uphold the President's constitutional power to use force and take other actions that violate customary international law.[41] However, important separation of powers concerns, the early constitutional history of our nation, and the contemporary situation in the world suggest a reconsideration of these recent rulings.

LIMITING THE EXECUTIVE'S POWER

Proponents of the position that there is no constitutional bar to the Executive's use of force in violation of international law make several arguments. First, they argue that even if the President has no general constitutional power to override international law, as Commander in Chief of the armed forces and "sole organ of foreign affairs" he has independent or plenary constitutional authority to take actions which are controlling executive acts. For example, the President's power as Commander in Chief permits him to decide which weapons or tactics to use in warfare and therefore, Executive advocates argue, to use certain weapons that are proscribed by international law.

This argument has been amply answered by Professor Glennon who notes that plenary power refers to the power of the President to act even if Congress prohibits that act.[42] As Justice Jackson's opinion in *Youngstown* points out, when the President acts in derogation of the expressed or implied will of Congress, his power is at its lowest ebb, and his actions can only be sustained if he has the constitutional power to act in disregard of the congressional will.[43] Since the twin principles that international law is part of our law and that congressional statutes are to be interpreted consistently with international law reflect a presumptive congressional intent that such law be followed, the President can only act if he has independent power to act in derogation of a congressional will.

But the Constitution certainly permits Congress to prohibit such acts as mining another nation's harbors, launching a first strike tactical nuclear attack during a war against another nation, using chemical weapons to repulse an enemy attack, shooting prisoners of war, assassinating civilians, or covertly intervening in another nation's affairs by assassinating its leader. Would the President be bound to comply with any of these hypothetical congressional prohibitions? Article I, § 8, cl. 10 explicitly grants Congress the power to define and punish violations of the law and nations. Thus, Congress could constitutionally define any of these actions as violations of the law of nations and make them crimes under U.S. law. Since the President could not violate any of these laws, and since international law is also the law of the land and presumed to reflect Congress's intent, the President has no plenary or sole power to conduct warfare in violation of international law. Even if the President's role as Commander in Chief gives him the sole power to generally choose which tactics and weapons to utilize in warfare, that power is limited by Congress's power to define offenses against international law; this power, even when unexercised, presumes that the Executive will follow international law, even if no criminal sanctions apply.

Moreover, it is simply not true that the President's powers as Commander in Chief or over foreign affairs gives him sole authority over the conduct of war or other forcible actions against foreign nations, even in the absence of the congressional power to define and punish international law violations. As the majority report on the Iran-Contra affair made clear, the Boland Amendment was a constitutional effort limiting the Executive's conduct of foreign affairs.[44] Certainly, the President could have been similarly restrained by a congressional statute prohibiting assassination of foreign leaders, mining Nicaraguan harbors, or forcibly kidnapping foreign citizens. If he can be restrained by statute, he can also be restrained by treaty or international law, both of which are equal in constitutional status to statutes.

Controlling the use of weaponry in wartime seems more problematic. As Professor Franck has argued, "while international law may help fill the Constitution's interstices, it cannot repeal its intent by deleting or altering the President's power to 'make' i.e. conduct war."[45] To Franck, international law may help define the circumstances in which the President may use nuclear weapons to initiate warfare; it cannot prohibit the use of such weapons once war has been authorized by Congress.

While the President's powers as Commander in Chief are enormous, they are not absolute. Apart from the limitations contained in the article I, § 8, cl. 10 power to define and punish offenses, Congress also has some power over the conduct of war. Congress has the power to raise armies and navies and "make rules concerning captures on land and water." The Supreme Court has noted that Congress could authorize hostilities which were "limited as to places, persons and things."[46] Thus while many tactical wartime decisions, such as which general should command an army, how many troops to use, or even generally what weaponry should be used, are within the President's sole control, Congress could establish certain rules of engagement pursuant to its war powers.[47] Professor John Norton Moore, a strong and effective advocate for according the Executive exclusive command powers over the conduct of a constitutionally authorized conflict, has recognized that Congress could prohibit the "use of internationally prohibited chemical or biological weapons" because of the "profound effects on international relations," the "grave risk of escalation," and the possibility of "unnecessary suffering."[48] That the President's power as Commander in Chief could be limited by Congress in certain respects, suggests that other forms of federal law such as treaty and customary international law also provide limitations.

A second objection to imposing international law limitations on the President's constitutional powers to use force abroad stems from the method by which customary international law changes. A new rule of customary international law often develops by one state or several states taking action departing from the old rule and seeking to replace it with a new one. According to some scholars, to impose a constitutional requirement that the President obey international law would handicap U.S. participation in the growth and development of international law.[49] William Barr, testifying before Congress on behalf of the Justice Department, stated that the need for the United States to play a role in shaping and changing customary international law supports providing the President, who has primary responsibility for the conduct of foreign affairs, with "discretion to depart from customary international law norms in the exercise of his constitutional authority."[50]

The United States would not be disabled from participating in changing international law if the President was without constitutional power to violate international norms. The Constitution only requires that the President seek congressional approval to take such action. The constitutional question involved in this issue is not whether the U.S. government has the power to take such action (although I believe that some peremptory norms of international law are so fundamental that even the two branches acting together cannot violate them—i.e., torturing prisoners),[51] but whether the President can do so alone. International law is not static, however; it is at a minimum entitled to enough respect to ensure that actions that violate the law are subject to the collective decision making that our separation of powers structure provides. A decision to violate international law ought to be suspect; it should at least require both branches acting together to decide that the United States cannot abide by a particular rule.

There are, of course, different degrees of clarity and strength of international law rules. The vaguer the rule, the more discretion the President will have in deciding whether a particular act violates international law. However, there are many clear rules of international law: a nation cannot use force to kidnap another nation's citizen within the other country's territory; a nation cannot intentionally bomb civilian targets; a nation cannot mine another country's harbors without notice; to attempt to assassinate another country's leader in peacetime constitutes unlawful intervention in that nation's affairs. To the extent that the U.S. government believes it is not in its benefit to follow any of these rules, that decision ought to be made by Congress, not the President.

A third objection questions the practicality of imposing international law restraints on the President. Only the President, as Commander in Chief, is in a position to determine whether nuclear weapons ought to be used, a particular target ought to be bombed, or a foreign leader should be targeted. These decisions often must be made quickly and secretly and often require a command of the facts that over 500 members of Congress could not possibly have. Moreover, this argument goes, the imposition of a limitation on the President who might be fighting an enemy which observes no such limitation impermissibly deprives him of the flexibility needed to win wars and successfully conduct foreign policy.

This argument suffers from a conflation of authorization of particular actions with the establishment of general policy. If the President wants to establish policies that permit the U.S. to introduce nuclear weapons into an armed conflict or to use chemical weapons, or to be able to assassinate foreign leaders or kidnap foreign civilians, those overall policies ought to be approved by Congress. The President, of course, has the discretion to decide when to use such tactics within the limits set by Congress. This chapter does not argue that particular military decisions—which might require speed or secrecy—ought to be made by Congress, but merely that overall policy should be approved by Congress if that policy violates international law.

Of course, in the absence of enactment by Congress of a policy permitting the use of any tactics set forth above, the President's flexibility is limited. But such flexibility should be limited if the President cannot convince Congress that the first use of nuclear weapons, or assassination of foreign leaders, is an appropriate tactic. In that case he ought not have the constitutional power to undertake such actions.

There may be rare occasions where the need is so overwhelming, emergency so great, and the time and secrecy concerns so pressing that the President must act on his own. For example, the Church Committee, in proposing an absolute ban on assassinations, recognized that there might be a national emergency, such as the threat posed by Adolf Hitler, where assassination might be the best course of action. Yet the committee believed that it would still be better to bar assassinations entirely, bringing any presidential authorization of such action into conflict with the law.[52] That position would ensure that only where such an action represented an "indispensable necessity" to the life of a nation could the President authorize it.[53] If the President decides to authorize an attack in violation of international law, he must do it with the recognition that such action violates his constitutional obligations— that standard can help ensure that such actions are not taken lightly.

The practical objections all assume that international law operates as a straitjacket which would impermissibly hamstring the President in conducting foreign policy or warfare. But in fact, the rules of international law generally are very flexible and often suffer more from vagueness than from stringent restrictions on conduct. It should be the rare case where the U.S. interest requires derogation— such rare cases require congressional assent.

Related to the practical objections are enforcement concerns—how can the courts enforce restrictions on Presidential powers stemming from international law. In some cases they will not be able to, as courts may be inappropriate institutions to determine whether the President's bombing of another country violates international law. But many international law issues can and have been adjudicated by the courts in appropriate cases. Moreover, even without judicial intervention, our Constitution has meaning if Congress and the American people believe in it and are committed to its principles. For example, while the courts refused to order President Bush to seek congressional assent before attacking Iraq in January 1991,[54] the political climate in both Congress and among the public eventually forced the President to obtain that approval.

A fifth objection has been made to the reliance on history to support international law restrictions on the Executive's constitutional authority. As Professor Stewart Jay has eloquently argued, "[n]otwithstanding the fascination we may feel for the events of the early Republic in regard to international relations, their contextual differences from world affairs today should lead us to view the various statements about the law of nations from that era as having no bearing on modern controversies."[55] Similar statements have also been made in connection with congressional war powers. For the America that drafted and ratified the Constitution and took its place as an independent nation was a weak nation, which sought to ensure that its leaders did not take precipitous action that could lead to its destruction. To be sure, America has now, as Professor Jay argues, "reached its place in the sun." An imperial America has led to an imperial President that is not restrained by either international nor constitutional limitations on power. But the distortion that empire has wrought on the Constitution is not a positive development. As Henry Steele Commager once wrote, the "abuse of power by Presidents is a reflection, and perhaps a consequence, of abuse of power by the American nation."[56] In the long run, "abuse of executive power cannot be separated from abuse of national power. If we subvert world order and destroy world peace, we must inevitably subvert and destroy our own political institutions first."[57]

The rise of American power that led to the submersion of international law norms in domestic U.S. law has also led to an evisceration of congressional war power. The end of the Cold War opens an opportunity to revitalize both international law and congressional war powers constraints on the President. Abiding by our original constitutional design is not warranted by a recognition of weakness—as was the case in 1787—but rather from an acceptance of the limitations of power.

INTERNATIONAL LAW, THE CONSTITUTION AND THE END OF THE COLD WAR

The end of the Cold War and President Bush's purported search for a "new world order" raises new possibilities for rediscovering the original interrelationship between constitutional and international law restraints. First, the rationales utilized over the past half century for removing restraints on the President's conduct of foreign policy no longer apply with the same force. Those justifications were most clearly stated in the 1954 Hoover Commission on Government Organization: "We are facing an implacable enemy whose avowed objective is world domination by whatever means and at whatever cost. There are no rules in such a game. Hitherto acceptable norms of human conduct do not apply."[58] In that ideological context it was unlikely that the Executive would accept or the Congress and Judiciary would impose constitutional limitations on the President's use of force based on international law.

While the United States still faces many enemies in the world, and dangerous dictators, terrorists, and drug traffickers abound, the "implacable enemy" seeking "world domination" has disintegrated. In the wake of the Soviet Union's demise, perhaps the time is ripe to rethink our own constitutional commitment to abide by international law. While it may be too idealistic to suppose that the U.S. government will accept constitutional restraints on its ability to violate international treaties or customary international law as some of our European allies now have adopted, it doesn't seem a particularly radical step to at least impose separation of powers restraints to ensure that any such violation is agreed to by both Congress and the President.

Second, in the coming era some commentators have noted that establishing better enforcement mechanisms for international law will occupy an important place in the conduct of international relations. David Scheffer, a former Senior Associate with the Carnegie Endowment for International Peace, has argued that the Gulf War represented a "transition from an age of norm creation in international law to one of enforcement of international law."[59]

If in a future, less divided world, the international community focuses more heavily on enforcing and not merely defining or creating international law, it would seem that one key area of change would likely be the creation of better domestic enforcement mechanisms. For the world community needs not only international organizations to enforce international law, but also the incorporation of international law into domestic legal systems to place limitations on unlawful governmental conduct. Perhaps, as Professor Richard Bilder has suggested, as the United States finds itself more "committed to the international legal order, we may even wish to re-examine our strongly dualist tradition regarding the incorporation of international law into our own domestic law."[60]

Finally, while the Bush Administration has proclaimed a "new partnership of nations" and rhetorically supported a "new world order, in which the rule of law supplants the rule of the jungle,"[61] it is clear that we are unwilling to accept that law when it limits our own foreign policy options. The post-Cold War invasion of Panama, the kidnapping of foreign nationals for trial here in violation of basic norms of international law, and the interdiction of Haitian refugees in derogation of the international norm of nonrefoulment all suggest a rhetoric of international law unmatched by a real willingness to abide by its rules.[62]

This hypocrisy stems from a longstanding tension in American perspectives on international law, one which is evident even in the Hamilton-Madison debates in the 1790s. That tension is between international law as a sword and a shield, between law providing government power versus law as a limitation of power.

International law, as all law, performs both functions. In the recent Persian Gulf crisis the Bush Administration recognized the useful aspect of international law as a sword, as legitimating power. The question now is whether the U.S. Executive will also recognize that law as a limitation on power. Integrating international law into our own constitutional separation of powers framework would be one step in that direction.

NOTES

1. *See, e.g.*, Louis Henkin, *The Constitution and United States Sovereignty: A Century of Chinese Exclusion and Its Progeny*, 100 Harv. L. Rev. 853, 882 (1987) (enunciating, although not necessarily espousing this view); Louis Henkin, *The President and International Law*, 80 Am. J. Int'l L. 930, 936 (1986) ("Perhaps an act within the President's constitutional authority as sole organ or as commander-in-chief is controlling [even if violative of international law]."); Thomas Franck, *The President, The Constitution, and Nuclear Weapons*, 363, 366 *in* Nuclear Weapons and Law (Arthur Miller & Martin Fernrider eds., 1984) (international law cannot alter President's power to conduct war); Frederic L. Kirgis, *Federal Statutes, Executive Orders and Self-Executing Custom*, 81 Am. J. Int'l L. 371, 374 (1987).

2. *Covert War and Congressional Authority: Hidden War and Forgotten Power*, 134 U. Pa. L. Rev. 1035 (1986).

3. *See Committee of United States Citizens Living in Nicaragua (CUSCLIN) v. Reagan*, 859 F.2d 929, 941 (D.C. Cir. 1988) (Such basic norms of international law as the proscription against murder and slavery . . . may well restrain our government in the same way that the Constitution restrains it."); Jules Lobel, *The Limits of Constitutional Power: Conflicts Between Foreign Policy and International Law*, 71 Va. L. Rev. 1071 (1985).

4. 1 *The Records of the Federal Convention of 1797* 316 (Max Farrand ed., 1911) (J. Madison).

5. *Id.* at 319 (J. Wilson).

6. *Id.* (G. Mason).

7. Op. Sec'y of State (May 16, 1793) (Thomas Jefferson), *reprinted in* 7 John Bassett Moore, *A Digest of International Law* 123 (1906).

8. *The Federalist* No. 75 at 506 (Jacob Ernest Cooke ed., 1961) (A. Hamilton).

9. Alexander Hamilton, Pacificus 1 in 15 *Papers of Alexander Hamilton* 40 (Harold Syrett ed., 1961).

10. Michael J. Glennon, *Can the President Do No Wrong?*, 80 Am. J. Int'l L. 923, 927–28 (1986).

11. *United States v. Alvarez-Machain*, 504 U.S. _____, 112 S. Ct. 2188, 119 L. Ed. 2d 441 (1992).

12. *The Nereide*, 13 U.S. (9 Cranch) 388, 423 (1815); Restatement (Third) of Foreign Relations Law § 111 (1986).

13. Article II, § 3 ("he shall take care that the laws be faithfully executed").

14. *Murray v. The Schooner Charming Betsey*, 6 U.S. (2 Cranch) 64, 118 (1804); *see also* Restatement (Third) of Foreign Relations Law § 134 (1986).

15. *Youngstown Sheet & Tube Co. v. Sawyer*, 343 U.S. 579, 637 (1952) (Jackson, J., concurring).

16. Quincy Wright, *The Power of the Executive to Use Military Forces Abroad*, 10 Va. J. Int'l L. 43, 49 (1969).

17. 15 *The Papers of Alexander Hamilton*, *supra* note 9, at 40.

18. Madison, Helvidius, No. II *reprinted in* 2 *Writings of James Madison* 159–60 (Gaillard Hunt ed., 1906).

19. *Id.* at 313.

20. 5 *Annals of Cong.* 1807 (1798) (Rep. Robert Williams); *id.* at 1806 (Rep. Abraham Venable).

21. 12 U.S. (8 Cranch) 110 (1814).

22. *Id.* at 125.

23. *Id.*

24. *Id.* at 128.

25. *Id.*

26. Jonathan I. Charney, *The Power of the Executive Branch of the U.S. Government to Violate Customary International Law*, 80 Am. J. Int'l L. 913 (1986).

27. 12 U.S. (8 Cranch) at 128.

28. *Id.* at 129.

29. *Id.* at 153.

30. 1 Op. Atty. Gen. 566, 570 (1822).

31. 11 Op. Atty. Gen. 297, 299–301 (1865).

32. 78 U.S. (11 Wall.) 268 (1870).

33. *Id.*

34. *Id.* at 316.

35. 175 U.S. 677 (1900).

36. *Id.* at 700.

37. 788 F.2d 1446, 1453–55 (11th Cir. 1986). *But cf. Fernundez v. Wilkinson*, 505 F. Supp. 787 (D. Kan. 1980), *aff'd on other grounds*, 654 F.2d 1382 (10th Cir. 1981) for a contrary view.

38. Hearings on FBI Authority to Seize Suspects Abroad before the House Subcommittee on Civil and Constitutional Rights, 101st Cong., 1st Sess., at 5 (Nov. 8, 1989). That opinion conflicted with the Carter Administration's view of Executive Power. *See* Extraterritorial Apprehension by the Federal Bureau of Investigation, 4B Op. Off. Legal Counsel 543 (1980).

39. *Id.*

40. *United States v. Alvarez-Machain*, 504 U.S. _____, 112 S. Ct. 2188, 119 L. Ed. 2d 441 (1992).

41. *See, e.g.*, Restatement (Third) of Foreign Relations Law § 115 (Reporters Note 3) (1986).

42. Glennon, *supra* note 10, at 925.

43. 343 U.S. at 637.

44. H. Rep. No. 100–433, S. Rep. No. 100–216, 100th Cong., 1st Sess., at 406 (Nov. 1987).

45. Franck, *supra* note 1, at 366.

46. *Bas v. Tingy*, 4 U.S. (4 Dall.) 37 (1800).

47. On the debate over the breadth of the President's Commander in Chief power compare Arthur Schlesinger, *The Imperial Presidency* 6 (1973), Raoul Berger, *Executive Privilege* 77 (1974), and Gary J. Schmitt, *Executive Privilege, Presidential Power to Withhold Information, in* The Presidency in the Constitutional Order 171 (Joseph M. Bessette & Jeffrey Tulis eds., 1981).

48. John Norton Moore, *Law and the Indo-China War* 566 (1972).

49. Charney, *supra* note 26; Arthur M. Weisburd, *The Executive Branch and International Law*, 41 Vand. L. Rev. 1205, 1253–55 (1988).

50. *See* Testimony of Assistant Attorney General William Barr, Hearings on FBI Authority to Seize Suspects Abroad before House of Representatives, Judiciary Committee Subcommittee on Civil and Constitutional Rights, 101st Cong., 1st Sess., at 7–8 (Nov. 8, 1989).

51. *See CUSCLIN v. Reagan*, 859 F.2d 929, 941 (D.C. Cir. 1988).

52. S. Rep. No. 94–465, 94th Cong., 1st. Sess., at 282–84 (Nov. 20, 1975) (Church Committee Interim Report on Alleged Assassination Plots Involving Foreign Leaders).

53. *The Intelligence Community* 810 (Tyrus Fain, Katharine Plant, & Ross Milloy, eds., 1977).

54. *Dellums v. Bush*, 752 F. Supp. 1141 (D.D.C. 1990); *Ange v. Bush*, 752 F. Supp. 509 (D.D.C. 1990).

55. Stewart Jay, *The Status of the Law of Nations in Early American Law*, 42 Vand. L. Rev. 819, 849 (1989).

56. Henry Steele Commager, *The Defeat of America* 57 (1968).

57. *Id.*

58. Quoted in S. Rep. No. 94–755, 94th Cong. 2d Sess., at 9 (1977) (Church Committee Report).

59. 1991 *Friedmann Conference Proceedings*, 29 Col. J. of Transnat'l L. 487, 518 (1991).

60. Richard Bilder, *International Law in the "New World Order": Some Preliminary Reflections*, 1 J. Transnat'l L. & Pol'y 1, 20 (1992).

61. Transcript of President's Joint Address to Joint Session of Congress, N.Y. Times, Sept. 12, 1990, at A20.

62. *See, e.g.*, John Quigley, *The New World Order and The Rule of Law*, 18 Syracuse J. Int'l L. & Com. 75 (1992).

6 Judicial Constraints: The Courts and War Powers

Harold Hongju Koh[1]

When it comes to the war powers, courts are now treated like small children at a wedding—there to be seen and not heard—while the main players, Congress and the President, busily command center stage. Many have made the case for judicial passivity, usually expressing their fears as a blurred concern about separation of powers and judicial incompetence. Our constitutional structure of separated powers, they say, does not allow judges to usurp the role of generals, much less assume the role confided to our Commander in Chief. Nor, in their opinion, are judges and their law clerks competent to make the factual or legal evaluations necessary to assess the legality of executive action, much less "to specify, monitor, and enforce an injunction circumscribing the President's use of . . . military force."[2] Others, I among them, have taken pains to suggest that in war powers cases, courts have played and should continue to play a useful role that is not merely constitutionally permissible, but constitutionally required.[3]

This chapter seeks not to recapitulate this all-too-familiar debate, but to sharpen it: by identifying those issues that commonly arise in war powers cases, and then briefly suggesting which ones ought to be uncontroversial at this advanced stage in our constitutional history. Nearly all of the most controversial questions were discussed in Judge Harold Greene's now famous opinion in *Dellums v. Bush*,[4] an effort by 54 Members of Congress to enjoin President Bush from initiating war against Iraq without prior congressional authorization.

Although Judge Greene held that request unripe, he also rejected the Government's requests that the suit be dismissed for lack of congressional standing or remedial discretion. He further held that the political question doctrine did not bar a federal court from deciding the constitutional question in an appropriate case and controversy. On the question of relief, Judge Greene issued what amounted to an unappealable declaratory judgment *against* the government, stating without equivocation that the Constitution did not permit the President to order U.S. Armed Forces to make war without meaningfully consulting with Congress and receiving its affirmative authorization. He went on to declare that "in principle, an injunction may issue at the request of Members of Congress to prevent the conduct of a war which is about to be carried on without congressional authorization," clearly laying the groundwork for future requests for injunctive relief.[5]

Despite its flawed ruling on ripeness,[6] Judge Greene's *Dellums* opinion sets the analytic framework within which any debate over the role of the courts in war powers cases should now proceed. I close by suggesting that disputants in that debate would best proceed by focusing more closely on the relatively few issues regarding which they truly differ: in particular, congressional standing, scope of judicial review, and injunctive relief.

POINTS OF AGREEMENT

Our first, and most fundamental point of agreement, should be with regard to history. As I have argued at length elsewhere, in the early years of our constitutional history, the courts played an important and active role in delineating and delimiting the Executive's authority to conduct warmaking, particularly when Congress had made an effort to regulate that authority.[7] Such rulings continued even into the 1960s,[8] but grew fewer and farther between after the Supreme Court recognized the President's unenumerated "sole organ" power in 1936 in *United States v. Curtiss-Wright Export Corp.* which promoted an increasingly deferential judicial attitude toward presidential power in foreign affairs.[9] The Court checked the trend toward both deference and nonreviewability in the 1952 *Steel Seizure* case, which reiterated limits upon exclusive presidential powers in foreign affairs and specified (particularly in Justice Jackson's classic concurrence) the roles that congressional consultation and judicial review should play in distributing concurrent constitutional authority.[10]

But in the decades since, particularly after the Vietnam War, the pendulum has swung back as the federal courts have adopted an increasingly deferential attitude toward presidential warmaking.[11] Even when Congress finally responded to the President's Vietnam-era abuses by embedding the *Youngstown* vision into a statute—the War Powers Resolution of 1973[12]—the courts have responded by invoking *Curtiss-Wright* to claim both that the President has inherent powers over foreign affairs and that his conduct is largely unreviewable (a proposition for which that case most assuredly does not stand).[13]

A second point over which there should now be little dispute, is that—despite these recent precedents—the legality of governmental decisions regarding war, are not, by their nature, *political questions* inherently unfit for judicial resolution. In *Baker v. Carr*, which most fully explicated the political question doctrine—in the context of legislative apportionment, not foreign affairs—the Court called it "error to suppose that every case or controversy that touches foreign relations lies beyond judicial cognizance." The Court further asserted that the nonjusticiability doctrine is one "of 'political questions,' not one of 'political cases.' "[14] That statement rested on Justice Brennan's recognition that, since the beginning of the Republic, federal judges have reviewed the legality of military seizures, retaliatory strikes, and covert actions ordered under claims of delegated and inherent presidential power to conduct warfare.[15] While several of these cases reviewed executive conduct on the merits and even sustained its legality, none found such actions immune from judicial scrutiny.[16]

Judge Greene definitively, and in my view, correctly rejected the political question approach in *Dellums*. Even before *Dellums*, his view had been shared even by strongly pro-executive judges, ranging from Antonin Scalia to Robert Bork to Malcolm Wilkey. All have expressed some form of the view that the "political question" doctrine is "a tempting refuge from the adjudication of difficult constitutional claims[, whose] shifting contours and uncertain underpinnings make it susceptible to indiscriminate and overbroad application to claims properly before the federal courts."[17]

Third, we should also be able to agree that *prudential factors* do not invariably weigh against judicial review in war powers cases.[18] A claim oft made here is that judges and their law clerks are somehow incapable of resolving the questions of fact or law most commonly raised in war powers cases. Yet in most open warfare situations, like the recent Gulf War at issue in *Dellums*, the facts are simply undisputed, and the case can be adjudicated on the public record. Similarly, the claim that the courts lack expertise and information to conduct a national security review function is totally self-fulfilling. One need look no further than Judge Gesell's handling of the Oliver North trial, Judge Greene's conduct of the Poindexter case, or the recent trial of Manuel Noriega to surmise that even cases involving massive amounts of classified information can be fairly adjudicated by a competent and conscientious judge, particularly if the parties provide the crucial information to the court *in camera*.

Nor in the war powers context is there much to the claim that courts cannot derive principled legal standards to decide the cases. To the contrary, questions of interpretation of treaties, executive agreements, and customary international law have long been held justiciable.[19] Nor is it clear why a court should be able to evade interpretation of a statute of Congress—whether the War Powers Resolution or any other joint resolution—simply because the legality of acts of war may be called into question. As the Court recently declared, "[u]nder the Constitution, one of the judiciary's characteristic roles is to interpret statutes, and we cannot shirk from this responsibility merely because our decision may have significant political overtones."[20] Even when the war powers clauses of the Constitution are at stake, the notion that the courts cannot derive principled standards to adjudicate is belied by their demonstrated ability to derive workable standards from even the vaguest constitutional provisions. If the Court can derive detailed rules of criminal procedure from the Fifth Amendment and elaborate standards of personal jurisdiction from the due process clause of the Fourteenth Amendment, then surely it can construe the more determinate terms of the Declare War and the Commander in Chief Clauses.

Equally insubstantial is the prudential argument that the courts should not rule for fear that the political branches will ignore their judgment, a fear that presidential compliance in *Youngstown* and *U.S. v. Nixon*[21] should have put to rest. A final prudential claim is that courts should not rule for fear that their rulings might "embarrass" the President, confusing the rest of the world as to who is in charge of our foreign policy.[22] If this claim rests on foreign confusion, it denigrates our allies' intelligence and falsely assumes that they cannot comprehend a constitutional system of shared powers.[23] Nor does it make sense to condone illegal executive conduct simply to avoid embarrassing the President, particularly if the unlawful actor should be embarrassed.[24]

Fourth, few would deny that in times of actual and threatened hostilities, the courts bear a special responsibility to scrutinize government conduct that allegedly infringes upon *individual rights* (particularly individual rights at home).[25] If anything, meaningful judicial review is even more constitutionally necessary in the war powers cases than in traditional domestic cases, given the Framers' decision largely to remove the states as a political check against executive action in foreign relations. One outgrowth of this conclusion is that as hostilities proceed, someone (most likely an American soldier under orders to report to a war zone) will have *standing* to bring suit challenging the conduct of the war.[26]

Fifth, in nearly all war powers cases, at some point, the legality of the executive conduct in question should be *ripe* for judicial examination. Perhaps there are rare cases—such as the President pushing the "nuclear button"—where a legal challenge would never be ripe until after the event, at which point it would be moot. But notwithstanding Judge Greene's incorrect ruling on this point in *Dellums*, ripeness should not pose a major barrier to judicial review so long as the Executive branch has clearly committed itself to a course of action and the two political branches have reached a political impasse regarding whether that course of action would be legal.

Sixth and finally, considerable agreement exists about the kinds of *judicial relief* that might appropriately be granted in a war powers case. Few deny that those who lose property interests as a result of war should be able to claim compensatory damages after the fact.[27] Even critics of a judicial role generally do not protest issuance of declaratory relief.[28] Nor does the D.C. Circuit's doctrine of equitable discretion deny federal courts their power to order coercive or injunctive remedies against executive branch representatives, an authority that has been settled at least since *Marbury v. Madison.* Even injunctions that have some extraterritorial effect against U.S. officials should be permitted if we presume, as the D.C. Circuit did in condoning the possibility of injunctive relief against American military movements in Honduras, that "the defendants, all officials of the United States government present in Washington, D.C., will obey an order of the district court."[29] At the same time, no one would seriously suggest that "federal judges, contemporary successors to the practical men that sat as courts of equity of old, should issue orders to end a war or drop (or not drop) a bomb."[30]

In sum, reasonable people should be able to agree that: (1) courts have historically decided war powers cases; (2) neither the legal nor the factual questions in such cases are inherently incapable of judicial resolution; (3) such disputes are not invariably barred from the courts because of standing or timing concerns; and (4) there are some forms of meaningful relief—short of day-to-day micro-management of the conduct of a war—that courts can give, particularly to individuals who are adversely affected by warmaking decisions.

POINTS OF CONTROVERSY

If so many fundamental points are settled, to what, then, do we owe the continuing controversy over the judicial role in war powers cases? In my judgment, all three branches of government are to blame.

To say that none of these hurdles should pose an absolute barrier to judicial action in war powers cases does not determine whether a court will choose to act in any particular case. In case after case, the Executive branch has invoked each of these barriers as a separate and independent reason to block judicial review, even in circumstances where a judicial finding of legality would have strengthened the President's hand.

Other culprits are Congress and its creature—the War Powers Resolution—both because of what that statute says and what it does not say. What the Resolution does is to seek to limit *overt sustained conflicts* by placing a 60-day durational limit upon future troop commitments. But to the extent that the Resolution has stimulated the Executive to resort to short-term military strikes of less than sixty days and to substitute sustained covert for overt operations, it has made it more difficult for private parties or Members of Congress to bring challenges to executive actions, which may now be either concluded before the action can be fully adjudicated[31] or driven underground into covert activity, and hence inherently less susceptible to judicial scrutiny.[32]

More seriously, what the Resolution does not specifically say is that the courts should enforce it.[33] This statutory silence has played into the perverse incentives of all three branches: the President's incentive to act, Congress's incentive to avoid responsibility, and the courts' incentive to defer.[34] Acting together, all three branches have effectively rendered the War Powers Resolution's 60-day time limit nonself-executing, thus denying that time limit any real power to push the President toward consultation or Congress toward voting a prompt resolution of ratification or disapproval of his troop commitment. As a consequence, the Resolution has largely failed to promote either the interbranch dialogue or the legislative-executive cooperation with regard to war powers that it was originally intended to produce.

A third and final culprit has been the judiciary itself. Despite the arguments surveyed above, since Vietnam, judges have suffered collective amnesia about their historical role in war powers cases and grown increasingly timid about deciding such cases, even when they have been asked to do so, and even when such decisions plainly fall within their competence.[35] Even in *Dellums*, for example, Judge Greene pulled back from granting injunctive relief at the last moment, relying upon strained ripeness reasoning to avoid a decision on the merits.

The convergence of these institutional factors has led to a near-total withdrawal of the federal courts from the war powers arena. Yet upon reflection, the real dispute over the current role of courts in war powers cases centers around three basic issues: congressional standing, the scope of judicial review of political action, and injunctive relief. Despite its dispositive role in *Dellums*, the issue of ripeness was badly muddled with these three questions, and does not in fact pose a separate controversy.[36]

With regard to congressional standing, I think Judge Greene in *Dellums* got it just about right. He recognized that Members of Congress have their own cognizable interest in challenging violations of the War Clause or the War Powers Resolution that is distinct from the general public. In *Dellums*, "[t]he right asserted by the plaintiffs . . . is the right to vote for or against a declaration of war."[37] The threat of injury to that right posed by the President's proposal to go to war without securing congressional approval was sufficient to give each individual Member a cognizable stake in going to court.

The D.C. Circuit's requirement of specific "vote-nullification" as a prerequisite to recognizing congressional standing, articulated in *Kennedy v. Sampson*,[38] ensures that legislators will not run to court simply because a statute they supported has been misconstrued or because they have been denied information that might help them generally to legislate. The vote-nullification rule also recognizes that legislator-plaintiffs, like class action plaintiffs, play a representative function that presidential vote-nullification specifically impairs and that such legislators, like named plaintiffs, tend to be better informed and better positioned to protest illegal executive action than a private citizen or even an individual serviceman.

With regard to the second issue—scope of judicial review—John Hart Ely has argued persuasively that courts can adjudicate in war powers cases, without engaging in day-to-day management of the war. Ely suggests that courts should act as "Congress-prodders," assuming the relatively limited function of forcing Congress to perform its constitutionally-contemplated functions, and to "remand" difficult decisions to Congress when it has not been meeting its obligations.[39]

Applied to *Dellums*, this logic would have required Judge Greene to state that an imminent likelihood of war existed (overcoming concerns about ripeness) and to issue an injunction that the President may not conduct a war absent constitutionally required congressional authorization. In effect, such an order would have remanded the matter to the political branches to do their constitutional duty. The order would have forced the President and his subordinates to decide whether to go to Congress to obtain its approval or to conduct an illegal war in the face of an unambiguous court order. Equally important, the order would have forced Congress to face up to its constitutional duty to decide whether it had in fact approved the war in question. Applied to the War Powers Resolution, the same role-definition would entitle judges to construe and define statutory terms—what constitutes "hostilities," when statutorily required reports are due, etc.—as well as to enforce requirements expressly created by the statute—for example, to order the President to submit a hostilities report (of the kind requested in *Lowry v. Reagan*) and thereby to start the clock that the Resolution was intended to embody.

Perhaps the most controversial lingering issue regards a court's "equitable discretion" to issue an injunctive remedy, an amorphous remedial doctrine that has now gained substantial headway in the D.C. Circuit.[40] The doctrine combines the equitable notion of "no other adequate remedy"—that congressional plaintiffs must exhaust their political remedies before turning to the courts for equitable relief—with an anomalous concept of discretionary jurisdiction—that federal courts have some kind of free-floating discretion to decline to issue injunctions even against illegal military operations if separation of powers concerns would render such an injunction inappropriate.[41]

The doctrine potentially has broad impact. Indeed, the Executive branch has recently begun to urge application of this doctrine outside the war powers context, most recently in the Haitian Refugee litigation, with which I have been involved.[42] On this point, too, I believe that Judge Greene made the proper assessment in *Dellums*: that federal courts have a duty to grant injunctions, so long as plaintiffs meet the well-established standards for such relief.[43] It is true that the status of plaintiffs as legislators may affect whether they have available through the political process other adequate remedies short of injunctive relief from a court. But Judge Greene correctly concluded that an injunction should issue so long as the plaintiffs "cannot gain 'substantial relief' by persuasion of their colleagues alone."[44] To hold otherwise would be to create a *de facto* certiorari jurisdiction in the lower federal courts, permitting them to avoid exercising jurisdiction based upon *ad hoc* and standardless determinations of when injunctions are or are not "appropriate."

CONCLUSION

Given that another *Dellums* is not likely soon to come along, how can we best address these lingering controversies over standing, scope of judicial review, and equitable relief? The recent Byrd-Nunn-Warner-Mitchell proposal to amend the War Powers Resolution[45] contained the seeds of a new legislative strategy to deal with the war powers problem, a central element of which is frank acceptance that courts must be forced to decide such cases.[46] By explicitly permitting "[a]ny Member of Congress [to] bring an action in the United States District Court for the District of Columbia for declaratory judgment and injunctive relief on the ground that the President or the United States Armed Forces have not complied with any provision," the bill not only conquers the standing problem, by allowing individual Members to seek judicial enforcement of the Act, but also codifies the remedy of declaratory and injunctive relief. More fundamentally, by laying venue in the D.C. Circuit, the bill begins to attack prudential concerns regarding lack of judicial expertise or familiarity with war powers issues by developing a counter-arena of legal expertise in a particular federal circuit with regard to war powers issues.

The result in *Dellums* only confirms the continuing need for this legislative revision. In ways not fully appreciated by the public, Judge Greene's decision in *Dellums* helped break the looming impasse between the political branches in Iraq. In the weeks preceding that decision, the nation had witnessed a now-familiar dance: the President had threatened to make war without seeking congressional consent, Congress had avoided taking a stand, and the courts had declined to pass on the legality of an unauthorized war.[47] Although Judge Greene held the congressional claim unripe, by declaring that the Constitution did not permit the President to order U.S. Armed Forces to make war without meaningfully consulting with

Congress and receiving its affirmative authorization, he put all parties on notice that other suits would soon follow. Had President Bush proceeded to wage war without congressional authorization, he undoubtedly would have faced scores of servicemen suits citing that proposition, claiming (unquestionably ripe) rights *not* to fight and die in an unconstitutional, unauthorized war.[48]

I cannot but think that this unsavory prospect helped persuade the President to request, and Congress to grant, an eleventh-hour joint resolution authorizing the war. By promoting that resolution, *Dellums* established a piece of "quasi-constitutional custom" around which future institutional expectations will likely coalesce.[49] All three branches effectively acknowledged Congress's constitutional right to approve the war.[50] After Iraq, we will not likely hear our President again claim such a broad inherent constitutional authority to commit U.S. forces to such a large-scale, premeditated, potentially sustained war.[51]

Thus, *Dellums* demonstrates that judicial participation in war powers cases, judiciously undertaken, need not be self-perpetuating. To the extent that such participation—particularly when required by statute—forces interbranch dialogue and spurs creation of legally binding or customary norms around which future institutional expectations can converge, the judicial role in war powers cases can remain limited, sporadic, umpireal, and appropriately tailored to the judiciary's institutional expertise.

NOTES

1. This chapter grows out of and builds upon Harold H. Koh, *The National Security Constitution: Sharing Power After the Iran-Contra Affair* (1990) [hereafter "The National Security Constitution"].

2. J. Gregory Sidak, *To Declare War*, 41 Duke L.J. 27, 113 (1991).

3. *See generally The National Security Constitution, supra* note 1; John Hart Ely, *Suppose Congress Wanted a War Powers Act that Worked*, 88 Colum. L. Rev. 1379 (1988); and Harold H. Koh, *The Coase Theorem and the War Power: A Response*, 41 Duke L.J. 122 (1991).

4. 752 F. Supp. 1141 (D.D.C. 1990).

5. *Id.* at 1149.

6. Although Judge Greene held the claims unripe, he did not dismiss the suit, suggesting that his real concern was not about ripeness, but that the equitable prerequisites for injunctive relief had not yet been met.

7. *See, e.g., Bas v. Tingy*, 4 U.S. (4 Dall.) 37 (1800) (upholding John Adams' undeclared war with France based on declarations that Congress had intended to authorize limited hostilities by means other than formally declared war, not on findings of plenary presidential power); *Talbot v. Seeman*, 5 U.S. (1 Cranch) 1, 28 (1801) (finding that Congress had authorized an American commander's capture of neutral ship, reasoning that "[t]he whole powers of war being, by the constitution of the United States, vested in congress, the acts of that body can alone be resorted to as our guides in this inquiry"); *Little v. Barreme*, 6 U.S. (2 Cranch) 170 (1804) (naval officer who had executed presidential order during undeclared war was nevertheless liable to those he had injured in violation of a duly enacted statute); *Brown v. United States*, 12 U.S. (8 Cranch) 110 (1814) (invalidating executive seizure of British property shortly before Congress declared the War of 1812,

ruling on merits that Executive was powerless to confiscate enemy property without legislative authorization); *The Prize Cases*, 67 U.S. (2 Black) 635, 665–71 (1862) (sustaining Union seizure of ships trading with Confederacy after Lincoln's blockade of southern ports). *See generally The National Security Constitution, supra* note 1, at 134–49.

8. *See* cases cited in Lawrence R. Velvel, *The War in Viet Nam: Unconstitutional, Justiciable, and Jurisdictionally Attackable*, 16 Kan. L. Rev. 449, 480–81 n.138 (1968).

9. *United States v. Curtiss-Wright Export Corp.*, 299 U.S. 304 (1936).

10. *Youngstown Sheet & Tube Co. v. Sawyer*, 343 U.S. 579, 635 (1952) (Jackson, J., concurring).

11. For a listing of the Vietnam cases, see Velvel, *supra* note 8; Robert P. Sugarman, *Judicial Decisions Concerning the Constitutionality of United States Military Activity in Indo-China: A Bibliography of Court Decisions*, 13 Colum. J. Transnat'l L. 470 (1974) (collecting cases).

12. 50 U.S.C. §§ 1541–48.

13. *See generally The National Security Constitution, supra* note 1, at 67–100 (collecting cases).

14. 369 U.S. 186, 211–13 (1962). *Accord INS v. Chadha*, 462 U.S. 919, 942 (1983) ("Resolution of litigation challenging the constitutional authority of one of the three branches cannot be evaded by the courts simply because the issues have political implications.").

15. *See generally* cases cited in *Baker v. Carr*, 369 U.S. 186, 211–13 (1962); Charles A. Lofgren, *War-Making under the Constitution: The Original Understanding*, 81 Yale L.J. 672, 701 (1972).

16. *See, e.g., The Prize Cases*, 67 U.S. (2 Black) 635, 666–71 (1862) (sustaining President's authority to order blockade in Civil war pursuant to Commander in Chief power or legislative ratification); *Martin v. Mott*, 25 U.S. (12 Wheat.) 19, 30 (1827) (sustaining President's authority to call forth militia to repel invasion); *United States v. Curtiss-Wright Export Corp.*, 299 U.S. 304 (1936) (reviewing and sustaining presidential action on merits, relying on authority delegated from Congress).

17. *Ramirez de Arellano v. Weinberger*, 745 F.2d 1500, 1514 (D.C. Cir. 1984) (en banc) (Wilkey, J.), *vacated on other grounds*, 471 U.S. 1113 (1985); *see id.* 745 F.2d at 1551 (Scalia, J., dissenting); *Tel-Oren v. Libyan Arab Republic*, 726 F.2d 774, 798 (D.C. Cir. 1984) (Bork, J., concurring).

18. For an enumeration of these prudential concerns, see generally Alexander M. Bickel, *The Least Dangerous Branch: The Supreme Court at the Bar of Politics* 183–98 (1962); Jesse H. Choper, *Judicial Review and the National Political Process: A Functional Reconsideration of the Role of the Supreme Court* 217–315 (1980).

19. *See, e.g., Sumitomo Shoji America v. Avagliano*, 457 U.S. 176 (1982) (construing treaty); *U.S. v. Belmont*, 301 U.S. 324 (1937) (construing executive agreement); *The Paquete Habana*, 175 U.S. 677 (1900) (customary international law). This point was graphically made in *Mora v. McNamara*, 389 U.S. 934 (1967), where Justice Stewart, joined by Justice Douglas, dissented from denial of certiorari to three draftees' petition requesting an injunction and declaratory judgment regarding the illegality of U.S. military activity in Vietnam. Justice Stewart identified the following "questions of great magnitude" raised by the petition, all of which he suggested involved standard questions of judicial interpretation:

I. Is the present United States military activity . . . a "war" within the meaning of Article I, Section 8, Clause 11, of the Constitution?

II. If so, may the Executive constitutionally order the petitioners to participate in that military activity, when no war has been declared by the Congress?

III. Of what relevance to Question II are the present treaty obligations of the United States?

IV. Of what relevance to Question II is [any] Joint Congressional . . . Resolution [passed with regard to such activity]?

(a) Do present United States military operations fall within the terms of the Joint Resolution?

(b) If the Joint Resolution purports to give the Chief Executive authority to commit United States forces to armed conflict limited in scope only by his own absolute discretion, is the Resolution a constitutionally impermissible delegation of all or part of Congress's power to declare war?

Id. at 934–35.

20. *Japan Whaling Ass'n v. American Cetacean Soc'y*, 478 U.S. 221, 230 (1986).

21. 418 U.S. 683 (1974).

22. *See, e.g.*, Fritz W. Scharpf, *Judicial Review and the Political Question: A Functional Analysis*, 75 Yale L.J. 517 (1966).

23. As Professor Redish has noted, the same argument could be made when the Senate refuses to ratify a treaty that the President has negotiated: "In that instance, other nations are asked to understand our complex constitutional system of checks and balances, and we somehow manage to survive as a nation." Martin H. Redish, *Judicial Review and the "Political Question,"* 79 Nw. U.L. Rev. 1031, 1052 (1985).

24. As the Iran-Contra Affair revealed, embarrassing information will almost certainly emerge anyway, during subsequent executive, legislative, and criminal investigations. To bar civil adjudication on this ground while the illegal conduct is occurring merely heightens the likelihood that the unscrutinized conduct will cause even greater embarrassment for the country. *See generally The National Security Constitution, supra* note 1, at 11–37, 101–16.

25. *See, e.g., New York Times Co. v. United States*, 403 U.S. 713 (1971); *Kent v. Dulles*, 357 U.S. 116 (1958). Even the Supreme Court's infamous and thoroughly discredited decision in *Korematsu v. United States*, 323 U.S. 214 (1944), did not deny the justiciability of the challenged governmental conduct.

26. *See, e.g., Massachusetts v. Laird*, 451 F.2d 26 (1st Cir. 1971); *Berk v. Laird*, 429 F.2d 302 (2d Cir. 1970).

27. Although the parties might well dispute whether certain types of interests—for example, extinguished claims against foreign governments—constitute protected property taken without just compensation for a public purpose. *See, e.g., Shanghai Power Co. v. United States*, 4 Cl. Ct. 237 (1983), *aff'd*, 765 F.2d 159 (Fed. Cir. 1985), *cert. denied*, 474 U.S. 909 (1985).

28. *See, e.g.*, Sidak, *supra* note 2, at 113.

29. *Ramirez de Arellano v. Weinberger*, 745 F.2d 1500, 1531 (D.C. Cir. 1984) (en banc), *vacated on other grounds*, 471 U.S. 1113 (1985). For a discussion of the rule in *Marbury*, see Akhil R. Amar, *Marbury, Section 13, and the Original Jurisdiction of the Supreme Court*, 56 U. Chi. L. Rev. 443, 448 (1989).

30. Louis Henkin, *Constitutionalism, Democracy, and Foreign Affairs* 88 (1990).

31. *See, e.g.*, Libya, Grenada, Panama, discussed in *The National Security Constitution, supra* note 1, at 39.

32. *See, e.g.*, Angola, Laos, El Salvador, discussed in *The National Security Constitution, supra* note 1, at 58–66.

33. As Professor Ely has trenchantly observed, under the current Resolution, courts have inexplicably claimed separation-of-powers or judicial incompetence rationales for refusing to decide whether "hostilities" exist for purpose of triggering the War Powers Resolution, even while they "are routinely called upon, without incident, to decide insurance cases in which the existence or nonexistence of hostilities must be judicially determined for purposes of giving effect to a war risk clause." Ely, *supra* note 3, at 1409.

34. *See The National Security Constitution, supra* note 1, at 117–52.

35. *See, e.g.*, Robert M. Cover, *Justice Accused: Antislavery and the Judicial Process* Forward (1975).

36. In *Dellums*, Judge Greene reasoned that for the case to be ripe "the plaintiffs [must] be or represent a majority of the Members of the Congress: the majority of the body that under the Constitution is the only one competent to declare war, and *therefore also the one with the ability to seek an order from the courts to prevent anyone else, i.e., the Executive, from in effect declaring war.*" 752 F. Supp. at 1151 (emphasis added). In fact, since the Constitution requires *Congress* affirmatively to declare war, far less than a majority of Congress as a whole (fifty-one Senators, for example) may prevent the Executive from "declaring" war. Under Judge Greene's own reasoning, that smaller number should also be able to obtain a court order enjoining an unauthorized war.

As I have suggested in this chapter, the ripeness question that should have been asked was whether the Executive branch had clearly committed itself to a course of action and the two political branches had reached a political impasse regarding whether that course of action would be legal. Under this test, Judge Greene still could have found the case not ripe, but because Secretary Baker had not yet met with Iraqi Foreign Minister Tariq Aziz, a meeting that might have altered the course the Executive would ultimately pursue.

37. 752 F. Supp. at 1147.

38. 511 F.2d 430 (D.C. Cir. 1974).

39. *See* Ely, *supra* note 3, at 1406; John Hart Ely, *Another Such Victory: Constitutional Theory and Practice in a World Where Courts Are No Different from Legislatures*, 77 Va. L. Rev. 878–79 (1991).

40. *See, e.g.*, *Riegle v. FOMC*, 656 F.2d 873 (D.C. Cir. 1981), and its progeny.

41. For an influential statement of this view, see *Ramirez de Arellano v. Weinberger*, 745 F.2d at 1561 (Scalia, J., dissenting).

42. In *McNary v. Haitian Centers Council*, 969 F.2d 1350 (2d Cir. 1992), *rev'd*, 61 U.S.L.W. 4684 (June 21, 1993), the Solicitor General has recently claimed that 5 U.S.C. § 702(1)—a subsection of the Administrative Procedure Act which provides that "[n]othing" in this section "affects other limitations on judicial review or the power or duty of the court to dismiss any action or deny relief on any other appropriate legal or equitable ground"— grants lower federal courts free-floating equitable power to find immigration injunctions "inappropriate," even when actions of INS and other executive officials plainly violate statute and treaty.

43. *See, e.g.*, *Resolution Trust Corp. v. Elman*, 949 F.2d 624, 626 (2d Cir. 1991) ("The party seeking the [preliminary] injunction must demonstrate (1) irreparable harm should the injunction not be granted, and (2) either (a) a likelihood of success on the merits, or (b) sufficiently serious questions going to the merits and a balance of hardships tipping decidedly toward the party seeking injunctive relief.").

44. 752 F. Supp. at 1149. Judge Greene concluded that "[t]he 'remedies' of cutting off funding to the military or impeaching the President are not available to these plaintiffs either politically or practically [and] would not afford the relief sought by the plaintiffs— which is the guarantee that they will have the opportunity to debate and vote on the wisdom

of initiating a military attack against Iraq before the United States military becomes embroiled in belligerency with that nation." *Id.*

45. *See* S.J. Res. 323, 100th Cong., 2d Sess., 134 Cong. Rec., May 19, 1988, at S6239 (daily ed.).

46. The bill's strategy has three other key elements. First, by creating core consultative groups, the bill attempts to devise centralized repositories of political expertise within Congress with continuing responsibility to deal with the war powers problem. Second, by requiring the President to consult with those groups, the bill both directly fosters inter-branch dialogue and attempts to equalize access to sensitive information that would other-wise lie exclusively within the President's control. In the process, the consultation requirements seek to ensure that Congress will become involved earlier in the decision-making process, so that the President cannot simply commit troops first, then present Congress with a *fait accompli.* Third, the bill attempts to short-cut the problems of ineffective legislative tools and insufficient political will by employing a variety of legal devices that allow Congress to declare its opposition to presidential commitment of troops by less than a two-thirds vote in each house: *e.g.,* a fast-track procedure, an automatic appropriations cutoff device, and a judicial review provision. *See generally The National Security Constitution, supra* note 1, at 185–207.

47. *See generally The National Security Constitution, supra* note 1 (arguing that recur-rent pattern of executive initiative, congressional acquiescence, and judicial tolerance pervades foreign affairs).

48. A similar claim was made in *Ange v. Bush,* 752 F. Supp. 509 (1990), which was dismissed by Judge Lamberth on the same day that Judge Greene decided *Dellums.*

49. *See The National Security Constitution, supra* note 1, at 70 (defining "quasi-consti-tutional custom" as a set of institutional norms generated by the historical interaction of two or more federal branches with one another . . . [that] represent informal accommodations between two or more branches on the question of who decides with regard to particular foreign policy matters"); *see also* Chapter 2 (discussion by Peter Raven-Hansen on "cus-tomary national security law").

50. Judge Greene found that "the forces involved are of such magnitude and signifi-cance as to present no serious claim that a war would not ensue if they became engaged in combat, and it is therefore clear that congressional approval is required if Congress desires to become involved." 752 F. Supp. at 1145. Congress's authorizing resolution expressly invoked the War Powers Resolution, and the House's Bennett-Durbin Resolution reaf-firmed that "[a]ny offensive action against Iraq must be explicitly approved by the Con-gress of the United States before such action may be initiated." H. Con. Res. 32, 102d Cong., 1st Sess. (Jan. 12, 1991). Most telling is that, despite his disclaimers, President Bush came to Congress and asked it to approve the war. Thus, Iraq joins the two World Wars and Vietnam as four of five relevant historical instances in this century in which the President has sought such formal congressional approval.

51. President Bush's subsequent deployment of troops into Somalia pursuant to a U.N. Security Council resolution but without seeking congressional authorization suggests that some Presidents still believe they have such authority for lesser uses of force.

7 Constraints on "Covert" Paramilitary Action

Gregory F. Treverton

The use of covert action has caused deep divisions in the United States, ones that seem likely to outlive the end of the Cold War. On one hand, America's opponents, especially its former mortal foe, the Soviet Union, have not always played by Marquis of Queensberry rules; countering them has thus compelled the U.S. government to act in ways just as nasty as they act. On the other hand, if doing so entails violating principles that the nation holds dear, the United States risks looking no different than those enemies.[1]

Absent the Soviet bear, the national security grounds for covert operations may erode, but the world will still seem a dangerous place where democracy's enemies continue to resort to unsavory tactics. Covert actions—including paramilitary operations or secret warfare—will in all likelihood remain on the agenda, and with them the question: can they be squared with open democracy at an acceptable price, which in turn requires asking, how effective have they been?

Over the last two decades the Executive branch and Congress have argued their way toward a means of handling secret operations between the two branches. That process has meant that Congress is, most of the time and paradoxically, more a partner in decisions about secret warfare than about open uses of force. The War Powers Resolution (WPR), enacted to deal with the latter is widely agreed to have been a failure; indeed, the WPR resulted from and contributed to precisely what it was intended to avoid—a built-in confrontation between the branches. Yet the existing process for handling covert warfare stops well short of open deliberation in advance of the decision to act. Nonetheless, I would suggest that we cannot expect to do much better, and that indeed it may be unwise to try.

This chapter focuses on "covert" *paramilitary action*, supposedly secret operations designed to provide military aid and training to foreign parties, generally though not always on a large scale. This discussion excludes covert *political actions*, which are by far the largest type of covert action; political actions attempt to change the balance of political forces in another country, most often by secretly providing money to particular groups.

The categories are hardly tidy, for it goes without saying that *who* gets paramilitary assistance has political effects; it was critical, for instance, to the balance of power among competing Afghan factions when the U.S. provided clandestine aid to rebels following the 1979 Soviet invasion. Moreover, political operations often begin, accompany, or follow secret warfare—or open war for that matter: in Panama, no fewer than four separate covert plans were designed to oust Manuel Noriega before American GIs were called upon to do the job overtly in 1989.

Before unleashing war against Iraq, for example, the Bush Administration had considered and rejected as infeasible covert projects to overthrow Saddam Hussein. In late 1991 and 1992, after open war in the Gulf could not unseat him, the Administration, under Saudi pressure, revisited those plans, including for U.S. air support to a coup, while continuing to lay most of its emphasis on overt pressure through the United Nations if Saddam obstructed U.N. inspectors trying to find Iraqi weapons. Both Saudi Arabia and Kuwait were reported ready to help fund covert operations and to support whatever military or paramilitary operations might then ensue. In June 1992, though, a U.S. National Intelligence Estimate, ostentatiously leaked in Washington, concluded that despite all the pressure, Saddam's hold was stronger than a year earlier.[2]

OVERT-COVERT ACTION

Paramilitary operations are now for the most part open secrets, with open congressional debates on most and open votes on several. These so-called "overt-covert" actions, with antecedents dating to Laos in the 1960s, began to take on their current shape in the wake of the first congressional investigations of intelligence abuses in the mid-1970s. In 1974 Congress passed the Hughes-Ryan Act, the operative paragraph of which reads:

No funds appropriated under the authority of this or any other Act may be expended by or on behalf of the [CIA] for operations in foreign countries, other than activities intended solely for obtaining necessary intelligence, unless and until the President finds that each such operation is important to the national security of the United States and reports, in a timely fashion, a description and scope of such operation to the appropriate committees of Congress.[3]

From the verb "finds" came the noun "finding"—a written document bearing the President's signature. Hughes-Ryan required the President to put his name and his reputation on the line. The "appropriate committees" were originally six—the Intelligence subcommittees of Armed Services and Appropriations in both houses plus House Foreign Affairs and Senate Foreign Relations. The six became eight when Congress created permanent intelligence committees in both the House and Senate in the mid-1970s, and then two when Congress passed the 1980 Intelligence Oversight Act. The Act required the President to notify the two committees of all covert actions in advance, or in a "timely fashion" when advance notice was not possible.[4] Following the Reagan Administration's claim in the Iran-Contra Affair that the statute allowed the President to delay notice for as long as he felt necessary, Congress revised the Act in 1991 to strengthen the reporting and oversight requirements for covert actions.[5]

Covertness has now come primarily to mean discretion, such that the activity can be "plausibly denied" by the United States vis-a-vis foreign governments. The United States and other nations, including the target, could thus act officially as though it were not happening if they chose. They could continue diplomatic discussion if they thought it useful, much as Elizabeth I of England and Philip II of Spain did while each was doing the best to "destabilize" the other. That was most apparent in the instance of Afghanistan, where only in the final Geneva negotiations did the United States openly acknowledge that it had been supporting the Mujahedeen since 1979.

The 1985–1986 covert arms sales to Iran stand in lone contrast. When President Reagan's assistants John Poindexter and Oliver North sought to protect him by keeping him ignorant of some critical details of the Iran operation, they corrupted plausible denial in a way reminiscent of CIA officials who, during attempts to assassinate Fidel Castro two decades earlier, apparently kept President Kennedy ignorant to protect him.

In contrast, the "correct" form of plausible denial is ambiguous in its effect on international order—diplomacy continues while destabilization proceeds, and the first can be seen as an encouragement of the second—but is less corrupting of American democracy than real secrecy. It now means, as it rarely did in the past, that the American people and their representatives will often be able to know of and debate about the underlying operations. In the future, too, major covert actions, especially paramilitary ones, will be for all intents and purposes overt. The controversy over them will spill into the public domain if they are not propelled there by the Executive branch in the first place. If some options are thereby foreclosed, at least the choices will be openly debated at some point during their occurrence.

However, although paramilitary operations become overt-covert once they are large, they usually do not start large. Thus, there is the question of whether covert operations, even paramilitary ones, are not just a "middle option," more than nothing but less than open war, but also an "easier option" because they are initially secret. Do officials in the Executive branch—and increasingly, perhaps, Members of Congress—find it easier to say "yes" than if the initial decision were more public? If so, is that dangerous for constitutional governance?

The question turns on the constitutional standard for approval. In the largest recent case, Afghanistan, the reasons for discretion were in Pakistan, not Washington, and aid to the Mujahedeen plainly would have been authorized openly by Congress; indeed, after the beginning it was so authorized as part of the miltary construction budget. In that case and the others (save Iran), the statutory procedure for covert actions was observed—the congressional oversight committees were informed, usually in advance but in any event near the time actions began, they asked questions, and registered their approval or at least their acquiescence.

Congress did not formally approve in advance, but it had not asked for that responsibility.

CASE STUDIES

The Iran-Contra Affair

Nicaragua. The Iran-Contra affair most vividly displays the issues, both practical and constitutional, inherent in secret warfare. At its pinnacle, it crossed profits from covert arms sales to Iran with efforts by White House operatives to support the Contras in Nicaragua during the period when Congress had cut off covert funding for them. The extended debate over aiding the Contras has been well-told elsewhere.[6] It began with the end of the long reign of the Somoza family in 1979, bringing to power the armed opposition, the Sandinista National Liberation Front, in uneasy—and temporary—partnership with a range of non-military opposition groups. The Reagan Administration then sought to unite and support the Sandinista's armed opponents, dubbed the Contras. Yet the purpose of that covert support seemed a moving target, which suggested to Congress either confusion or deception.

The aims of America's covert intervention remained in dispute while the war intensified. Any limited objective seemed less and less plausible after revelations early in 1984 that the CIA itself had mined Nicaraguan harbors. Gaps in the Administration's consultation with the congressional intelligence committees angered even Senator Barry Goldwater, the Republican committee chairman and a man not known for his opposition to covert action.

The sequence illustrates the problems Congress has in confronting a popular—and determined—President, especially if it is divided or ambivalent. The Senate had a fairly consistent majority in support of aid to the Contras; the majority of the House, however, was prepared to support aid only on the condition that the Administration actively pursue a negotiated peace in Central America. Yet since the negotiating lever was in the control of the Administration, the House was left to exhort or to vote "no" on aid to reinforce its unhappiness with administration policy. The House had voted three times against paramilitary aid only to have the operation rescued by House-Senate conferences.

Finally, in the fall of of 1984, the Congress had adopted the Boland Amendment that cut off all funding for paramilitary activities against Nicaragua. In early 1985 the House again voted down a request for aid; but in August agreed to $27 million in so-called "nonmilitary" aid to the Contras, although barring the CIA from administering the aid and from direct contact with the Contras or assisting in their training. Congress did not restore CIA funding until October 1986.[7]

This off-again-on-again funding, deeply frustrating to those in the Reagan Administration most committed to the Contras, bred circumventions of the congressional restrictions. Some in the Administration felt that congressional language did not bar the National Security Council staff and other "nonintelligence" officials from seeking aid elsewhere. In early 1984, the President directed the NSC staff, in the words of national security adviser Robert McFarlane, to keep the Contras together "body and soul." William Casey, the Director of Central Intelligence (DCI) and other officials began to approach governments ranging from Israel to Brunei to Saudi Arabia, and quietly canvassed private sources in the United States, South Korea, Taiwan, and Latin America. That private support totalled some $34 million during the period of the aid cut-off.[8]

By the spring of 1984, as congressional appropriations were running out, Oliver North, the NSC staff's deputy director for political-military affairs, had become coordinator of the private support, dubbed "the Enterprise" by those involved. In October when Congress barred any CIA involvement, the Agency issued a "cease and desist" order to its stations. Nevertheless, about a dozen CIA officers remained involved in North's operation, apparently construing his role to signify White House authorization.

By the fall of 1985, North was overseeing the shipping of privately-purchased arms to the Contras and the construction of a secret airfield in Costa Rica—operations North dubbed "Project Democracy." But a year later a Beirut newspaper printed a bizarre account of a trip to Teheran by McFarlane in connection with secret arms sales to Iran, and the clutch of secret operations labelled "Iran-Contra" began to unravel—details trailing through executive and congressional investigations and ensuing criminal trials. In February 1990 the Sandinistas were voted out of office in elections where international observers practically outnumbered voters.

Iran. The arms sales to Iran illustrate the untidiness of trying to distinguish between political and paramilitary operations, for they used military means but for explicitly political purposes. The United States did not transfer arms to revolutionary Iran to help it win a conflict, or to give one faction a military advantage over another. Rather, the point, in so far as one can be inferred, was some combination of establishing the *bona fides* of American negotiators, giving a boost to their Iranian interlocutors, and bribing them to press Iran's Lebanese allies to release American hostages. Instead of providing money or technical assistance along with their advice, the United States furnished arms.

North sought and received CIA help in November 1985 when, in a comedy of errors, North's operatives could not get one shipment through Portugal to Israel. When he heard of the CIA involvement, John McMahon, the Agency's deputy director, angrily barred any further CIA involvement without a presidential finding. The next month President Reagan signed one finding to provide retroactive approval for the shipments; the new national security adviser, Admiral John Poindexter, destroyed that finding a year later because, he subsequently testified, it would have been embarrassing to the President.[9]

The President approved another finding on January 17, 1986, but it remained unknown to Congress until the next autumn when the scandal broke.[10] It expressed the operation's purposes "to establish contact with moderate elements within and outside the government of Iran by providing these elements with arms equipment." However, the accompanying background paper, prepared by North, was explicit about the link to getting U.S. hostages out of Lebanon: "this approach may well be our *only* way to achieve the release of the Americans held in Beirut. . . . If all the hostages are not released after the shipment of the first 1,000 weapons, further transfers would cease" (emphasis in the original).[11]

In February 1986 American arms were first shipped directly from the United States by the CIA to Israel for transfer to Iran. Three other shipments were made, the last in late October. In all, some 2,000 TOW antitank missiles, as well as other weapons and spare parts were sold to Iran. Three U.S. hostages were released, but three more were taken during the course of the operation.

Post Mortem. What is striking about the Contra side of the operation is how little of a secret it was, as has been the case with other recent "secret" wars. The intelligence committees had doubts aplenty about what kind of operations they were approving or permitting against Nicaragua. The language of the President's first finding submitted to the committees "engage in paramilitary . . . operations in Nicaragua and elsewhere"[12]—seemed to permit almost anything. The purpose of aid to the Contras was ever changing: it would slow the infiltration of arms from Nicaragua to the rebels fighting the American-backed government of El Salvador, or it would focus the Sandinistas inward, away from the export of their revolution, or it would pressure the regime into serious negotiations with its neighbors and the United States.

Surely, however, the Contras themselves did not have limited purposes, much less ones that suited American convenience. They wanted not to constrain the Sandinista government, but to replace it. Likewise, toppling the Sandinista regime was the Reagan Administration's purpose that everyone suspected but no official would utter. At the same time, public opinion surveys in the United States suggested what congressional votes on aid to the Contras indicated: Americans did not like or trust the Sandinistas but were not prepared to pay the price of sending the Marines to rid the hemisphere of them.[13]

And, so, most likely, the Administration dissembled, turning, as Robert McFarlane subsequently admitted, "to covert action because they thought they could not get congressional support for overt activities."[14] If the Administration was intentionally being duplicitous, it was not the first one to take half a loaf from Congress when it couldn't get a whole one. Nor, if it weren't, would it be the first to set off down a path without knowing where it might lead.

That latter problem—choices made now leading to later consequences that acquire a momentum of their own—is a particular one for covert action because the stakes get acquired when the operation is most secret, at the beginning. It is, however, not unique to covert action; rather it runs through all policies, secret and open, foreign and domestic. Small actions create stakes and expectations which then weigh on subsequent choices; "throwing good money after bad" is the frequent result.

On the other hand, the arms sales to Iran *were* successfully concealed from Congress for nearly a year explicitly because the Administration feared opposition. (That this most secret covert action was the least successful may be a telling caution.) The sales operation, also managed day to day by North, was so closely held that even the CIA was at first cut out, though Casey himself was central.

Critical meetings were held with no analytic papers prepared beforehand and no record of decisions kept afterward.

Afghanistan

The biggest recent overt-covert operation was U.S. assistance to the Afghan rebels—or freedom-fighters, depending on your taste—which began in the last year of the Carter Administration and escalated sharply in the mid-1980s, to over $300 million per year, mostly for small arms, clothing, and supplies.[15] Americans, in and out of Congress, broadly supported the cause. The secret was an open one; the American role was not so much covert as, by tacit agreement, unacknowledged. Indeed, Egyptian President Anwar el-Sadat said on NBC news two weeks before he was killed: "Let me reveal a secret: the first moment that the Afghan incident [the 1979 Soviet invasion] took place, the U.S. contacted me here and the transport of armaments to the Afghans started from Cairo on U.S. planes."[16]

The reason for circumspection was the touchy position of the Pakistani government, the only conduit for American supplies to the rebels. Pakistan was prepared to support them but unwilling to be too visible in doing so lest it antagonize its powerful neighbor, the Soviet Union. In those circumstances, the resort to the CIA, rather than the American military, was more a matter of being discreet than of keeping the whole affair secret. Congress was sometimes in front of the Executive, appropriating unrequested money in 1983 and pressing the Administration to deliver more sophisticated weaponry.

As the fighting dragged on and Mikhail Gorbachev took power, the Soviet Union agreed to what few expected—to withdraw its troops from Afghanistan, by February 15, 1989. It did so even after the United States insisted on symmetry—i.e., Washington would feel free to help the rebels, the Mujahedeen, as much as Moscow helped the government. The Soviet withdrawal brought one surprise and one predictability: the Soviet-installed government in Kabul did not collapse, and the Mujahedeen could not unify.

The Soviet departure ended neither the American operation nor Afghanistan's agony, but it did diminish Congress's enthusiasm for what had been an anti-Soviet crusade. The Mujahedeen remained fragmented, and reports accumulated that they were involved in drug trafficking and arms dealing. Meanwhile, the United States and the Soviet Union edged toward a compromise that might leave the Kabul government in power during a transition. In 1990 Congress reportedly cut $50 million from the Administration's request for $300 million.[17]

An abortive Mujahedeen offensive in November 1990 underscored the differences between the U.S. State Department, which sought to disengage from Afghanistan, and the CIA operators, who thought a rebel victory still possible. In September 1991 Washington and Moscow agreed to stop arms shipments to the combatants by the end of the year, leaving the issue to U.N. mediation. The United States continued humanitarian aid, in the range of $60–80 million per year.

By March 1992 the United Nations had put together a plan to pull the factions into an interim government, which would then hold free elections. In April, though, the Mujahedeen took control of Kabul. The United States continued providing relief supplies, while quietly supporting U.N. mediation and a peaceable end to Afghanistan's turmoil. At the same time it sought to retrieve some of the advanced arms that remained in Mujahedeen arsenals.

Angola

In two other recent cases, involving Angola and Cambodia, the process did seem to provide for a tolerably thorough debate close to the time an operation was initiated. In Angola, the CIA had provided covert support to Jonas Savimbi, leader of Angola's insurgent UNITA (Union for the Total Independence of Angola, in its Portuguese acronym) during the Angolan civil war of the mid-1970s ("Angola I"). By the mid-1980s, with a Marxist government in Angola that was supported by thousands of Cubans, the Reagan Administration debated whether to resume significant aid to Savimbi's anti-government forces ("Angola II").

Both Secretary of State George Shultz and the congressional intelligence committees were reluctant to get reinvolved. Aiding UNITA would increase the threat to the Angolan government and thereby justify its retaining Cuban cadres. That argument was overturned by Savimbi's January 1986 visit to Washington, which generated rave reviews especially from American conservatives. The CIA was authorized $15 million in weaponry for UNITA, which grew to some $50 million in 1989.[18] It included Stinger hand-held anti-aircraft missiles, a subject of special controversy because of their attractiveness to terrorists should they fall into the wrong hands.

Nothing about the aid was very secret. Lee Hamilton, then chairing the House Intelligence Committee, took his opposition to the program to the floor of the House, where he lost. In an open hearing in 1989, Assistant Secretary of State Herman Cohen labelled U.S. aid "an open secret."[19]

Just weeks before George Bush took office, the Reagan Administration managed to broker a deal in which South Africa cut off support for UNITA and promised independence for Namibia in return for the withdrawal of all 50,000 Cuban troops supporting the leftist government of Angola. Namibia became independent in early 1990, and the last Cuban troops departed Angola in 1991.

When South Africa cut UNITA loose, the CIA had to resupply it through Zaire, geographically awkward but conferring leverage on Zaire's leader, Mobutu Sese Seko, who had arranged a truce in June 1989 between Savimbi and Angolan President Jose Eduardo dos Santos. Savimbi pulled out of the truce in September, Mobutu stopped the flow of arms in October, and fighting broke out again in January 1990. Savimbi turned back an Angolan offensive, and cease-fire talks resumed, with both Washington and Moscow working behind the scenes. The administration requested supplemental covert aid for Savimbi in mid-1990, and in the fall the House and Senate agreed, but held back $25 million of a total aid package of $60 million for 1991 in order to entice Angola to reach a settlement and Moscow to withdraw its aid. The $25 million was to be released at the President's request with the assent of the two intelligence committees.[20]

In May 1992 Savimbi and the government reached an agreement, with Washington and Moscow again urging from behind the scenes. At the same time, gathering reports of UNITA human rights abuses marked a cooling in Washington's long on-again-off-again connection to Savimbi. The man who had seemed a freedom fighter, especially to American conservatives, when there were Soviets and Cubans to oppose, looked different with the end of the Cold War. Elections in autumn 1992 produced a narrow defeat for Savimbi, and violence broke out again. Ironically, observers seemed to predict a peaceable transition in part because they presumed the election and its aftermath were "wired," yet if the Cold War's end provided the wirers—Washington and Moscow—incentive to agree, it also diminished their influence with their previous clients. In May 1993, the United States formally recognized the government of Angola under the declared winner, dos Santos.

Cambodia

In Cambodia, the United States supplied both overt and covert aid to "non-communist" rebels fighting the government installed after Vietnam's invasion of that country. Overtly, American aid for supplying and transporting nonlethal material totalled some $5.5 million in (fiscal year) 1989 and increased the next year.[21] By the end of 1989 the covert component of American policy was estimated at more than $15 million.[22] The mechanism for aid was the ASEAN-sponsored Working Group, officially made up of Thailand, Malaysia, and Singapore, but also including American military and intelligence officials.

The program was controversial from the start, for as with other covert actions, circumstances abroad frustrated tidy distinctions made in Washington. The United States sought to build up non-communist rebels by comparison to their uneasy ally, the Khmer Rouge, whose bloody rule brought on Vietnam's occupation in the first place. But aiding the Khmer Rouge's allies without helping it was no mean feat.

In late spring 1989, after a visit to Washington by the son of exiled Cambodian leader Prince Sihanouk, the United States debated providing weaponry covertly. By fall it was reported that American arms, including Dragon antitank weapons, were reaching the rebels at their bases in Thailand, although it remained unclear whether any of the U.S. aid actually went for weapons, or whether the weapons were purchased by others (Singapore, for instance), with American aid taking up the slack by providing uniforms, food, vehicles, and training.[23] Congressional leaders remained leery of sending weapons and reportedly stipulated, against executive objections, that CIA contingency funds could not be used for that purpose without explicit congressional approval.[24]

One American objective was achieved in the autumn of 1989 when Vietnam ended its decade-long occupation of Cambodia. The next year all the Cambodia parties agreed to a U.N. framework for a peace settlement—another fruit of warming superpower relations. In July 1990 the United States had reversed policy and withdrawn recognition of the guerrilla coalition, again largely because of concern over the Khmer Rouge. Congress then acted to end the *covert* support, and instead voted for $20 million in open assistance, to be allocated by the State Department, and again stipulated that no aid go to the Khmer Rouge.[25]

In October 1991 the Cambodian factions signed a comprehensive peace treaty in Paris, agreeing to disarm and move toward free elections under U.N. auspices—the most ambitious U.N. program ever undertaken. By mid-1992 the U.N. had collected pledges of nearly $1 billion in reconstruction aid for the country, with the United States committed to provide $135 million. The Khmer Rouge's failure to comply with the disarmament provisions of the treaty, however, continues to hang over Cambodia's future. Free elections were held in May 1993, and threatened violence by the Khmer Rouge never materialized. The opposition party led by Prince Sihanouk won.

CONTROVERSY AND CONSTITUTIONAL GOVERNANCE

The degree of controversy over the goals of specific covert actions directly affects the way in which they are conducted. Afghanistan was hardly controversial at all; in the words of former DCI William Colby: "Afghanistan was a two-column headline in the *Washington Post* for one day, then almost nothing."[26] This was so because most members of Congress thought it made sense, as did most Americans who knew or thought about it—and, no doubt, most of the journalists who reported it.

At the other end was Nicaragua, controversial from start to finish. It is plain that covert pieces of larger, controversial policies will not remain secret. In this case neither proponents nor opponents had much interest in secrecy. Overt debate no doubt foreclosed some alternatives and produced inconsistent American policy. Yet the policy was inconsistent not because no one knew what was afoot but rather because they could not agree. Nicaragua was a far cry from some covert actions of the 1960s and early 1970s—from Laos to Chile—which were secret from the American people and the Congress but hardly a secret in the country that was the target.

Similarly, many in government—at both ends of Pennsylvania Avenue—had doubts about the Angolan operation. However, once the Executive had decided what he wanted, Congress acceded to his demands. Presidents usually get their way in foreign policy, if they are determined. Unless they are badly out of step with public opinion, Congress is permissive. So it has been in the realm of covert action, as in the case of Angola.

In the future, too, Administrations will have to make evident that covert programs are consistent with publicly announced policies. And because major covert actions will not remain secret, Presidents will be well advised, before the fact, to ask themselves whether the covert action could bear the test of disclosure: would it still seem sensible once it were public, and, most likely, public before it was over?[27]

The views of congressional overseers can give Presidents a reading of what the public would think if it knew of the operation. If the operation is not controversial, as with Afghanistan, it will go forward discreetly. If the Administration is out of step with what the public will accept, as in the case of arms sales to Iran, it may learn that in advance, rather than being punished by Congress after the fact. If the public is divided or confused, as with aid to the Contras, the Administration probably can have its way but will be well advised to think twice. Congress indicated, about as clearly as it could, that it did not like the course of administration policy. Yet in the crunch Congress found it difficult to vote against a popular President with respect to the "covert" piece of that policy—aid to the Contras. The result, in American democracy, was gridlock, no clear sense of policy, and a large degree of frustration on both sides.

Success or Failure?

Judgments about the effectiveness of these operations cannot settle the constitutional issue, but they are relevant. It plainly would make no sense to strain constitutional governance if the results abroad were minimal or negative. On its face, the Afghanistan operation was a success, or certainly cannot be labelled a failure: the Soviet Union departed.

In retrospect, though, it does seem that the form of the covert funding was partly responsible for what ensued after the Soviet departure—testimony to the inevitable costs of focusing on proximate objectives. To minimize the CIA role, American aid was channeled through Pakistan's Directorate of Inter-Services Intelligence (ISI). For reasons Pakistani and not American, ISI was closest to the more radical of the fundamentalist parties within the Mujahedeen, hardly the groups the United States would have liked to advantage.[28]

Plainly, aid to the Contras failed against the objective widely suspected of it—dislodging the Sandinistas from power. It had a number of intangible costs as well as tangible ones. It justified siege economics and politics by the Sandinistas, made the United States a handy bogey-man for internal failings, and justified almost any relationship with the Soviets and Cubans that Managua chose to pursue. It also was deemed excessive, if not improper, by most of America's friends in Europe and Latin America (even if some of the latter privately whispered urgings that the United States take care of the Sandinistas with force of arms). It is also fair to observe that in the year before the election, not to mention after it, the Contras were more trouble than any pressure on the Sandinistas they applied.

Yet the Sandinistas would not hold a completely fair election in 1984 when they would have won and did so in 1990 only under extraordinary external pressure. That same pressure may have made the Sandinista regime more repressive, hence less attractive than it might otherwise have been. Whether the Contras were a significant part of that pressure or marginal by comparison to other factors—the Central American peace process itself, the U.S. economic blockade, and the international distaste for the Sandinistas—is a matter for argument. My own conclusion, one I come to reluctantly, is that the aid did make a difference, especially given the fecklessness of internal opposition to the Sandinistas.

For Angola, the question is whether aid to UNITA was instrumental, marginal, or hurtful to getting both the deal by which Namibia became independent and the

Cubans departed Angola and an internal cease-fire in Angola. At this short distance from events, the aid seems marginal to the first agreement, one way or the other. With superpower relations warming, Cuba accepted American mediation, and Moscow seems to have argued for settling; its own resource drain was significant, perhaps $2 billion in 1988, and about half that for arms in 1989.[29]

Both Cuba and South Africa came to see strong reasons for agreement—fighting each other was a costly draw, all the more expensive for Cuba because as Angola's oil revenues dried up, so did the country's ability to pay Cuba; for South Africa, with domestic opposition to fighting a distant war growing, the argument for shrinking its defense perimeter by letting Namibia go became compelling. Whether the violence will be subdued, given UNITA's dissatisfaction with the 1992 election results, remains in doubt. To the extent, though, that American arms precluded the Angolan government from defeating UNITA prior to the election, it would count as a success. Now that the United States has recognized Angola, UNITA may be more compelled to cease its resistance.

Vietnam's withdrawal from Cambodia occurred before American weapons were sent, and so that part of American aid seems not to have been a factor. Although the non-Khmer Rouge opposition did score a victory in the May 1993 elections, at this distance, again, the American role does not seem to have been a significant factor in achieving that result.

Overall, the tally is one clear success (Afghanistan), one troubling partial success (Nicaragua), and two no-decisions (Angola and Cambodia). Those results can be viewed either as modest or as modestly impressive. Judgments of older cases would be similar.[30] The successes of the 1950s in overthrowing Mossadeq in Iran and Arbenz in Guatemala were almost too easy.[31] They obscured both how tenuous the successes were and how vulnerable the opponents. In so doing, they laid the basis for the debacle of the Bay of Pigs. In Angola I in the 1970s as well, the United States was seen both to intervene and to fail.

There is the risk that this accounting excludes successes that remained secret. That is possible but not likely: if success has a thousand fathers, one of them is likely to boast publicly even if the success is clandestine; CIA director Allen Dulles carefully leaked the two 1950s successes to the *Saturday Evening Post*. If any successes have remained secret, they are likely to be small ones.

OPTIONS FOR THE FUTURE

Banning Covert Paramilitary Action

On this record of success, why not ban paramilitary covert operations entirely? Given the fuzziness of the categories, this would probably require banning most covert actions lest there be arguments over which was which and who defined them. Logically, the end of the U.S.-Soviet confrontation erodes the justification for covert action; no longer does the Soviet Union serve as a bogey behind every regional conflict, one that argues for doing *something*, with covert action often a handy something.

Alas, such a ban is impractical and probably unwise. There is little sentiment for it in Congress. More to the point, in the chaotic world beyond the Cold War, foreswearing covert action is unwise. Terrorists, would-be nuclear proliferators, drug traffickers—all of these potential threats evoke plausible arguments for stealthy options and for not proclaiming American intentions in advance for all the world to see. In these circumstances, a ban on covert action would be likely to breed just the circumventions of Congress that are the most troubling feature of Iran-Contra. Presidents will be able to find someone, somewhere, to do their bidding. If covert actions are to be undertaken, better that they be the responsibility of the Director of Central Intelligence, who is confirmed by and thus accountable to Congress.

The alternative is the "Enterprise," the most troubling piece of the entire Iran-Contra story and one the congressional investigations paused over far too briefly. It was an attempt to escape congressional oversight entirely, to construct a CIA outside the American government. As North put it: "Director Casey had in mind . . . an overseas entity that was . . . self-financing, independent of appropriated monies."[32] The idea was dangerous, but the price the Administration paid for entertaining it was ultimately very high.

In circumventing the ban on aid to the Contras, the Reagan Administration's approach to Congress was more contemptuous than excluding. An isolated act or two of aiding the Contras would have been a close call given the ambiguity of the Boland Amendment. But close congressional votes do not excuse establishing the Enterprise. Poindexter and North were explicit in their later testimony before Congress: "I simply did not want outside interference," and "I didn't want to tell Congress anything," they said, respectively.[33]

Making Paramilitary Actions Formally Overt

If, then, banning paramilitary operations is impractical but if the main success, Afghanistan, was hardly covert, why not deny the covert option initially, as Halperin and Stern suggest?[34] Presidents could run paramilitary operations through the CIA but only after they had been approved openly by Congress, in some process akin to that of the War Powers Resolution. The practical problems, daunting on their face, may be less than they seem. Authorization in general terms could permit some discretion in implementation. Reasons for stealth are also less than they seem—after all, Afghanistan was a success in part surely because the Soviet Union *knew* that the United States was behind the funding of the Mujahedeen. And in cases of overt force, like Panama or Libya, the fact of force was hardly a surprise to the target, only its timing; authorization in advance would therefore have been possible, even through open congressional deliberations.

The rub is that it is precisely the operational details that matter, and so advance authorization is a recipe for subsequent arguments over what has been authorized. To be sure, the existing restricted—and secret—process is no guarantee that operational details will not fall between the cracks of relations between the President and Congress, even with goodwill on both sides. A case in point was the mining of Nicaragua's harbors by the CIA in January 1984. The mining was a new phase in the covert war, itself an act of war and one that threatened the shipping of both American allies and the Soviet Union. With a few mumbled words by Casey in the midst of a long briefing to one intelligence committee, the Administration honored the letter of the law but only just, and the episode angered even Senator Goldwater. When he learned about the operation, he was furious. His letter to Casey, which leaked into the press, was as notable for its unsenatorial prose as well as for its displeasure: "It gets down to one, little, simple phrase: I am pissed off!"[35]

CONCLUSION

Overall, existing constitutional arrangements have not worked badly, Iran-Contra notwithstanding. Congress neither desires nor is able to approve every covert action in advance; it can, however, exercise greater control over the CIA reserve for contingencies, a preauthorized fund from which the CIA can finance covert actions pursuant to a presidential finding. In the case of Cambodia, for example, Congress passed a statute prohibiting use of the reserve without explicit approval of the intelligence committees. Congress's reticence in insisting on advance approval of covert actions is, in my reading, not just political prudence but constitutional wisdom as well.

Historically, in Europe covert actions were accountable only to the sovereign. In the United States, the people are sovereign, and thus covert war-making, like open war, is the *shared* responsibility of the Executive branch and Congress. Declarations of overt war have been sparing, and their purpose has been to ratify a state of hostilities, not to initiate them. Congress is required to be a partner but not the ultimate decider. In the circumstances of the late twentieth century, as opposed to the eighteenth, congressional approval of standing intelligence services, like standing armies, is a recognition of changed circumstances.

And as in other areas of policy, the Constitution does not require Congress to exercise its role as partner through open votes of the full Houses. Congress can decide how to participate—it can choose to delegate at least some of its responsibility to a committee—in this case the intelligence committees.

If the existing process is not bad, it still can be improved. Several refinements would build the shared responsibility.[36] The most important is bringing Congress, through its intelligence committees, into the process at the earliest stage before an operation starts. Prior approval by Congress may not always be feasible, or even sought. But prior information is almost always possible, giving Presidents the benefits of the views of elected officials who are not his or her subordinates. President Bush accepted such notification in practice, in a letter to Congress, but rejected it as a matter of law as an infringement of presidential prerogatives.[37]

That expansive view of the President seems to me overreaching; for him to withhold, indefinitely, notifying anyone outside of the Executive branch abridges the accountability of Congress and misconstrues the President's own authority. Prior notification should be the law of the land, with notification delayed only when fast-moving circumstances make it impractical, and then for no more than a day or two.[38] When sensitivity is extreme, current law lets the President notify only the "gang of eight"—the chairmen and ranking minority members of the two intelligence committees, the majority and minority leaders of the Senate, and the Speaker and minority leader of the House.

No process can legislate wisdom or prevent circumvention. Process is, as we have seen, no guarantee against stupid presidential decisions or the resulting public scandals. But a requirement for advance notification—coupled with a ban on covert operations by any entity, public or private, other than the CIA, and with specific civil and criminal penalties for violators—would take the United States further in managing the inherent tension between secrecy and open government that is the root of American ambivalence about covert action.

If the Congress saw fit to create a *single* focal-point for engaging the Executive in discussion about both overt and covert uses of force, so much the better. If doing so contributed to the kind of real consultation between politicians not dependent on one another that was the point of the process for setting in motion covert action, better still. Surely, the first task is to give Congress something like the consultative role in open war-making that it now has in covert.

NOTES

1. *See, e.g.,* the colloquy between Ray Cline and George Ball in *Should the U.S. Fight Secret Wars?*, Harpers, Sept. 1984, at 33–47.

2. *See* reports in the Washington Post, Nov. 25, 1992, and the N.Y. Times, Feb. 7, 9, and June 16, 1992.

3. 22 U.S.C. § 2422 (1988), section 622 of the Foreign Assistance Act of 1974, repealed in 1991 as part of the Intelligence Oversight Act of 1991, Pub. L. No. 102–88, 105 Stat. 441.

4. 50 U.S.C. § 413 (1988), amended in 1991.

5. 50 U.S.C. § 413 (1991), Pub. L. No. 102–88. The new law retained the term "timely fashion" (in the face of a presidential veto), but Congress made clear in its legislative history that it intends the language to mean no more than a couple of days. S. Rep. No. 102–85, at 39–41, *reprinted in* 1991 U.S. Code Cong. & Admin. News 232–34.

6. My version is in *Intelligence: Welcome to the American Government*, in *A Question of Balance: The President, the Congress and Foreign Policy* (Thomas E. Mann, ed., 1990); *see also* the congressional investigation, Report of the Congressional Committees Investigating the Iran-Contra Affair, H. Rep. No. 100–433, S. Rep. No. 100–216, 100th Cong., 1st Sess. (1987) ("Iran-Contra Report"); and the earlier Report of the President's Special Review Board, known as the Tower commission after its chairman, former Senator John Tower, reprinted by Bantam and Times Books in 1987 ("Tower Commission Report").

7. *See* Iran-Contra Report, *supra* note 6, at 41, 59–61, 72–75.

8. The quote and the estimate are both from the Iran-Contra Report, *supra* note 6, at 37 & 4.

9. Id. at 7.

10. It was this delay that the Justice Department's Office of Legal Counsel stated was in the confines of the 1980 Intelligence Oversight Act. "The President's Compliance with the 'Timely Notification' Requirement of Section 501(b) of the National Security Act" (known as the Cooper Memorandum), *reprinted in* Hearings on Oversight Legislation

before the Senate Select Committee on Intelligence, 100th Cong., 1st Sess., at 126–52 (1987) (S. Hearing 100–623).

11. The finding is printed in the Tower Commission Report, *supra* note 6, at 215–17.

12. Washington Post, Mar. 19, 1982.

13. This point is developed in my *U.S. Strategy in Central America*, 28 Survival 128 (March/April 1986).

14. Joint Hearings before the House Select Committee to Investigate Covert Arms Transactions with Iran and the Senate Select Committee on Secret Military Assistance to Iran and the Nicaraguan Opposition, 100th Cong., 1st Sess., at 9 (May 8, 1987) (testimony of Robert McFarlane).

15. As reported by the N.Y. Times, July 29, 1986, and Oct. 24, 1990.

16. As quoted in Jay Peterzell, *Reagan's Secret Wars* 9 (1984).

17. As reported in the N.Y. Times, Sept. 30 & Oct. 24, 1990.

18. *See, e.g.,* Washington Post, Nov. 30, 1989.

19. Quoted in the Washington Post, Oct. 4, 1989.

20. *See* Washington Post, June 18, 1990; N.Y. Times, Oct. 24, 1990.

21. As reported in Department of State, "Update on Cambodia," May 1, 1989.

22. *See* N.Y. Times, July 21 & Sept. 13, 1990.

23. *See* Washington Post, Sept. 25, 1989; N.Y. Times, Nov. 15, 1989, at A15.

24. N.Y. Times, Nov. 15 & 16, 1989.

25. N.Y. Times, Oct. 24, 1990.

26. Interview with author, Jan. 9, 1986.

27. This is the emphasis of a recent Twentieth Century Fund Task Force on covert action, in which I participated. *See The Need to Know: The Report of the Twentieth Century Fund Task Force on Covert Action and American Democracy* (1992).

28. For background, see Barnett R. Rubin, *The Fragmentation of Afghanistan*, 68 Foreign Aff. 150 (Winter 1989–90).

29. Washington Post, Oct. 23, 1989; N.Y. Times, Oct. 2, 1990. *See also* Gillian Gunn, *A Guide to the Intricacies of the Angola-Namibia Negotiations*, CSIS Africa Notes, at 90 (Sept. 8, 1988).

30. I provide evidence for this judgment in my book, *Covert Action: The Limits of Intervention in the Postwar World* (1987).

31. I discuss Iran and Guatemala along with Angola 1975–76 (Angola I) in *Covert Action*. Arrangements for approving and overseeing covert operations have changed dramatically since, partly in response to those earlier cases.

32. *Id.* at 333.

33. Iran-Contra Report, *supra* note 6, at 19.

34. *See* Chapter 8.

35. The letter was dated April 9; *see* the Washington Post, Apr. 11, 1984.

36. These have been suggested by a number of people, including me. The Twentieth Century Fund report, *supra* note 27, elaborates them.

37. Letter, *reprinted in* 1991 U.S. Code Cong. & Admin. News 233.

38. For my argument to this effect, see testimony in Hearings on H.R. 3822, to Strengthen the System of Congressional Oversight of Intelligence Activities of the United States before the Subcommittee on Legislation of the House Permanent Select Committee on Intelligence, 100th Cong., 2d Sess., at 316–23 (Feb. 24 & Mar. 10, 1988).

8   "Covert" Paramilitary Action and War Powers[1]

Gary M. Stern and Morton H. Halperin

The Iran-Contra affair was the most recent demonstration of the deep incongruity and danger that unauthorized covert action poses in a democracy. In a country founded on the principle of a shared foreign affairs power, the President has come to assert a unilateral authority over all use or support of military force by the United States, especially through covert action. The officials who ran the Iran-Contra affair completely bypassed every democratic check placed upon the Executive branch. This abuse by the Reagan Administration suggests that we take another look at the role of such activities in U.S. foreign policy.

The term "covert action" comprises a range of activities, from those verging on diplomacy to those verging on war. This chapter focuses exclusively on covert paramilitary actions, or "secret wars"—clandestine activities intended to provide lethal support to participants in a foreign military conflict without officially revealing the role of the United States. We argue that maintaining the official "deniability" of such actions serves no necessary foreign policy objective while it significantly undermines a fundamental constitutional check on Executive branch action. Accordingly, we propose that the officially "covert" aspect of such activities be eliminated by requiring prior congressional authorization in accordance with procedures that should be followed for overt wars.

THE ADVENT OF OVERT/COVERT ACTIONS

Over the last few decades, Presidents have come to use covert action largely to avoid congressional involvement; they fear that Congress will ask too many questions and might actually oppose the operation. Robert McFarlane said it pointedly when he testified at the Iran-Contra hearings: the President and his advisors "turned to covert action [in Nicaragua] because they thought they could not get Congressional support for overt activities."[2] Yet it is rarely the case that congressional participation would jeopardize the success of the operation or under-mine the effectiveness of our foreign policy.

On the contrary, we assert that congressional participation enhances, and is essential—constitutionally as well as practically—to a successful American foreign policy. The benefits of public consensus on military activity far outweigh the conceivable loss of some opportunities because of the requirement of public debate and congressional approval. Not only does our democratic system demand, as a matter of constitutional law, that the government make all major policy decisions—especially decisions concerning war—publicly and through the legislative process, but it is also the case that no major military policy will succeed without public and congressional approval. Former Secretary of Defense Caspar Weinberger accepted this latter tenet when he articulated six predicate standards requiring clear congres-sional and public support before the overt engagement of any U.S. troops.[3] His standards should apply to covert paramilitary operations as well as to overt war. But these standards should be secured in a legal framework that ensures some form of congressional participation in every kind of military involvement.

The Iran-Contra affair illustrates what can, and invariably does, happen when a President tries to circumvent the need for public debate and approval. The covert effort to supply the Contras, in the face of an express congressional ban on such activity, led to a near constitutional crisis. A cornerstone of our democracy is that the government shall be accountable to the people for all it does. Yet President Reagan fostered a policy and environment where he was not accountable to the Congress or the people, and where his advisors in the National Security Council and the Central Intelligence Agency were not even accountable to him.

The NSC operated outside of the law and the Constitution to implement a policy that Congress had specifically rejected through its undisputed power of the purse. And the NSC staff performed the operation covertly not because the foreign policy objectives required that the U.S. role remain undetected; rather, as McFarlane confessed, the activities were kept covert simply to keep Congress from learning about them.

Yet when, in November 1986, the covert diversion and assistance to the Contras did became public, as such paramilitary operations generally do, the operation against Nicaragua was not immediately stopped. Rather, the recently approved $100 million in aid flowed unhindered, and U.S. support continued for another two years. One lesson from this and other experiences is that public exposure and congressional approval do not necessarily hinder foreign policy objectives (even though these factors may change the means by which those objectives are pursued) where there is adequate political support for that policy; but where there is no such public support, a protracted covert paramilitary operation has little chance of success and is, in any case, inappropriate.

Robert McFarlane learned the truth of this lesson as well; he testified that "it was clearly unwise to rely on covert activity as the core of our policy . . . [because] you cannot get popular and Congressional support for such policy." This is so, he confirmed, because "it is virtually impossible, almost as a matter of definition, to rally the public behind a policy you cannot even talk about."[4]

The Iran-Contra affair resurfaced the issue of whether covert action is an effective and worthwhile instrument of U.S. foreign policy. For its part, the Report of the Congressional Committees Investigating the Iran-Contra Affair, while raising the question of whether "covert action [can] be authorized and conducted in a manner compatible with the American system of democratic government and the rule of law," never analyzed that fundamental problem. Instead, the Iran-Contra Report simply asserted that "covert operations are a necessary component of our Nation's foreign policy."[5]

Indeed, covert action retains a certain romantic attractiveness among both the populace and politicians that squarely contradicts the reality of their failure in policy and practice. Not only do they require the use of unsavory tactics by our own agents, but covert actions have tended to promote and maintain regimes that practice the worst kinds of repression.

In 1976 the Church Committee conducted the most thorough analysis of covert paramilitary operations following revelations of widespread abuse, both at home and abroad, by the CIA, the FBI, and other U.S. intelligence agencies. The Church Committee's review of almost 30 years of secret wars concluded that "[o]n balance, . . . the evidence points toward the failure of paramilitary activity as a technique of covert action." While finding it difficult to make judgments as to "success" or "failure," the Committee found that only "when covert operations have been consistent with, and in tactical support of, policies which have emerged from a national debate and the established processes of government, these have tended to be a success."[6]

The Church Committee also reiterated testimony given it that "covert action can be a success when the objective of the project is to support an individual, a party, or a government in doing what that individual, party or government wants to do—and when it has the will and capacity to do it. Covert action cannot build political institutions where there is no local political will to have them."[7] Additionally, the Committee pointed out that the long-term cumulative effect of a covert action tended to undermine whatever short-term success it may have achieved, and noted that the U.S. operatives and policy makers rarely considered the long-term consequences of past or pending operations.

Upon final consideration, the Church Committee, fell just short of making the ultimate proposal of "a ban on *all* forms of covert action." In preserving the covert action option, the Committee stressed, as its "most basic conclusion," that "covert action must be seen as an exceptional act, to be undertaken only when the national security requires it and when overt means will not suffice."[8] But Congress's failure to enact this standard into law enabled the Reagan Administration to initiate a whole new wave of precisely those kinds of operations the Church Committee had sought to prevent.

The decade and a half since the Church Committee issued its final report has only served to confirm its primary conclusion that "the evidence points toward the failure of paramilitary activity as a technique of covert action."[9] From a constitutional perspective, such operations are objectionable if only because they fail to adhere to the procedures established in the Constitution that guarantee an open and accountable system of government. Since covert paramilitary operations are by their very nature secret, they are not open to the normal process of full public debate by the people, the Congress, and the media; they avoid precisely the democratic process in this country that most of them are at least ostensibly designed to promote in the countries towards which they are targeted.

Secret wars not only violate the constitutional demands of our democratic government, they also make for bad foreign policy. The result of even our "successful" secret wars has been the empowerment of dictators wholly inimical to our political values. Our greatest "successes," Iran in 1953, Guatemala in 1954, and Chile in 1973, spawned some of the worst oppression of the postwar era. Clearly it was not intended, nor is it necessary, that we, in the words of the Church Committee, "adopt tactics unworthy of a democracy [or] . . . reminiscent of the tactics of totalitarian regimes" in order to maintain our national security.[10] The continued popular and political support in the United States for covert action belies the actual failure experienced at home and the damage done abroad.

THE CASE FOR PUBLIC AUTHORIZATION OF PARAMILITARY ACTIONS

There is virtually unanimous agreement among foreign policy makers and experts that covert actions should not proceed, and likely will not succeed, unless they are a part of and consistent with publicly approved foreign policy objectives.[11] We believe that the truth of this statement increases exponentially in relation to the magnitude of the proposed operation. A secret war, being of the highest magnitude, is virtually certain to fail at a very high cost to U.S. policy and influence if attempted outside of this prescription.

Unfortunately, covert paramilitary operations have come into favor in large part to avoid giving Congress any such control over that decision. For the same reasons that Congress passed the War Powers Resolution—to restore its constitutional role, which had been diminished as a result of presidential end-runs—it is imperative that Congress take steps to institute its full share of authority over paramilitary operations, by taking the "covert" out of covert action.

The common understanding of such a prohibition on paramilitary operations focuses on the operational level—stopping the CIA (or any other intelligence agency) from engaging in covert paramilitary activities. However, we approach the issue purely from a procedural standpoint—requiring that any "covert" paramilitary activity be constitutionally authorized by Congress and the President. The new phenomenon of "overt/covert" paramilitary operations—as in Nicaragua and Afghanistan in the 1980s—complies in general with this understanding, to the extent that the operational details of those activities have been kept secret while the policy objectives have been publicly debated and authorized. These operations would have fully conformed to our proposal if there had been public debate and congressional authorization *prior* to their initiation.

Thus, we suggest that paramilitary operations, as instruments of war, should not be initiated or supported without public debate and congressional approval on the substantive objectives of the proposed action. This requirement would not prevent the President from conducting paramilitary operations whose operational details need to be kept secret, once the approval of Congress was obtained. But it would ensure a democratic basis for the policy objective of the operation. The quantity and quality of the assistance, as well as the names of third countries who do not want their identities revealed can remain secret, or, at least, not be officially confirmed. The same standards that currently apply to all other national security secrets—a balance between the government's legitimate interest in secrecy and the public's right to know, with a presumption in favor of disclosure—should apply here.

Supporters of covert operations assert that the concern for constitutional procedure is irrelevant when vital issues of national security are at stake. Their primary objection to any kind of public acknowledgement of covert action is that it would inhibit our ability to conduct necessary foreign policy initiatives. But, in the first place, inadvertent, and intentional, leaks have occurred on almost every major covert action carried out over the last forty years. It is now virtually certain that all significant and prolonged paramilitary operations will become public early in the course of the operation. If the press alone does not ferret it out, then the operatives themselves (U.S. government officials or the people in the field) will be hard pressed not to reveal the policy. As then Representative Wyche Fowler commented with respect to the Nicaragua operation, "a paramilitary operation of the size being conducted was impossible to be kept covert. . . . We knew that from the beginning, and we found that within 3 or 4 weeks the participants were themselves announcing their thanks to the people of the United States for giving them the resources to try to overthrow a government down there."[12]

Second, notwithstanding the certainty of such exposure, covert operations are not stopped simply because they are made public; they are stopped only when they have no popular or congressional support. As noted above with respect to Nicaragua, where support was widespread, or opposition indifferent, such exposure did not force an end to the project. The main result for this and other operations is that the President must make a stronger case to the Congress to gain support for its activities.

In 1975, the United States began to provide covert assistance to one side in Angola following decolonization and a subsequent three-sided civil war. President Ford, following the rules of the time, made a "finding" and notified the appropriate committees of Congress. But because it was impossible to keep the operation secret (due both to public pronouncements in the field and to greater press coverage), the effect of plausible denial was completely lost. With the operation already public, Ford simply went to Congress for public authorization, as he should have done in the first place. At that time, Congress saw fit to deny the President such funds and stop the operation; it also imposed an absolute ban on all covert assistance directed against Angola, the so-called Clark Amendment.[13]

Congress thus played an instrumental role in assessing whether the United States should continue to intervene in Angola. The decision to do so was not the President's alone to make. The covert program was cut off in 1976 after careful consideration by Congress. In 1985, Congress repealed the Clark Amendment with the express understanding that it was not authorizing renewed covert assistance to Jonas Savimbi's UNITA forces, and that the Reagan Administration would not request such aid. The Administration, however, then went ahead and initiated a covert operation to provide paramilitary support to UNITA. In response, Senator Bill Bradley (D-N.J.) introduced a bill in July 1987 that would "require that any United States Government support for military or paramilitary operations in Angola be openly acknowledged and publicly debated."[14] A parallel effort was made in the House to add similar language to the Intelligence Authorization Act. Although these legislative proposals were not enacted, they demonstrated that public knowledge of the fact of clandestine U.S. involvement in Angola did not undermine the operation itself. The action continued unabated until 1991.

In yet another relevant example, the CIA had been funneling hundreds of millions of dollars of "secret" military assistance to rebel forces in Afghanistan—the Mujahedeen—opposing the Soviet invasion up until the Soviet Union began to withdraw its troops from Afghanistan. Details of the operation—sources and methods, shipment times, and the means of implementation—were kept secret, but the fact of U.S. involvement was well known to Congress, the media, and the public, as well as to the Soviet Union, the government and people of Afghanistan, and anyone else in the world who wanted to know about it. Similarly, Pakistan's participation in the effort, while not officially acknowledged by the American government, was widely known. Despite the assertion that this was a covert action, the CIA operation was publicly authorized on October 4, 1984, by a concurrent resolution of Congress, which expressed Congress's opposition to the Soviet invasion of Afghanistan and called for "effective support" for the Afghan rebels.[15]

Although the Afghan assistance began as a secret covert action shortly after the Soviet invasion in 1979, it provides the most useful insights into the proper means through which the United States should now engage in or support paramilitary operations. What was significant is that Congress debated the issue and publicly authorized the Reagan Administration to aid the rebels who opposed the Soviets; this public debate and authorization, far from preventing the United States from supporting the Mujahedeen, in fact led to a larger and more effective operation.

Critics also object to the expansion of congressional control over covert actions as an intrusion, practical if not constitutional, into the President's ability to conduct foreign policy. They state the old phrase that there cannot be 535 secretaries of state trying to run the country. This argument is buttressed by the general state of inefficiency that pervades congressional action, especially on foreign policy matters.[16]

But Congress would not be so inefficient in responding to presidential initiatives if the President, as a practical matter, included Congress in the decision-making process. And as a constitutional matter, the President cannot exclude Congress simply to ensure himself a freer hand in implementing his desired policy. Unquestionably, covert actions are attractive to Presidents largely because they are a convenient shortcut around the procedural hassles inherent in our democratic system. But mere convenience, unlike threats to the nation's survival, does not excuse unconstitutional or illegal conduct. As the Supreme Court stated in *INS v. Chadha*:

There is no support in the Constitution for the proposition that the cumbersomeness and delays often encountered in complying with explicit constitutional standards may be avoided, either by the Congress or by the President.... With all the obvious flaws of delay, untidiness, and potential for abuse, we have not yet found a better way to preserve freedom than by making the exercise of power subject to the carefully crafted restraints spelled out in the Constitution.[17]

Nevertheless, the temptation for Presidents to use covert actions mounts in the face of protracted congressional resistance to a favored policy, especially following that first instance of success in avoiding the procedural morass through covert means. Yet covert actions were not intended to shield the President from domestic accountability. They have come into such favor, however, precisely because they are one of the President's last vestiges of unfettered power. They offer the President a tempting opportunity to avoid all the constraints Congress is able to impose on the President's policy.

These congressional tactics, however, have developed in large part in response to presidential efforts to minimize Congress's role, which is essential in our system of checks and balances. Indeed, congressional opposition need not be dismissed as an intrusion upon the operation; rather, it should be seen as a barometer on the political efficacy of the plan.

The Church Committee and the Iran-Contra investigations should have taught us that even the strictest provisions controlling the use of covert actions are inevitably abused. The only way to stop this pattern of abuse is to impose an absolute requirement of public approval as a way of prohibiting *covert* paramilitary operations. But such a prohibition does not mean that we have to stand by in the face of a real threat to our national security and let the Republic crumble simply because the only means of defense is unconstitutional or illegal. Where the President feels he must take paramilitary action in an emergency situation, he could do so in conformity with the War Powers Resolution or under his implied constitutional power to "repel sudden attacks."[18]

Finally, critics contend that the inclusion of Congress in the use of paramilitary operations will inhibit agents in the field from acting for fear that congressional leaks will expose the operation and risk their lives. They say that Congress does not have a "need to know." On the contrary, Congress, as the legislative body, has an essential need to know the substance of all military or paramilitary initiatives. Again, this does not mean that Congress must know of the operational details—who is going exactly where, and when. But it must know, and approve, the substantive goals of the operation. Furthermore, given the political and legal fallout that ensues when a secret war is exposed, it is in the interest of agents in the field to know that the operation is fully authorized before it begins. Few agents would risk their careers, and possible criminal prosecution and conviction, to conduct an operation without clear legal authority.

RECENT EXAMPLES OF OVERT/COVERT ACTIONS

The three major paramilitary operations of the 1980s, at least in their latter stages, comport with this approach. The United States conducted major paramilitary operations to overthrow or repulse sitting governments in Afghanistan, Angola, and Nicaragua. Although there were initial attempts to keep each operation covert in whole or in part, they were quickly revealed in the media and by the foreign operatives themselves. All three then continued unhindered from an operational perspective, although they did engender varying degrees of public and congressional opposition. Those local governments who wished to assist us without officially revealing their involvement were not constrained to do so, even though their involvement was well known. In all, no operational purpose was served by pursuing these operations "covertly."

While the operations in Afghanistan, Nicaragua, and Angola are useful models for instituting a procedural prohibition on covert paramilitary actions, they are also indicative of the problems endemic to the existing system of conducting covert operations. Both the Contra and Afghan operations were initiated as covert actions, and received public approval only afterwards. Congress gave its assent only with the momentum of the operations already in full swing. The Reagan Administration presented Congress with a *fait accompli*, and left Congress with the ominous burden of bearing the blame for whatever "failure" might ensue should it stop the operation.

As is also the case when U.S. forces are overtly committed abroad, it is very difficult for Congress to pull the plug once U.S. commitments and resources are on the line. Our proposal, like the War Powers Resolution before it, is designed to give Congress its opportunity to act before the operation begins and before the political pressure mounts. Indeed, the Intelligence Oversight Act of 1991 requires *prior* notification of all covert actions, except in the most extreme circumstances, for precisely the same reason.[19]

Congress has the constitutional authority and the statutory means to prohibit the use or support of covert paramilitary actions for conducting major foreign policy initiatives. What it lacks is the political will. The present sentiment on Capitol Hill continues to favor retaining the covert option. Even the strongest advocates of tighter congressional oversight have not been willing to go the next step in support of a procedural ban on paramilitary operations. That reluctance stems in part from the fear of giving up a policy tool that has come to be seen as a middle ground between military intervention and diplomacy. But as David Aaron, former Deputy Assistant National Security Adviser to President Carter, stated, "one of the tragedies about covert action is that it is often an excuse for doing something without really doing it. It is something that a policy maker does because he does not have anything else [to] do. . . . "[20]

This practice, reinvigorated by the Reagan Administration, violates the Church Committee conclusion that covert actions should only be used in extreme situations. We assert that once covert paramilitary operations are removed from common practice and relegated to last-resort status, requiring that they be publicly approved will not seem so drastic. Moreover, public authorization will not necessarily eliminate the "middle option" from our foreign policy retinue; it will simply place it in the public sphere where all major policy decisions of a democratic society belong.

CONCLUSION

The legislature, and the people of this country, have a right, if not an obligation, to be skeptical when the President takes it upon himself to commit the United States to war or any other military action. While he may ultimately have good cause to do so, recent history—the Vietnam War and the Iran-Contra affair alone—invites us to exercise significant caution before supporting such a commitment. If the President cleared his action with Congress before carrying it out, he could avoid the rancorous and disruptive reaction that could otherwise ensue. By overcoming internal division in advance, the President can more effectively focus attention on the military objective at hand.

Advance congressional approval also legitimizes the policy to the outside world once an operation has actually begun. Policy makers have always striven for a bipartisan foreign policy. It allows us to present to allies and adversaries alike a unified front fully committed to achieving its goals; and it would further undermine any attempts by the adversary to try to defeat the President through the Congress.

Finally, advance approval will help to prevent the political backlash from Congress that invariably follows upon a foreign policy failure. Indeed Congress's investigation into the Iran-Contra affair focused extensively on the President's failure to keep Congress informed about the Iran operations, as was required under the intelligence oversight procedures in effect. (The President's violation of the funding restrictions on the Nicaragua operation was a wholly separate problem.) Had the appropriate Members of Congress been so informed, they would have had far less to complain about once the ensuing operation was exposed. While Congress may still have voiced strong objection to the intent and effect of the Iran operation, the President would have at least satisfied all of the existing legal requirements. Of course, we believe that the existing legal requirements are deficient, and should be further tightened, because they allow the President to proceed with a military operation even in the face of congressional opposition.

NOTES

1. This chapter is based on portions of an article entitled *Lawful Wars* that appeared in Foreign Policy, No. 72, at 173 (Fall 1988). Copyright 1988 by the Carnegie Endowment for International Peace. Reprinted with permission.

2. Hearings before the House Select Committee to Investigate Covert Arms Transactions with Iran and Senate Select Committee on Secret Military Assistance to Iran and the Nicaraguan Opposition, 100th Cong., 1st Sess., Testimony of Robert McFarlane, at 9 (May 11, 1987) [hereafter Iran-Contra Hearings].

3. *See* N.Y. Times, Nov. 30, 1984, at A5 (reprinting text of Weinberger's speech: "Fifth, before the U.S. commits combat forces abroad, there must be some reasonable

assurance we will have the support of the American people and their elected representatives in Congress.")

4. Iran-Contra Hearings, *supra* note 2, at 9.

5. Report of the Congressional Committees Investigating the Iran-Contra Affair, H. Rep. 100–433, S. Rep. 100–216, 100th Cong., 1st Sess., at 383 (Nov. 1987).

6. Senate Select Committee to Study Government Operations with respect to Intelligence Activities, S. Rep. No. 94–755, 94th Cong., 2d Sess., Book I, at 154–55 (Apr. 26, 1976) (Church Committee Report, Foreign and Military Intelligence).

7. *Id.* at 154.

8. *Id.* at 159–60.

9. *Id.* at 155.

10. S. Rep. 94–755, 94th Cong., 2d Sess., Book II, at 3 (Apr. 26, 1976) (Church Committee Report, Intelligence Activities and the Rights of Americans).

11. *See, e.g., The Need to Know: The Report of the Twentieth Century Fund Task Force on Covert Action and American Democracy* at 8 (1992) ("Covert action should be undertaken only in support of *publicly articulated* policy." [emphasis in original]).

12. Hearings on Congressional Oversight of Covert Activities before the House Permanent Select Committee on Intelligence, 98th Cong., 1st Sess., at 120 (Sept. 20–22, 1983) [hereafter 1983 Congressional Oversight Hearings].

13. Pub. L. No. 94–329, Title IV, § 404 (June 30, 1976), 90 Stat. 757 (commonly known as the Clark Amendment). This law was repealed in 1985, Pub. L. No. 99–83, Title XII, § 1211(a)(4) (Aug. 8. 1985), 99 Stat. 279.

14. S. 1474, 100th Cong., 1st Sess. (July 8, 1987). This language conforms exactly to our proposal to eliminate the "covert" aspect of paramilitary operations.

15. S. Con. Res. 74, 98th Cong., 2d Sess. (1984).

16. For example, Congress was incapable of applying the War Powers Resolution to the President's order to escort the reflagged Kuwaiti ships in the Persian Gulf in 1988. But in January 1991, Congress did formally authorize the use of force against Iraq. Congress was still debating a resolution to authorize the deployment of troops to Somalia, in May 1993, five months after they were first sent over and well after the majority of troops had been withdrawn. S.J. Res. 45, 103d Cong., 1st Sess. (passed Senate on Feb. 4, 1993; passed House on May 25, 1993).

17. 462 U.S. 919, 959 (1983).

18. And if he has to resort to illegal, unauthorized action, he would then be obliged to explain the reasons for his actions immediately after their completion, and then accept the political consequences, be they a drop in his opinion rating, an election loss, or even impeachment; it is equally likely, however, that if the President did come clean in this way, there would be minimal, if any, political fallout. Such is what both Presidents Lincoln and Roosevelt did in actions taken during the Civil War and World War II, respectively.

19. 50 U.S.C. § 413(c)(1) (1991) (The President shall ensure that any finding . . . shall be reported to the intelligence committees as soon as possible after such approval *and before the initiation of the covert action* authorized by the finding, except as otherwise provided for in paragraph (2) and paragraph (3).) (emphasis added).

20. 1983 Congressional Oversight Hearings, *supra* note 12, at 157–58.

9   Emergency War Powers

John Norton Moore

> At the conclusion of the Constitutional Convention, Benjamin Franklin was
> asked, "What have you wrought?"
> He answered, "[A] Republic, if you can keep it."[1]

The President of the United States has broad authority to employ military force in
emergency settings engendered by attacks against the United States or its interests,
allies, forces, or citizens, at home or abroad. In developing this broadly supported
proposition, though not in all its elements a unanimously supported proposition,
this chapter will briefly examine the debate about the general scope of the war
powers, the relevant issues in constitutional interpretation, the goals at stake in
constitutional decision about the war powers, and the war powers in settings of
emergency and immediate engagement. Most importantly, this chapter will develop
an argument that we need to incorporate "new thinking" about war avoidance into
policy considerations in the war powers debate: "new thinking" suggesting that
major wars in the twentieth century have resulted in substantial part from a synergy
between aggression by totalitarian, or at least nondemocratic, nations and settings
of system-wide failure to deter such aggression. If this paradigm is correct, then it
may suggest, as one way of enhancing deterrence, greater presidential authority in
initial commitment decisions, always subject to congressional checks through the
power of the purse and the ability to legislatively (through the normal law-making
process) prohibit or terminate specific major foreign wars.

BACKGROUND: THE DEBATE ABOUT THE GENERAL
SCOPE OF THE WAR POWERS

Throughout American constitutional history, the proper allocation of authority
between Congress and the executive in the use of the armed forces has been
surrounded by controversy. This controversy has been invited by a skeletal consti-

tutional structure giving Congress the power "to declare War" and to "raise and support Armies" but making the President the "Commander in Chief" and the principal representative of the nation in foreign affairs. That this controversy has persisted suggests that there is a great deal to be said for both the executive and the congressional roles. It also suggests that the issue is not simply the triumph of the views of either Pacificus or Helvidius,[2] but is instead the far more difficult quest for reasonable lines which will optimize the strengths of both Congress and the executive.

At the outset we should note that intellectual clarification in debate about the war powers requires recognition that we are dealing with not one issue but many issues encompassing a range of activities from the stationing of forces abroad, through initial commitment to hostilities and the conduct of hostilities, to the termination of hostilities, among other major headings. Today, however, as we examine the debate about decisions to initially commit U.S. armed forces to hostilities, there seem to be at least four macro positions (having many variations) among which there can be substantial agreement on certain sub-issues such as the "emergency setting" subject of this chapter. These four macro positions are as follows.

First, there is a position which might be summarized as one of "concurrent presidential authority" which would regard the President as having concurrent constitutional authority initially to commit U.S. armed forces to hostilities abroad, at least absent a specific prior or subsequent legislative enactment (passed by the normal legislative process) directing nonengagement or withdrawal of U.S. forces. This position is supported by a textual argument that the power of Congress is simply "to declare War"; that few wars, including those in the seventeenth and eighteenth centuries, have been formally declared; and that the powers of Congress enumerated in Article I, section 8, should be construed narrowly, or, at least, not beyond their own terms, when the issue is one of initial authority of the President in foreign affairs absent specific congressional direction to the contrary in a particular case. Concurrent presidential authority, which in general terms has been supported by the Executive branch through many administrations, is also given support by an overwhelming number of practice examples throughout American history, including, most importantly, President Truman's commitment of a quarter of a million U.S. troops to hostilities in Korea without prior congressional authorization.

Second, on the other end of the spectrum there is a position—popular in the academic community and particularly in the segment strongly supporting congressional authority generally—that views the Declaration of War Clause as *removing* any presidential concurrent authority, even in the first instance and absent an expression of congressional intent to the contrary, except in a narrow range of "minor" or "limited" uses of force and in cases of direct attack against the United States or its forces at home or abroad. With some qualifications, it is this congressional view that has been adopted in the War Powers Resolution, which is now under intense policy and constitutional attack.[3]

A third and intermediate position, developed and espoused by myself in testimony on the War Powers Resolution twenty years ago,[4] is that congressional authorization might be required in all cases where regular combat units are committed to sustained hostilities, with provision for subsequent congressional authorization in emergency settings requiring speed and decisiveness. This view, although like all approaches somewhat frayed at the edges, is an effort to be responsive to a policy test of congressional authorization in major wars most likely to place at risk the nation's blood and treasure. It would, however, give substantial weight to the need for presidential flexibility and the rich "common law tradition" of practical experience in presidential authority in this area over the years.

The fourth major, and also intermediate, position—and there may be others—is the view espoused over the last decade by Robert F. Turner, a former Deputy Assistant Secretary of State for Legislative Affairs with many years experience as a congressional staff member on Capitol Hill, that the President has authority to commit the armed forces to *defensive* as opposed to *offensive* settings. Defensive and offensive in Mr. Turner's view are defined as they would be under the United Nations Charter, that is, aggressive attack is illegal, but actions in individual or collective defense against aggressive attack are lawful.[5] Under this view, not only would the President have authority in a wide variety of emergency and "minor coercion" settings, but the President would also have authority to engage U.S. forces in major hostilities, such as in Korea, provided they were defensive under the U.N. Charter.

One practical difficulty with the second, or what might be called the "restrictive" view, is the reality that, in a nuclear age, Presidents will inevitably have enormous authority concerning major conflict settings, and, as many scholars have observed, throughout our history, Presidents have had the power to shape events so as to make war largely inevitable. A second, critical point, largely ignored in the debate, is that war powers authority concerning the initial deployment decision is *not* the only point in the process where effective checks on presidential authority are possible. Among many other such checks, including hearings and the power of the purse, is the potentially powerful check of specific legislation, passed *before* or *after* an initial deployment of forces by the President, directing noninvolvement or protective withdrawal. In exercising this check, Congress would be required to operate through the normal legislative process.

A BRIEF NOTE ON CONSTITUTIONAL INTERPRETATION

I will not at this point seek to definitively engage in the lively, ongoing, and diverse debate about constitutional interpretation. But it may be helpful, in candor and fairness in permitting appraisal by others, to briefly set out parameters and criteria that I would regard as useful in interpreting the war powers. We should also maintain our role as *independent appraisers* to comment on whether we believe a particular constitutional interpretation, even if constitutionally correct, is necessarily the optimum constitutional policy choice. That is, we are always free to argue for constitutional change if we feel it is warranted by the policies at stake.

I believe that a range of factors are important in constitutional interpretation. First, the language of the Constitution, the totality of information about the intent of the language, and particularly its purpose, are important. The extreme view that would dismiss the intent of the framers as an irrelevant, dead hand from the past both fails to understand the political genius of the American Constitution and fails to understand the fundament of "constitutionalism" itself in establishing certain elemental checks and balances *against* governmental action. If constitutions were simply infinitely variable and subject to change with shifting majority opinion, then they could not serve their purpose as checks, where needed, against governmental and even majority actions. A First Amendment guarantee that protected only speech deemed "politically correct" by a changing majority certainly would not be much of a guarantee.

Second, one of the great geniuses of the common law has been reliance on, and learning from, concrete experience. Thus, while not decisive on its own, as *INS v. Chadha* properly shows,[6] constitutional experience can substantially assist in interpretation, and a strong pattern of practice should be set aside only as a result of substantial clarity to the contrary in the underlying constitutional language or purpose. Thus, as Justice Frankfurter pointed out in his concurring opinion in the *Steel Seizure* case: "It is an inadmissibly narrow conception of American constitutional law to confine it to the words of the Constitution and to disregard the gloss which life has written upon them."[7] Justice Holmes was making much the same point when he said that "the life of the law has not been logic: it has been experience."[8]

Finally, constitutions are not like statutes or administrative regulations. A constitution is intended to serve as a fundamental charter for the relation of a people to its government. Among other consequences, this means that in implementing the major purposes and first principles of a constitution, it is relevant to interpret ambiguities in its construction in the light of changed circumstances and contemporary conditions. As such, a knowledge of relevant circumstances and the policies sought to be effectuated in those circumstances are also of importance in interpretation.

THE COMPLEXITIES OF WAR AVOIDANCE: RETHINKING THE GOALS AT STAKE

The Constitution, of course, reflects an important range of policies and principles in the foreign affairs process generally, and the war powers more specifically. Thus, it is clear that the Constitutional Convention wanted the power to formally declare war to be located in the Congress, rather than in the Senate or the Executive branch. This seems to have been intended as one of a variety of checks, including the power of the purse and the provision against standing armies, against largely uncontrolled presidential war-making. On the other hand, we know that the framers changed the originally broader phrase "to make war" to the final, narrower phrase "to declare war" (in a setting in which they must have known that declarations of war were not the norm—even then—in international relations); they clearly expressed a not otherwise limited intention that the President should have "the power to repel sudden attacks"; and they gave the President "the executive Power" (which included the general foreign affairs power), the "Commander in Chief" power and the power to "take care that the laws [including "Treaties made"] be faithfully executed." In general, it might be said that they sought to ensure ultimate congressional control of the power to engage in major or formal war, while recognizing the need for flexibility, broad executive authority over the armed forces (particularly as Commander in Chief), and the need for dispatch in defensive settings.

Perhaps in terms of Benjamin Franklin's admonition that the framers had created "a Republic, if you can keep it," the framers were aware of two competing threats from military force against such a republic. The first was unfettered presidential discretion to commit the nation to major or formal war. And the second was the risk that, in the absence of broad presidential authority over the armed forces, the republic could be lost through the hostile actions of others.

It may well be that competing conceptions of the war powers are heavily influenced by which of these two is regarded as the greatest threat and is most relevant to war avoidance. If one holds a world-view that the principal experience shows we are most at risk of major war as a result of adventurism on the part of American Presidents, then, not surprisingly, one would likely favor toughening the constraints under the War Clause. If, however, one believes that the principal threat to democracy emanates from dangerous regimes elsewhere in the world in settings of deterrence failure, then, also not surprisingly, one would likely favor greater presidential authority (within some system of still effective congressional checks) in order to assist deterrence and better enable the protection of freedom (the republic) and the avoidance of war.

If these competing perceptions of threats to the nation are of importance in shaping views of the war powers, and I believe that they are, then it may be relevant to introduce the underlying debate—particularly that about newer models or paradigms on this basic issue—into the war powers debate. Although debate rages as broadly, if not more so, on these underlying issues as on the war powers, I believe that there is a significant body of data now suggesting that major wars in the twentieth century frequently have resulted in substantial part from a synergy between aggressive attack from a totalitarian (or nondemocratic) regime and a setting of overall deterrence failure. Where there has been no aggressive nondemocratic regime, there has been no *major* war, nor even concern about war despite copious weapons. Canada does not arm its borders or develop a nuclear retaliatory capability against the United States. Similarly, where there has been effective deterrence of potentially aggressive totalitarian regimes, there has been no war, as with NATO and the former Soviet Union. On the other hand, many examples exist where the two parts of the synergy come together, resulting in war. Thus, I believe that there is persuasive evidence that the principal international wars of the twentieth century—among them, World War II, the Korean War, the Iran-Iraq War, and the recent Gulf conflict—did not arise principally because of unresolved disputes (although they were a factor), accidents, or "arms races," but rather because of this synergy between two critical and necessary sets of conditions.

More specifically, the first set of conditions involves a totalitarian or nonde-mocratic regime bent on the use of aggressive force to alter the contemporary value map in fundamental violation of the U.N. Charter. The second set of conditions is a system-wide failure of deterrence, considering here systemic deterrence in its broadest sense of, among other factors, the effect of contemporary levels of international organization against aggression, balances of power, military capabili-ties, defensive alliances, clarity or lack thereof about intentions to respond, the state of effectiveness of the international legal system, and economic interdependencies or lack thereof.

Importantly, we should also note that the overwhelming majority of aggressive regimes in this century have been totalitarian, or at least nondemocratic, and that they tend to exhibit what I have elsewhere called "the radical regime syndrome" of a one-party political system with a repressive internal security system.[9] Indeed, one of the most interesting connections in this respect, is that these regimes are not only aggressors in initiating major wars, but they are also engaged in slaughtering their own people. One current researcher believes that these regimes, in perpetrating such "democide," may have killed two to four times the number of people as have been killed in all of the major wars of the twentieth century combined.[10] Hitler's Third Reich, Stalin's Soviet Union, and Pol Pot's Kampuchea are examples. In contrast, democratic nations almost never attack other democratic nations or commit demo-cide against their own people.

If this model of a synergy between an aggressive regime (typically a radical regime that is also engaged in democide or other massive human rights violations against its own people) and a system-wide deterrence failure *is* the principal model of major international conflict in our time, then the policies most useful in seriously working for peace are quite different than those which flow from the "conventional" legal, arms control, or peace studies models. The most useful policies include overall political engagement strategies (such as the Conference on Security and Cooperation in Europe [CSCE] process) to seek to promote more democratic regimes around the world—as a major component of the foreign policy of demo-cratic nations—and a variety of means to *strengthen* system-wide deterrence against aggressive threats from radical regimes.

In turn, if this model of an aggressive regime/deterrence failure synergy is correct, then it may give powerful impetus to the conclusion that the second set of policy assumptions about the war powers is more accurate and that excessive constraints resulting in reduced deterrence may pose a higher risk of American involvement in major war than any risk from somewhat broader presidential authority. This line of analysis would, then, support the first, third, and fourth general approaches in the war powers debate and would point out that, paradoxi-cally, the second or "restrictive" view, and statutory efforts built on that premise, such as the War Powers Resolution, may have the opposite effect of what was intended. That is, they may increase the risk of American involvement in major wars.

Let me again point out the assumption in this discussion that there are *major* potential congressional checks on presidential authority to engage the nation in war other than the check of requiring *prior* congressional authorization. The U.S.

Congress has major checks on the war powers, including the appropriations power, the hearings and impeachment power (in an extreme case of aggressive war), and, most importantly, the normal legislative process by which *prior* or *subsequent* congressional action can prevent or terminate presidential commitment of U.S. armed forces to major hostilities abroad.

EMERGENCY AND IMMEDIATE ENGAGEMENT

Whatever the competing approaches to the underlying general war powers, there is broad support, although not unanimous in all settings, for presidential authority in emergency settings to respond to aggressive attacks against the United States, its interests, allies, forces, or citizens, whether at home or abroad, and whether low-level or high-level force is required to repel the attack. Examples include initial actions in the Civil War, initial actions in the Mexican War, and President Truman's action in the Korean War. We all recognize, as other examples, that any American President would have taken appropriate, immediate action, if needed, in response to an attack on NATO, a nuclear strike against the United States, an aggressive attack against an American warship on the high seas (if a response would still be helpful), an attack against South Korea or Japan today, or other sudden, aggressive attacks requiring an immediate response for defense to be effective.

It might be noted here that this "emergency" or "immediate engagement" authority is clearly incorporated in approaches one, three, and four concerning the war powers. Even the second approach would recognize at least some emergency presidential authority. After all, one thing clearly known from the constitutional debate is that the executive was to have "the power to repel sudden attacks." Interestingly, in the history of the Constitutional Convention, this phrase was *not* limited by the additional wording "on the United States or United States forces," although certainly such attacks would be the clearest constitutional examples.

CONCLUSION

There is broad presidential authority to use the armed forces, at home or abroad, in emergency or immediate engagement settings, in response to aggressive attack.[11] By at least one newer model of the causes of major war and democide in this century, any other constitutional interpretation would likely have the opposite effect than that intended and would increase rather than decrease the risk of American involvement in war. Of greater interest in examining constitutional authority for the use of force more broadly, perhaps we should reflect on the competing war powers approaches with reference to, at least as one relevant factor, the best evidence and theory now available about the causes of major war and democide in the twentieth century.

NOTES

1. From the introductory pages in *The Constitution of the United States* (Bicentennial Commission).

2. *See generally* the debate between Alexander Hamilton (Pacificus) and James Madison (Helvidius) concerning the war powers and separation of powers in foreign relations generally, cited in Abraham D. Sofaer, *War, Foreign Affairs, and Constitutional Power: The Origins* 112–14 (1976).

3. In 1991 I testified that "[t]he War Powers Resolution is, at least in major part, unconstitutional, and if we take the rule of law seriously, as we should, the Resolution should be repealed. Its continued invocation after the *Chadha* decision demeans the Congress." Hearings on the War Powers of Congress and the President in the Gulf Crisis before the Senate Committee on the Judiciary, 102d Cong., 1st Sess., at 14 n.13 (Jan. 8, 1991) (testimony of J.N. Moore) (referring to *INS v. Chadha*, 462 U.S. 919 [1983]).

The specifics of my in-depth congressional testimony, with background citations on the constitutional issues, will not be repeated in this chapter. For further analysis, see Statement of J.N. Moore in Hearings on Congress, the President, and the War Powers before the Subcommittee on National Security Policy and Scientific Developments of the House Committee on Foreign Affairs, 91st Cong., 2d Sess. (June 25, 1970); and Statement by J.N. Moore, "Hearing of Federation of American Scientists," moderated by A. Frye (Jan. 7, 1991, Fed. News Service: "Capitol Hill Hearing About the Middle-East").

4. *See generally* Hearings on War Powers Legislation before the Senate Foreign Relations Committee, 92d Cong., 2d Sess., at 460 (1972) (statement of John Norton Moore, Apr. 26, 1971).

5. *See* Robert F. Turner, *Repealing the War Powers Resolution: Restoring the Rule of Law in U.S. Foreign Policy*, chs. 2 & 3 (1991).

6. 462 U.S. 919 (1983).

7. *Youngstown Sheet and Tube Co. v. Sawyer*, 343 U.S. 579, 610 (1952) (Frankfurter, J., concurring).

8. Oliver Wendall Holmes, *The Common Law* 1 (1886).

9. For an analysis of the radical regime syndrome, see John Norton Moore, *The Secret War in Central America* 153 n.2 (1987).

10. *See* R.J. Rummel, "The Rule of Law: Towards Eliminating War and Democide," Speech prepared for presentation to the American Bar Association Standing Committee on Law and National Security, Washington, D.C., Oct. 10–11, 1991. The principal scholar in this area believes that the figure is over 142 million killed, or roughly four times the number of persons killed in wars in the same time frame. R.J. Rummel, "Power Kills; Absolute Power Kills Absolutely," at 3 (Paper dated Oct. 20, 1991, Haiku Institute of Peace Research, Hawaii). See generally Professor Rummel's forthcoming book, tentatively entitled *Death by Government*, on democide in the twentieth century.

11. Even the War Powers Resolution seems to reflect a congressional assumption of substantial presidential "emergency" or "immediate engagement" authority. Thus, section 5(b) of the resolution purports to terminate presidential use of U.S. armed forces only after the first 60 days from submission of the required report to Congress and makes provision for extending this period another 30 days. 50 U.S.C. § 1544(b). Interestingly, apparently for this reason, and perhaps others as well, the War Powers Resolution was not even invoked by those who sought to challenge the President's authority in the recent Gulf crisis. *See, e.g.*, the brief of plaintiffs in *Dellums v. Bush*, 752 F. Supp. 1141 (D.D.C. 1990).

10   Common Ground

Gary M. Stern and Morton H. Halperin

This book has explored the range of constraints that the government faces when contemplating the use of military or paramilitary force. The first nine chapters delineate the various legal requirements that must, or should, be met to satisfy the constitutional proscriptions on the use of force—e.g., the Constitution itself, "customary national security law," statutes such as the War Powers Resolution, treaties such as the U.N. Charter, international law, and the courts. The anomalies of covert action, in particular what have now become "overt-covert" paramilitary actions, also come under scrutiny within the war powers rubric.

The authors of these chapters also address essentially legal reforms within the context of each topic. Raven-Hansen, for example, sees the development of a "customary" war power based on "executive practice" and "knowing congressional acquiescence" as adequately satisfying the legal requirements for certain limited military deployments. Collier contemplates a number of amendments to the War Powers Resolution that would serve to bolster congressional participation in the process. Stromseth calls for the fulfillment of the "contracts" between member nations that were originally envisioned under the U.N. Charter. Lobel looks for a greater constitutional commitment to abide by international law through a requirement of joint congressional and presidential concurrence.

Koh recommends legislation to allow any Member of Congress to file suit to enforce the War Powers Resolution (or any successor, as well as, assumedly, the Constitution) against presidential noncompliance. Treverton calls for a further strengthening of the Intelligence Oversight Act to ensure prior congressional involvement in the conduct of covert operations. In focusing on "covert" paramilitary actions, we propose a melding of the Intelligence Oversight Act and the War Powers Resolution to incorporate such activities into the legal war powers framework. John Norton Moore argues for establishing unilateral authority in the President to take emergency or immediate actions, with major checks reserved to the Congress to deal with long-term engagements.

Any legal prescription along these lines requires both Congress and the President to confront and recognize, if not concede, one another's contested constitutional powers. Constitutional battles have ensued at every previous attempt at statutory reform. President Nixon vetoed the War Powers Resolution as a constitutional infringement of executive war powers. Although Congress then overrode his veto, subsequent Presidents have for the most part refused formal compliance with the law and have all maintained that they have full constitutional authority to act outside of its requirements. The Carter Administration had agreed that it would submit the appropriate report under the law if it ever used such force, but maintained that the President had independent power to act on his own.[1]

Similarly, the Intelligence Oversight Act, first enacted in 1980 and then substantially amended in 1991, was in both instances substantially scaled down from the preferred congressional version in the face of a presidential veto. The reporting provision of the 1980 Act was intentionally left ambiguous at the insistence of the Carter Administration; the Reagan Administration was thus able to argue that its actions during the Iran-Contra affair did not violate the oversight rules. Post-Iran-Contra efforts to amend the law faced stiff opposition first from President Reagan and then from President Bush. The result was a significantly mollified bill that President Bush still vetoed because of nonbinding report language. He finally signed the bill after further congressional acquiescence.

This constitutional conflict between the two branches is as old as the republic. It is rooted deep in their institutional processes and preferences and, especially throughout the Cold War, has depended little on party affiliation and political leanings. The fact that Democrats now control the White House as well as both Houses of Congress does not assure any reduction in the ongoing standoff between executive and legislative viewpoints. Yet the end of the Cold War presents a new opportunity to consider interbranch relations in this area. After all, the current arrangement is largely a construct of Cold War thinking.

Thus we believe that the climate is ripe for forging a new consensus between Congress and the President over war powers. But success will most easily come by avoiding the indeterminate fight about the meaning of the Constitution, the intent of the framers, and which powers were intended to go where. The congressional authorization of the Iraq War demonstrates that the two political branches can at least find "political accommodation," in Stromseth's words, in formulating and authorizing military policy despite their assertions of contradictory legal positions.

Accordingly, we propose here that Congress and the Executive should develop a voluntary mechanism for working together to authorize any use of military force simply on the basis of political prudence, because the current political and world situations allow it and require it.[2]

Many foreign policy experts will disagree with this emphasis on the process by which the decision to use force is made. For some, the appropriate focus is on the U.S. interests—either strategic or humanitarian—that justify the intervention. In their view, if the motive is correct, the President is free to act without the consent of Congress. Those who suggest, for example, that force is justified if, but only if, the nation's security is truly threatened assume that it is somehow possible to determine objectively when the security interests of the nation require or justify the use of force.

We argue a contrary position, which stresses the impossibility of constructing a hierarchy of values for the nation as a whole and relies on the virtue of process as a means of determining "truth" for a democratic society. Americans have many different values and a multitude of notions of how the world works and what the United States should be trying to accomplish in that world.[3] In a democratic society, these differences are sorted out and decisions are made by observing laws that dictate process. Nowhere is this principle more important than in debating the use of military force that risks the nation's resources and the lives of those who volunteer to serve in its armed forces.

SEEKING POLITICAL CONSENSUS ON AUTHORIZING USES OF FORCE

Our proposal is simple: there should be full debate within both the Executive and Congress and among the public any time the use of military force, whether overt or clandestine, is contemplated to consider differing views on the facts of the situation and of what U.S. interests are and objectives should be. Developing a consensus must begin with an open process within the Executive branch and must culminate in congressional hearings and debate, after which Congress should be forced to make a decision.[4] The President should insist on hearing from dissenters as well as supporters of the proposed policy, including domestic advisers as well as his national security team. The military should also be fully consulted, but it should not be given a veto or a green light to use force whenever it decides.[5]

The President should also make the case for intervention to the public, including the potential drawbacks and the issues in dispute. Public debate will unearth a variety of experts on the country in which troops are to be deployed, such as historians, humanitarian aid specialists, and others. These experts would then be available to testify before Congress and serve to enhance the congressional decision-making process. Moreover, having such public debate in Congress and across the country in no way means that nothing about the proposed operation can be kept secret. It goes without saying that a President does not have to make public the proposed date or precise form of an intervention (even if it is to be done clandestinely, as an "overt/covert" action). Thus a public debate about whether the nation should use force would not, as it did not in Iraq, prevent the launching of military operations with some element of tactical surprise and with full secrecy as to combat strategy.

Finally, even with the consent of the American people and Congress, the United States should not, except when faced with direct aggression across an international border aimed at the United States or its allies, use force without the consent of the U.N. Security Council or an appropriate regional organization. Interventions in the internal affairs of other nations are doomed to failure unless they have broad international support. In fact, consent of the public and the Congress is likely to require a commitment on the part of the President to secure international support.

Accordingly, we propose that the President and Congress establish a procedure whereby they can work together to discuss, formulate, and enact an appropriate authorizing resolution prior to the actual engagement of such forces, all the while keeping the public informed of their intentions. This procedure should be supplemented by having Congress preauthorize a limited number of forces for the President to use unilaterally in accordance with U.N. Security Council authorization.[6] To increase that limited allotment and in all other anticipated, or ambiguous, situations that may involve the use or support of military force, the President should consult with Congress, perhaps through a special committee, to draft the necessary legal authorization, which shall then be approved by the whole Congress. The President, of course, is constitutionally empowered to respond unilaterally in self-defense to repel sudden attacks.

Although we would like to see this arrangement codified so that it would be binding on future Presidents and Congresses, what we propose here is only that the two parties institute a set of interbranch accords by which they agree to act. Thus the proposal need not be scrutinized in accordance with standard statutory or constitutional parameters—e.g., can Congress by statute require the President to consult with it. Rather, the guiding principle should be whether in fact foreign and military policy objectives can be achieved, and perhaps even strengthened, under this approach—e.g., the President voluntarily consults with members of Congress and seeks their consent so as to ensure their support.

The substance of such a nonstatutory accord could look like the following (remembering that this should not be read as a formal statutory text):

(a) The President may use military force at any time (1) to defend against attack on the United States, its armed forces, or its citizenry, or (2) in response to a U.N. Security Council resolution in accordance with preauthorizing legislation as enacted under section (b);

(b) Congress agrees to authorize the President to use a limited number of military forces pursuant to the U.N. Participation Act to respond to an international crisis as authorized by the U.N. Security Council pursuant to the U.N. Charter, for which no further congressional authorization is required. The President agrees to consult and seek appropriate authorization from Congress, where required, to expand the preauthorized force level or the scope of any such U.N. mission.

(c) The President and Congress agree to consult on all events that might involve the use of U.S. military force, military assistance, or paramilitary assistance (i.e., "covert" paramilitary actions) to formulate authorizing legislation for such action or assistance beyond that exercised under sections (a) and (b);

(d) Congress agrees to establish a joint special committee with whom the President agrees to consult on these issues in all instances, and shall establish expedited procedures for voting on any measure developed under section (c).

This proposal follows on the "contract model" outlined in chapter 4 by Jane Stromseth and is consistent with the proposal developed several years ago by Senator Joseph Biden and John Ritch.[7]

Our proposal begins by acknowledging those areas in which the President has unilateral authority to use military force (sec. (a)(1)). These include the well known power "to repel sudden attacks" on U.S. territory or forces; it also includes the power to rescue American nationals held captive abroad. This latter power has some constitutional and statutory bases.[8] Subsection (a)(2) would extend such authority to situations authorized by the U.N. Security Council for which Congress has preauthorized specific forces, as mandated under section (b). The President could thereby respond to a crisis by deploying a limited number of troops anytime there is an established international consensus for such a need. This authority should apply primarily, if not exclusively, to emergency situations warranting an immediate response. Long-term or expanded deployments would warrant specific congressional authorization under section (c).

Section (b) calls on Congress to preauthorize a contingent of forces for the President to use in response to a U.N. call for military action. The U.N. Charter explicitly outlines this never used procedure. Article 43 calls on all member nations "to make available to the Security Council, on its call in accordance with a special agreement or agreements, armed forces . . . necessary for the purpose of maintaining international peace and security." Because of the Cold War, no such special agreement was ever negotiated with the Security Council by any country. With the Cold War over and the U.N. beginning to perform its original goal of collective security, no obstacles remain for the United States to make its forces available.

The U.N. Participation Act requires that a special agreement, which is negotiated by the President with the Security Council, be approved by both Houses of Congress.[9] It also makes clear that no further congressional authorization is required to use these forces in accordance with a Security Council request: "The President shall not be deemed to require the authorization of the Congress to make available to the Security Council . . . the armed forces, facilities, or assistance provided for. . . . "[10]

Stromseth proposes that Congress designate up to 4,000 troops for U.N. actions.[11] Senator Biden envisions between 3,000 and 8,000.[12] This number would depend in part on the number of troops provided by other member nations under similar special agreements, so as to ensure an adequate force size to deal with appropriate contingencies. The U.S. initiative should encourage other countries to negotiate similar agreements and to provide additional troops to form a sizable force.

The final part of section (b), calling for subsequent congressional authorization for an increase in the preauthorized force size, is also consistent with the U.N. Participation Act, which provides that "nothing herein contained shall be construed as an authorization to the President by the Congress to make available to the Security Council for such purpose armed forces, facilities, or assistance in addition to the forces, facilities, and assistance provided for in such special agreement or agreements."[13] Under our scheme, the President would agree to come back to Congress for any expansion of not only the size, but also of the duration and purpose beyond the scope of the U.N. authorization. The special agreement procedure could be seen as supplementing the President's ability to respond to attacks on the United States to include emergency situations where there is an international consensus.[14]

Thus in nonemergency or other U.N. situations, the President and Congress should in all cases work together to formulate the legal framework under which the use of force should proceed, as called for in sections (c) and (d). In the "spirit of mutual respect and comity," the President should sit down with a special bicameral committee of Congress[15] any time he or she contemplates using military or paramilitary force, whether or not it is required, to determine which statutory mechanism, if any, is best suited for accomplishing his or her goal—e.g., the War Powers Resolution, the Intelligence Oversight Act, or another procedure.[16]

The two branches can then draft the proper bill or resolution to provide the necessary authorization, which Congress would then consider under an expedited schedule, but which includes hearings and reports by the committees having jurisdiction.[17] Or these discussions may determine that no formal statutory authorization is needed and that the President is fully empowered to act on his own. But the President should make it a practice to consult in this way in any ambiguous situation where the authorizing requirements are unclear, even if he is legally not required to do so. This process should apply even to preauthorized U.N. deployments where a long-term, expanded conflict is anticipated.

The Iraq War resolution—P.L. 102–1—was just such a statute, although it came well after the emergency response had settled into a status quo; it specifically delimited the terms by which the President could use military force—i.e., only in defense of U.N. Security Council resolutions and only after showing that all diplomatic and other peaceful means of resolving the conflict had been exhausted. The law also made clear that it "constitute[s] specific statutory authorization within the meaning of section 5(b) of the War Powers Resolution." And it required the President to report to Congress every 60 days on the status of the efforts to obtain Iraq's compliance with the Security Council resolutions. Under our scheme, the President should also have gotten this type of authorization when he decided to increase the troop deployment in November 1990 beyond the initial level, from 240,000 to 450,000.

Similarly, President Bush could easily have come to Congress to work out an authorization proposal for the deployment of U.S. forces into Somalia in December 1992—an action that we believe falls within Congress's war power responsibilities. Although the initial Somalia deployment was not "war," it was a use of force less than war (and *not* for defensive purposes) covered by the Marque and Reprisal section of the War Clause. As Alexander Hamilton noted, "anything beyond [repelling force with force — i.e., self-defense] must fall under the idea of reprisals and requires the sanction of that Department which is to declare or make war."[18] These more restricted actions are commonly known as "limited" or "imperfect" wars, which the Supreme Court has held fall within Congress's powers.[19] In addition, Jules Lobel has forcefully demonstrated that the Marque and Reprisal Clause "referred to the power to authorize a broad spectrum of armed hostilities short of declared war."[20] He notes that at the time the Constitution was drafted, "the term 'letters of marque and reprisal' lost much of its technical meaning and came to signify any intermediate or low-intensity hostility short of declared war that utilized public *or* private forces."[21]

Even under the War Powers Resolution, the Somalia deployment met the standard of "imminent" hostilities based on an objective test of what the forces were instructed to expect and authorized to do to achieve their mission, thus warranting a presidential report and triggering the 60-day time clock.[22] In this case, Security Council Resolution 794, adopted on December 3, 1992, authorizes the military forces to use "all necessary means" under Chapter VII of the U.N. Charter to achieve their objective.[23] This is the same language that was used in the U.N. resolution authorizing the use of force against Iraq,[24] and it is intended to constitute U.N. authorization for aggressive military action where necessary, and not just for defensive purposes as would be the case with a peacekeeping operation.[25]

Not surprisingly, Congress itself refrained from asserting its war powers responsibilities at the time the troops were deployed. Most Members initially shied away from asserting that any kind of legal authorization was required under either the Constitution or the War Powers Resolution, apparently in large part because they supported the mission and therefore did not want to be perceived as interfering or undermining it. Subsequently, however, both the Senate and House passed separate resolutions authorizing the President "to use United States Armed Forces pursuant to United Nations Security Council Resolution 794 in order to implement the resolution."[26] We see no reason why the Congress could not have taken up such a measure prior to the deployment, nor why the President could also not have asked for such a resolution in order to square the operation fully against all legal and political obstacles.

Our proposal would not prevent the President from launching surprise military attacks or from protecting the official deniability of third countries who assist with clandestine operations.[27] It would only require that the President receive from Congress the general authority to commit U.S. resources to an overseas conflict before in fact doing so. It would not reveal when, by what means, or even whether for certain the President will in fact act.

Perhaps the clearest illustration of our approach comes in the form of an amendment offered by Senator Jesse Helms (R-N.C.) following the failed coup attempt against Panamanian President Manuel Noriega in October 1989. Helms asked the Congress to authorize the President "to use the armed forces of the United States to secure the removal of General Manuel Antonio Noriega from his illegal control of the Republic of Panama. . . ."[28] And had the President wanted to use a "covert" paramilitary operation to oust Noriega, the provision could have been amended further to authorize him to use clandestine intelligence means under procedures outlined in the Intelligence Oversight Act regarding covert action.[29] Although indicating to Noriega that the United States was contemplating either military or paramilitary action, this authority would not have tipped him off as to whether and when such an attack would actually occur any more than he already was forewarned, and indeed expected, just such an attack. This is the type of authorization the President should have received, and quite likely could have obtained, before launching his invasion two months later.

The Senate, however, rejected Helms's language and instead adopted an amendment offered by Senator Sam Nunn (D-Ga.) that stopped short of authorizing the President to use force to remove Noriega from power. Nunn's "sense of the Congress resolution" acknowledged that the President "has authority under the

Constitution . . . to protect United States citizens and property, to protect and defend the Panama Canal, and to enforce the laws of the United States." It then "support[ed] (A) the efforts of the President to restore constitutional government to Panama and to remove General Manuel Noriega from his illegal control of the Republic of Panama [and] (B) the President's utilization of the full range of appropriate diplomatic, economic, and the [sic] military options in the Republic of Panama."[30]

CONCLUSION

The preceding chapters of this book lend themselves in large part to the solution that we propose. John Norton Moore, for example, argues succinctly in favor of "greater presidential authority in initial commitment decisions."[31] He then goes on to acknowledge, however, that

congressional authorization might be required in all cases where regular combat units are committed to sustained hostilities, with provision for subsequent congressional authorization in emergency settings requiring speed and decisiveness. This view . . . is an effort to be responsive to a policy test of congressional authorization in major wars most likely to place at risk the nation's blood and treasure. It would, however, give substantial weight to the need for presidential flexibility and the rich "common law tradition" of practical experience in presidential authority in this area over the years.[32]

Jane Stromseth complements that view with a comprehensively developed proposal in favor of giving the President limited preauthorization to use U.S. military forces in certain defined circumstances. Stromseth holds that in preauthorized situations, Congress would nonetheless spell out by statute clear limits on both the number of forces and the types of U.N.-authorized operations in which they could participate. In situations beyond those expressly provided for, the President would still need to seek congressional approval on a case by case basis.

Louis Fisher, Jules Lobel, and Peter Raven-Hansen all present forceful legal arguments suggesting significant limits on a unilateral executive war power, each of which again counsels for defined procedures to guide relations between the branches. Fisher notes that the general principle embodied in the War Powers Resolution—requiring "explicit congressional approval if the President intends to engage the country in a long term military commitment"—"has received a broad endorsement from both parties, liberals and conservatives alike"; he cites Robert Turner for the proposition that "[r]egardless of legal analysis, . . . it is a 'political imperative' that Congress and the President cooperate in a spirit of mutual respect and comity."[33]

While Raven-Hansen concedes that the President's war power authority has been extended by custom and statute "to include the use of armed force abroad for rescue, evacuation, and protection of American nationals and their property, and hot pursuit of attackers," "customary law does not authorize the President to deploy combat forces where there is a risk of sustained hostilities or escalation."[34] Lobel argues that international law serves to limit domestic constitutional power as much as it authorizes it, and suggests that any governmental act in violation of international law should be subject to "separation of powers restraints."[35]

Treverton shies away from the proposal we make in Chapter 8 of formally incorporating covert paramilitary action into the war power rubric—on the ground that "[t]here is little sentiment for it in Congress"—but calls for prior notice of all such "overt/covert" operations to ensure congressional involvement from the start.[36] Should Congress decide that it does want more involvement, it is but a small step to formalize a prior approval procedure consistent with that established for overt war powers. Finally, Collier demonstrates both the effectiveness and limitations of the procedures created by the War Powers Resolution. While this law has certainly kept Congress abreast of presidential uses of force, it has not in and of itself brought the two branches together for the formulation of U.S. policy for such actions.[37]

Our proposal outlines a practical guide for reaching a new consensus between Congress and the President. It essentially ignores the legal claims made by both sides and seeks a workable approach that makes sense in the post Cold War world. Moreover, it is consistent with a proposal made by Warren Christopher in 1982:

At the most fundamental level, a government makes no more fateful decision than the decision to go to war. The President should want to share that decision with the Congress. When the President and the Congress stand together, the nation's commitment is clear.

On the other hand, steps short of war ought to require less collaboration and permit more Executive discretion. To be sure, a decision to provide arms to a country could lead, as in Vietnam, to a combat involvement. But it is not inevitably the same thing. Military aid or sales and other steps short of combat can be considered on their own terms—managed by the President, within general policy guidelines jointly designed. Indeed, after Vietnam, both the Executive and the Congress are probably more inclined to treat our security relationships not as slippery slopes, but rather as staircases, with delineated landings from which we must choose, deliberately, either to deepen or lessen our involvement.[38]

Because the Soviet/Russian threat has been significantly reduced, if not wholly eliminated, the President can no longer expect to garner public support for foreign intervention on the ground that he or she is combatting communist expansion. As the nation turns more inward, it is likely to be more skeptical of the President's lone battle cry.

Thus, to ensure that the country is behind any long-term military commitment abroad, the President should welcome congressional concurrence for any military action that extends beyond the limited deployment at his disposal in response to U.N. requests. He should recognize that congressional authorization offers enhanced credibility of his policy to both domestic and foreign audiences and is a reasonable exchange for the initial flexibility that U.N. special agreement authority would offer. Indeed, as President Eisenhower well understood, it is in the President's interest to insist on explicit congressional support before force is used. The President should therefore cut through the entire constitutional debate about war powers by simply asserting that, as a matter of prudence and policy, force will not be used except in a true emergency to repel an attack, without the passage of a congressional resolution.

Following these procedures will make it more difficult for the nation to go to war—a difficulty that the Framers intended. It will also make it more likely that we will stay the course once we decide to use force, and that we will do so without the acrimonious public debate that only weakens us abroad and tears at the fabric of our society.

NOTES

1. *See* Hearings on the War Powers Resolution: Review of the Operation and Effectiveness of the War Powers Resolution before the Senate Foreign Relations Committee, 95th Cong., 1st Sess., at 209 (1977) (statement of Herbert J. Hansell, Legal Adviser, Dept. of State); *see also* Hearings on Review of the War Powers Resolution before the Investigations Subcommittee of the House Armed Services Committee, 101st Cong., 1st & 2d Sess., at 320 (May 24, Sept. 26, 1989, & Jan. 29, 1990) (H.A.S.C. 101–80) (testimony of Jimmy Carter) ("I have never made any public condemnation of the War Powers Resolution. My position has been different than that of Gerald Ford, Richard Nixon, Ronald Reagan, and George Bush, who have expressed very strong views against the resolution. . . . Only once during my presidency was there an incident when the resolution seemed to apply. This was when the attempt was made to rescue the hostages in Iran. After the attempt, I immediately called in the House and Senate leadership and informed them of everything that had happened. I made a full report.").

2. Nonetheless, as a matter of constitutional law, we believe that Congress's power to declare war means that the President cannot initiate military action without specific congressional authorization, except "to repel sudden attacks." Congress could preauthorize the President to use forces for specific purposes, for example in response to U.N.-authorized actions, but such authority must be clear and explicit.

3. *See The Vietnam Legacy: The War, American Society, and the Future of American Foreign Policy* (Anthony Lake ed., 1976) (demonstrating that there was no consistent viewpoint on whether the Vietnam War constituted a threat to vital interests).

4. We use the term "forced" deliberately. Most members of Congress, including its leader, have usually supported Presidents when they initiated the use of force and asserted that Congress need not, and should not, be consulted. For example, rather than protesting Bush's decision to commit forces to Somalia without congressional authorization, many congressional leaders applauded his action and asserted they saw no reason for Congress to vote on the matter. Members of Congress prefer to avoid the responsibility for intervention. They try, above all else, to avoid a vote that can be used against them by opponents in the next election.

5. President Bush seems to have made both of these errors in dealing with Somalia and Bosnia—resisting military intervention in Bosnia and rejecting advice to intervene in Somalia for a long time because the Joint Chiefs were opposed. In so doing, he ignored the fact that from the Berlin blockade to Yugoslavia, the chiefs have almost always objected to the use of armed forces, especially when they were not given a free hand to do whatever they wanted. When the Chairman of the Joint Chiefs, Gen. Colin Powell, switched positions and agreed to use military force in Somalia, Bush also made the mistake of accepting the condition laid down by the military that a U.S. general command all American forces and be in full control of the situation.

6. *See* Chapter 4 by Jane Stromseth.

7. Joseph Biden & John Ritch, *The War Power at a Constitutional Impasse: A "Joint Decision" Solution*, 77 Geo. L.J. 367 (1988). Subsequently, Biden introduced a bill calling on the Administration to negotiate preauthorizing special agreements in accordance with the U.N. Participation Act. S.J. Res. 325, the Collective Security Participation Resolution, 102d Cong., 2d Sess. (July 2, 1992).

8. *In re Neagle*, 135 U.S. 1 (1890), is regularly cited as establishing the rescue power. The Supreme Court held that the President had a duty, not "limited to the enforcement of Acts of Congress or of treaties," but "growing out of the Constitution itself, our international relations, and all the protection implied by the nature of the government under the Constitution," to take appropriate measures to protect a Supreme Court Justice whose life had been threatened. 135 U.S. at 64. The so-called Hostage Act of 1868, as amended, 22 U.S.C. § 1732 (1990), authorizes the President to use "means not amounting to acts of war" to rescue Americans held abroad. Uses of force for the sole purpose of rescuing persons are arguably by definition not acts of war, although they may also be covered under the Constitution by the Marque and Reprisal Clause.

9. 22 U.S.C. § 287d.

10. *Id.*

11. Chapter 4.

12. *See* Cong. Rec., July 2, 1992, at S9854 (daily ed.).

13. 22 U.S.C. § 287d.

14. We disagree with those who argue that the Constitution requires Congress to authorize the use of force against a specific enemy, and therefore prohibits such open-ended preauthorizations. *See* the Introduction.

15. *See, e.g.,* proposal of Bird, Nunn, Warner, and Mitchell calling for creation of such a committee. S.J. Res. 323, 100th Cong., 2d Sess. (1988).

16. In Chapter 8 we argue that these statutes should be rewritten and conflated so that they comprise the exclusive means for authorizing the use of force, which includes requiring prior authorization for so-called "covert" paramilitary activities. A revised, comprehensive statute would also have to incorporate special agreements and U.N. authorization.

17. The War Powers Resolution already provides for expedited consideration of any war related legislation. 50 U.S.C. § 1545. That schedule could be amended to speed up the process even further.

18. Letter from Alexander Hamilton to James McHenry (May 17, 1798), *reprinted in* 21 *The Papers of Alexander Hamilton* 461–62 (Harold Syrett ed., 1974).

19. *Bas v. Tingy*, 4 U.S. (4 Dall.) 37, 45 (1800) ("[T]his modified warfare is authorized by the constitutional authority of our country. . . . As far as Congress tolerated and authorized the war on our part, so far may we proceed in hostile operations."); *Talbot v. Seeman*, 5 U.S. (1 Cranch) 1, 28 (1801) ("The whole powers of war being, by the constitution of the United States, vested in congress, the acts of that body can alone be resorted to as our guides in this inquiry. . . . [C]ongress may authorize general hostilities . . . or partial hostilities.").

20. Jules Lobel, *Covert War and Congressional Authority: Hidden War and Forgotten Power*, 134 U. Pa. L. Rev. 1035, 1046 (1986).

21. *Id.* at 1044–45.

22. Section 4(a)(1) of the War Powers Resolution, 50 U.S.C. § 1543(a)(1) (situations involving "hostilities or . . . where imminent involvement in hostilities is clearly indicated by the circumstances").

23. Chapter VII concerns nonconsenting, coercive "action with respect to the peace, breaches of the peace, and acts of aggression."

24. SC Res. 678 (Nov. 29, 1990).

25. Although the U.S. military has not revealed the precise rules of engagement for this operation, we presume that they authorized the forces to use military force even when not directly confronting imminent hostile action.

26. S.J. Res. 45, 103d Cong., 1st Sess., passed the Senate by unanimous voice vote on February 4, 1993. Cong. Rec., Feb. 4, 1993, at S1368 (daily ed.). The House passed a modified version of S.J. Res. 45 on May 25, 1993. Cong. Rec., May 25, 1993, at H2744–65 (daily ed.).

27. It would, however, end the charade of "covert" paramilitary actions, which cannot be kept secret and are therefore covert in name only. *See* Chapter 8.

28. Cong. Rec., Oct. 3, 1989, at S12447 (daily ed.).

29. 50 U.S.C. §§ 413–15.

30. Cong. Rec., Oct. 3, 1989, at S12685 (daily ed.) (the Senate Debate continues through S12693). Apparently the President also opposed the Helms language, assumedly because he believed he did not need congressional authorization to launch an invasion. However, had the President met with congressional leaders and explained his options and intentions concerning Panama, he could well have persuaded a majority of the Congress to provide him with broad authority to then act at his discretion. If the President could not convince Congress, then he should not have proceeded as he did.

31. Chapter 9. Moore premises his argument on the fact of "*major* potential congressional checks on presidential authority to engage the nation in war . . . including the appropriations power, the hearings and impeachment power (in an extreme case of aggressive war), and, most importantly, the normal legislative process by which *prior* or *subsequent* congressional action can prevent or terminate presidential commitment of U.S. armed forces to major hostilities abroad."

32. *Id.*

33. Chapter 1.

34. Chapter 2.

35. Chapter 5.

36. Chapter 7.

37. Indeed, this ongoing legal dispute will likely remain never-ending, and the conclusions made in this book will almost certainly prompt other scholars to publish rebuttals to their conclusions. Thus what Justice Jackson said 40 years ago in the *Steel Seizure* case still applies: "[P]artisan debate and scholarly speculation yields no net result, but only supplies more or less apt quotations from respected sources on each side of any question. They largely cancel each other." *Youngstown Sheet & Tube Co. v. Sawyer*, 343 U.S. 579, 634–35 (1952) (Jackson, J., concurring) (footnote omitted).

38. Warren Christopher, *Ceasefire Between the Branches: A Compact on Foreign Affairs*, 60 Foreign Aff. 899, 1002–03 (Summer 1982).

Appendix

CONFERENCE PARTICIPANTS

1. Barry Carter, Georgetown University Law Center
2. Blair Clark, Advisory Board, Center for National Security Studies
3. Ellen Collier, Congressional Research Service
4. Gregory Craig, Williams & Connolly
5. Lori Damrosch, Columbia Law School
6. Norman Dorsen, New York University School of Law
7. Stephen Dycus, Vermont Law School
8. John Hart Ely, Stanford Law School
9. Louis Fisher, Congressional Research Service
10. Michael Glennon, University of California at Davis Law School
11. Charles Gustafson, Georgetown University Law Center
12. Jeremiah Gutman, Levy, Gutman, Goldberg & Kaplan
13. Morton H. Halperin, Carnegie Endowment for International Peace
14. Harold Koh, Yale Law School
15. Lance Lindblom, J. Roderick MacArthur Foundation
16. Jules Lobel, University of Pittsburgh Law School
17. Mark Lynch, Covington and Burling
18. David MacMichael, Association of National Security Alumni
19. Kate Martin, Center for National Security Studies
20. John Norton Moore, Univ. of Virginia Law School
21. John Prados, author *Presidents' Secret Wars* (1986)
22. Christopher H. Pyle, Mount Holyoke College
23. Peter Raven-Hansen, George Washington University National Law Center
24. W. Taylor Reveley, III, author *War Powers of the President and Congress* (1981)
25. Steve Rickard, Senate Foreign Relations Committee
26. Eugene Rostow, National Defense University
27. Nicholas Rostow, National Security Council (Bush Administration)
28. David Scheffer, Carnegie Endowment for International Peace
29. J. Gregory Sidak, American Enterprise Institute

30. Gary M. Stern, Center for National Security Studies
31. Jane Stromseth, Georgetown University Law Center
32. Greg Treverton, Council on Foreign Relations
33. Don Wallace, Jr., Georgetown University Law Center
34. Peter Weiss, Center for Constitutional Rights
35. Edwin Williamson, State Department Legal Adviser (Bush Administration)
36. Jeanne M. Woods, Center for National Security Studies

Selected Bibliography

BOOKS

Abi-Saab, Georges, *The United Nations Operation in the Congo, 1960–1964* (Oxford: Oxford University Press, 1978).

Acheson, Dean, *Present at the Creation* (New York: Norton, 1969).

Adams, John Q., *Eulogy on Madison* (Boston: J. H. Eastburn City Printer, 1836).

After the Storm: Lessons from the Gulf War (J. Nye and R. Smith, eds.) (Lanham, Md.: Madison Books, 1992).

A Question of Balance: The President, the Congress and Foreign Policy (Thomas E. Mann, ed.) (Washington, D.C.: Brookings Institution, 1990).

Banks, William, and Peter Raven-Hansen, *The Sword and the Purse in American Law* (New York: Oxford University Press, 1994).

Berger, Raoul, *Executive Privilege* (Cambridge, Mass.: Harvard University Press, 1974).

Bickel, Alexander M., *The Least Dangerous Branch: The Supreme Court at the Bar of Politics* (New Haven: Yale University Press, 1962).

Blackstone, William, *Commentaries on the Laws of England* (St. George Tucker, ed.) (Philadelphia: William Young Birch & Abraham Small, 1803).

Blechman, Barry M., and Stephen S. Kaplan, *Force Withour War: The Use of Armed Forces as a Political Instrument* (Washington, D.C.: Brookings Institution, 1978).

Borchard, Edwin, *The Diplomatic Protection of Citizens Abroad* (New York: Banks Law Publishing Co., 1915).

Bowett, D. W., *United Nations Forces* (London: Stevens Publishing, 1964).

Carter, Barry, and Phillip Trimble, *International Law* (Boston: Little, Brown, 1991).

Choper, Jesse H., *Judicial Review and the National Political Process: A Functional Reconsideration of the Role of the Supreme Court* (1980).

Clausewitz, Carl von, *On War* (Howard & Paret, eds.) (Princeton, N.J.: Princeton University Press, 1976).

The Collected Works of Abraham Lincoln (R. Basler, ed.) (New York: Viking Press, 1953).

Commager, Henry Steele, *The Defeat of America* (New York: Simon and Schuster, 1968).

Corwin, Edwin, *Total War and the Constitution* (New York: A. A. Knopf, 1947).

Cover, Robert M., *Justice Accused: Antislavery and the Judicial Process* (New Haven: Yale University Press, 1975).

Cox, Henry B., *War, Foreign Affairs, and Constitutional Power: 1829–1901* (Cambridge, Mass.: Ballinger Publishing Co., 1984).

D'Amato, Anthony A., *The Concept of Custom in International Law* (Ithaca, N.Y.: Cornell University Press, 1971).

Durch, William, and Barry Blechman, *Keeping the Peace: The United Nations in the Emerging World Order* (Washington, D.C.: Henry L. Stimson Center, 1992).

Dycus, Stephen, Arthur L. Berney, William C. Banks, and Peter Raven-Hansen, *National Security Law* (Boston: Little, Brown, 1990).

Eisenhower, Dwight, *Waging Peace* (Garden City, N.Y.: Doubleday, 1965).

The Federalist (C. Rossiter, ed.) (New York: Mentor Books, New American Library, 1961).

First Use of Nuclear Weapons: Under the Constitution, Who Decides? (Peter Raven-Hansen, ed.) (Westport, Conn.: Greenwood Press, 1987).

Fisher, Louis, *Constitutional Conflicts between Congress and the President* (Lawrence: University of Kansas Press, 1991).

Friedman, Leon, and Burt Neuborne, *Unquestioning Obedience to the President: The ACLU Case Against the Legality of the War in Vietnam* (New York: Norton, 1972).

Glennon, Michael J., *Constitutional Diplomacy* (Princeton, N.J.: Princeton University Press, 1990).

Grob, Fritz, *The Relativity of War and Peace* (New Haven: Yale University Press, 1949).

Henkin, Louis, *Constitutionalism, Democracy and Foreign Affairs* (New York: Columbia University Press, 1990).

Henkin, Louis, *Foreign Affairs and the Constitution* (Mineola, N.Y.: Foundation Press, 1972).

The Intelligence Community (Tyrus Fain, Katharine Plant, and Ross Milloy, eds.) (New York: R. R. Bowker Co., 1977).

Keynes, Edward, *Undeclared War* (University Park: Pennsylvania University Press, 1982).

Koh, Harold H., *The National Security Constitution* (New Haven: Yale University Press, 1990).

Locke, John, *Two Treatises of Civil Government* (London: J. M. Dent & Son Ltd., 1962).

Moore, John Norton, *Law and the Indo-China War* (Princeton, N.J.: Princeton University Press, 1972).

Moore, John Norton, *The Secret War in Central America* (Frederick, Md.: University Publications of America, 1987).

The Need to Know: The Report of the Twentieth Century Fund Task Force on Covert Action and American Democracy (New York: Twentieth Century Fund Press, 1992).

Nuclear Weapons and Law (Arthur Miller and Martin Fernrider, eds.) (Westport, Conn.: Greenwood Press, 1984).

The Papers of Alexander Hamilton (Harold Syrett, ed.) (New York: Columbia University Press, 1974).

Peterzell, Jay, *Reagan's Secret Wars* (Washington, D.C.: Center for National Security Studies, 1984).

The Presidency in the Constitutional Order (Joseph M. Bessette and Jeffrey Tulis, eds.) (Baton Rouge: Louisiana State University Press, 1981).

Reveley, W. Taylor III, *War Powers of the President and Congress: Who Holds the Arrows and the Olive Branch?* (Charlottesville: University of Virginia, 1981).

Right v. Might: International Law and the Use of Force (New York: Council on Foreign Relations, 2d ed., 1991).

Rogers, James G., *World Policing and the Constitution* (Boston: World Peace Foundations, 1945).

Ronzitti, Natalino, *Rescuing Nationals Abroad Through Military Coercion and Intervention on Grounds of Humanity* (Boston: M. Nijhoff Publishers, 1985).

Schlesinger, Arthur, *The Imperial Presidency* (Boston: Houghton Mifflin, 1973).

Sofaer, Abraham D., *War, Foreign Affairs and Constitutional Power: The Origins* (Cambridge, Mass.: Ballinger Publishing Co., 1976).

Thomas, Ann V. W., and A. J. Thomas, Jr., *The War-Making Powers of the President* (Dallas: SMU Press, 1982).

Treverton, Gregory F., *Covert Action: The Limits of Intervention in the Postwar World* (New York: Basic Books, 1987).

Turner, Robert F., *The War Powers Resolution: Its Implementation in Theory and Practice* (Philadelphia, Pa.: Foreign Policy Research Institute, 1983).

Turner, Robert F., *Repealing the War Powers Resolution: Restoring the Rule of Law in U.S. Foreign Policy* (Washington, D.C.: Brassey's, 1991).

The Vietnam Legacy: The War, American Society, and the Future of American Foreign Policy (Anthony Lake, ed.) (New York: New York University Press, 1976).

The Writings of George Washington (J. Fitzpatrick, ed.) (Indianapolis: Liberty Classics, 1988).

The Writings of Thomas Jefferson (Paul L. Ford, ed.) (New York: Putnam's, 1892–1899).

The Writings of James Madison (Gaillard Hunt, ed.) (New York: Putnam's, 1900–1910).

Wormuth, Francis D., and Edwin B. Firmage, *To Chain the Dog of War: The War Power of Congress in History and Law* (Urbana: University of Illinois Press, 2d ed., 1989).

ARTICLES

Barr, William, Panel, *The Appropriations Power and Necessary and Proper Clause*, 68 Wash. U.L.Q. 626 (1990).

Bennett, Charles, et al., *The President's Powers as Commander-in-Chief Versus Congress' War Power and Appropriations Power*, 43 U. Miami L. Rev. 17 (1988).

Berger, Raoul, *War-Making by the President*, 121 U. Pa. L. Rev. 29 (1972).

Berger, Raoul, *Protection of Americans Abroad*, 44 Cinn. L. Rev. 741 (1975).

Biden, Joseph, and John Ritch, *The War Power at a Constitutional Impasse: A 'Joint Decision' Solution*, 77 Geo. L.J. 367 (1988).

Bilder, Richard, *International Law in the "New World Order": Some Preliminary Reflections*, 1 J. Transnat'l L. & Pol'y 1 (1992).

Bork, Robert, *Comments on the Articles on the Legality of the United States Action in Cambodia*, 65 Am. J. Int'l L. 79 (1971).

Casper, Gerhard, *An Essay in Separation of Powers: Some Early Versions and Practices*, 30 Wm. & Mary L. Rev. 211 (1989).

Celada, Raymond J., "Effect of the Legislative Veto Decision on the Two-House Disapproval Mechanism to Terminate U.S. Involvement in Hostilities Pursuant to Unilateral Presidential Action," C.R.S. Report (August 24, 1983).

Charney, Jonathan I., *The Power of the Executive Branch of the U.S. Government to Violate Customary International Law*, 80 Am. J. Int'l L. 913 (1986).

Christopher, Warren, *Ceasefire Between the Branches: A Compact on Foreign Affairs*, 60 Foreign Affairs 899 (Summer 1982).

Coase, Ronald H., *The Problem of Social Cost*, 3 J. Law. & Econ. 1 (1960).

Corwin, Edward S., *The President's Power*, The New Republic, Jan. 29, 1951, at 15.

Eagleton, Clyde, *The Form and Function of the Declaration of War*, 32 Am. J. Int'l L. 19 (1938).

Ely, John Hart, *Another Such Victory: Constitutional Theory and Practice in a World Where Courts Are No Different from Legislatures*, 77 Va. L. Rev. 878 (1991).

Ely, John Hart, *The American War in Indochina, Part I: The (Troubled) Constitutionality of the War They Told Us About*, 42 Stanford L. Rev. 877 (1990).

Ely, John Hart, *The American War in Indochina, Part II: The Unconstitutionality of the War They Didn't Tell Us About*, 42 Stanford L. Rev. 1093 (1990).

Ely, John Hart, *Suppose Congress Wanted a War Powers Act That Worked*, 88 Columbia L. Rev. 1379 (1988).

Emerson, J. Terry, *Making War Without a Declaration*, 17 J. Legis. 23 (1990).

Franck, Thomas, *The President, the Constitution, and Nuclear Weapons*, 363 *in* Nuclear Weapons and Law (Arthur Miller and Martin Fernrider, eds., 1984).

Franck, Thomas, and Faiza Patel, *UN Police Action in Lieu of War: 'The Old Order Changeth'*, 85 Am. J. Int'l L. 63 (1991).

Gardner, Richard, *Collective Security and the 'New World Order': What Role for the United Nations?*, *in* After the Storm: Lessons from the Gulf War (J. Nye and R. Smith, eds., 1992).

Gewirtz, Paul, *The Courts, Congress and Executive Policy-Making: Notes on Three Doctrines*, Law & Contemp. Probs. (Summer 1976).

Glennon, Michael J., *The Gulf War and the Constitution*, 70 Foreign Affairs 100 (Spring 1991).

Glennon, Michael J., *The Constitution and Chapter VII of the United Nations Charter*, 85 Am. J. Int'l L. 74 (1991).

Glennon, Michael J., *Two Views of Presidential Foreign Affairs Power: Little v. Barreme or Curtiss-Wright?*, 13 Yale J. Int'l L. 5 (1988).

Glennon, Michael J., *United States Mutual Security Treaties: The Commitment Myth*, 24 Colum. J. Transnat'l L. 509 (1986).

Glennon, Michael J., *Can the President Do No Wrong?*, 80 Am. J. Int'l L. 923 (1986).

Glennon, Michael J., *The Use of Custom in Resolving Separation of Powers Disputes*, 64 B.U.L. Rev. 109 (1984).

Halperin, Morton H. (and Gary M. Stern), *Lawful Wars*, Foreign Policy, No. 72, at 173 (Fall 1988).

Heindel, Richard et al., *The North Atlantic Treaty in the United States*, 43 Am. J. Int'l L. 633 (1949).

Henkin, Louis, *The Constitution and United States Sovereignty: A Century of Chinese Exclusion and Its Progeny*, 100 Harv. L. Rev. 853 (1987).

Henkin, Louis, *The President and International Law*, 80 Am. J. Int'l L. 930 (1986).

Henrikson, Alan K., *How Can the Vision of a 'New World Order' Be Realized*, 16 Fletcher Forum of World Affairs 63 (1992).

Jay, Stewart, *The Status of the Law of Nations in Early American Law*, 42 Vand. L. Rev. 819 (1989).

Koh, Harold H., *The Coase Theorem and the War Power: A Response*, 41 Duke L.J. 122 (1991).

Lobel, Jules, *Covert War and Congressional Authority: Hidden War and Forgotten Power*, 134 U. Pa. L. Rev. 1035 (1986).

Lobel, Jules, *The Limits of Constitutional Power: Conflicts Between Foreign Policy and International Law*, 71 Va. L. Rev. 1071 (1985).

Lofgren, Charles A., *War-Making Under the Constitution: The Original Understanding*, 81 Yale L.J. 672 (1972).

Mackinlay, John, and Jarat Chopra, *Second Generation Multinational Operations*, Washington Quarterly (Summer 1992).

Marks, Lee R., and John G. Grabow, *The President's Foreign Economic Powers after Dames & Moore v. Regan: Legislation by Acquiescence*, 68 Cornell L. Rev. 68 (1982).

Mathews, Craig, *The Constitutional Power of the President to Conclude International Agreements*, 64 Yale L.J. 345 (1955).

Meeker, Leonard, *The Legality of United States Participation in Defense of Viet-Nam*, 54 State Dept. Bull. 474, *reprinted in* 75 Yale L.J. 1085 (1966).

Mikva, Abner J., and Gerald L. Neuman, *The Hostage Crisis and the "Hostage Act*," 49 U. Chi. L. Rev. 292 (1982).

Monaghan, Henry, *Presidential War-Making*, 50 B.U.L. Rev. 19 (Special Issue 1970).

Note, *Congress, the President, and the Power to Commit Forces to Combat*, 81 Harv. L. Rev. 1771 (1968).

Note, *Congressional Control of Presidential War-Making Under the War Powers Act: The Status of a Legislative Veto After Chadha*, 132 U. Pa. L. Rev. 1217 (1984).

Peterson, Todd, *The Law and Politics of Shared National Security Power (Book Review)*, 59 G.W.U.L. Rev. 747 (1991).

Quigley, John, *The New World Order and the Rule of Law*, 18 Syracuse J. Int'l L. & Comm. 75 (1992).

Ratner, Leonard G., *The Coordinated Warmaking Power—Legislative, Executive and Judicial Roles*, 44 S. Cal. L. Rev. 461 (1971).

Ratner, Michael & David Cole, *The Force of Law: Judicial Enforcement of the War Powers Resolution*, 17 Loyola L.A. L. Rev. 715 (1984).

Raven-Hansen, Peter, *Remarks*, Am. Soc'y Int'l L. Proceedings of the 85th Annual Meeting 8 (1991).

Redish, Martin H., *Judicial Review and the "Political Question,"* 79 Nw. U.L. Rev. 1031 (1985).

Reveley, W. Taylor III, *Presidential War-Making: Constitutional Prerogative or Usurpation?*, 55 Va. L. Rev. 1243 (1969).

Rogers, William, *Congress, the President, and the War Powers*, 59 Calif. L. Rev. 1194 (1971).

Rostow, Eugene V., *Until What? Enforcement Action or Collective Self-Defense*, 85 Am. J. Int'l L. 506 (1991).

Rostow, Eugene V., *President, Prime Minister or Constitutional Monarch?*, 83 Am. J. Int'l L. 740 (1989).

Rostow, Eugene V., *"More Unto the Breach": The War Powers Resolution Revisited*, 21 Val. U. L. Rev. 1 (1986).

Rostow, Eugene V., *Great Cases Make Bad Law: The War Powers Act*, 50 Tex. L. Rev. 833 (1972).

Rubin, Barnett R., *The Fragmentation of Afghanistan*, 68 Foreign Affairs 150 (Winter 1989–90).

Schachter, Oscar, *United Nations Law in the Gulf Conflict*, 85 Am. J. Int'l L. 452 (1991).

Scharpf, Fritz W., *Judicial Review and the Political Question: A Functional Analysis*, 75 Yale L.J. 517 (1966).

Scheffer, David J., *Use of Force after the Cold War: Panama, Iraq and the New World Order, in* Right v. Might 156 (2d ed. 1991).

Schmitt, Gary J., *Executive Privilege, Presidential Power to Withhold Information*, in The
    Presidency in the Constitutional Order (Joseph M. Bessette and Jeffrey Tulis,
    eds., 1981).
Should the U.S. Fight Secret Wars?, Harpers (Sept. 1984).
Sidak, J. Gregory, *War, Liberty, and Enemy Aliens*, 67 N.Y.U. L. Rev. 1402 (1992).
Sidak, J. Gregory, *To Declare War*, 41 Duke L.J. 27 (1991).
Sidak, J. Gregory, *The Inverse Coase Theorem and Declarations of War*, 41 Duke L.J. 325
    (1991).
Stromseth, Jane, *Rethinking War Powers: Congress, the President, and the United Nations*,
    81 Geo. L. J. 597 (1993).
Sugarman, Robert P., *Judicial Decisions Concerning the Constitutionality of United States
    Military Activity in Indo-China: A Bibliography of Court Decisions*, 13 Colum. J.
    Transnat'l L. 470 (1974).
Treverton, Gregory F., *Intelligence: Welcome to the American Government*, in A Question
    of Balance: The President, the Congress and Foreign Policy (Thomas E. Mann,
    ed., 1990).
Van Alstyne, William, *Congress, the President, and the Power to Declare War: A Requiem
    for Vietnam*, 121 U. Pa. L. Rev. 1 (1972).
Velvel, Lawrence R., *The War in Viet Nam: Unconstitutional, Justiciable, and Jurisdic-
    tionally Attackable*, 16 Kan. L. Rev. 449 (1968).
Watson, Alan, *An Approach to Customary Law*, U. Ill. L. Rev. 561 (1984).
Weikert, Robert A., *Applying Chadha: The Fate of the War Powers Resolution*, 24 Santa
    Clara L. Rev. 697 (1984).
Weisburd, Arthur M., *The Executive Branch and International Law*, 41 Vand. L. Rev. 1205
    (1988).
Wright, Quincy, *The Power of the Executive to Use Military Forces Abroad*, 10 Va. J. Int'l
    L. 43 (1969).

GOVERNMENT DOCUMENTS

Congressional Records

Hearings on Crisis in the Persian Gulf Region: U.S. Policy Options and Implications before
    the Senate Committee on Armed Services, 101st Cong., 2d Sess. (Sept. 11–Dec.
    3, 1990) (S. Hearing 101–1071).
Hearings on Crisis in the Persian Gulf Region: U.S. Policy Options and Implications before
    the Senate Committee on Armed Services, 101st Cong., 2d Sess. (1990).
Hearings on Review of the War Powers Resolution before the Investigations Subcommittee
    of the House Armed Services Committee, 101st Cong., 1st & 2d Sess. (May 24,
    Sept. 26, 1989, Jan. 29, 1990) (H.A.S.C. 101–80).
Hearings on FBI Authority to Seize Suspects Abroad before the House Subcommittee on
    Civil and Constitutional Rights, 101st Cong., 1st Sess. (Nov. 8, 1989).
Hearings on the War Power After 200 Years: Congress and the President at a Constitutional
    Impasse before the Special Subcommittee on War Powers of the Senate Commit-
    tee on Foreign Relations, 100th Cong., 2d Sess. (1988) (S. Hearing 100–1012).
Hearings on War Powers: Origins, Purposes, and Applications before the House Commit-
    tee on Foreign Affairs, 100th Cong., 2d Sess. (1988).

The War Powers Resolution, Relevant Documents, Correspondence, Reports, Subcommittee on Arms Control, International Security, and Science, House Committee on Foreign Affairs, 100th Cong., 2d Sess. (May 1988).

Hearings on H.R. 3822, to Strengthen the System of Congressional Oversight of Intelligence Activities of the United States before the Subcommittee on Legislation of the House Permanent Select Committee on Intelligence, 100th Cong., 2d Sess. (Feb. 24 & Mar. 10, 1988).

Report of the Congressional Committees Investigating the Iran-Contra Affair, H. Rep. No. 100–433, S. Rep. No. 100–216, 100th Cong., 1st Sess. (Nov. 1987).

Hearings before the House Select Committee to Investigate Covert Arms Transactions with Iran and Senate Select Committee on Secret Military Assistance to Iran and the Nicaraguan Opposition, 100th Cong., 1st Sess. (1987).

Hearings on H.R. 1013 before the Subcommittee on Legislation of the House Permanent Select Committee on Intelligence, 100th Cong., 1st Sess. (Apr. 1, 8, & June 10, 1987).

"Strengthening Executive-Legislative Consultation on Foreign Policy," House Foreign Affairs Committee Print (October 1983).

Hearings on Congressional Oversight of Covert Activities before the House Permanent Select Committee on Intelligence, 98th Cong., 1st Sess. (Sept. 20–22, 1983).

Hearings on the U.S. Supreme Court Decision Concerning the Legislative Veto before the House Committee on Foreign Affairs, 98th Cong., 1st Sess. (July 19, 20, and 21, 1983).

Hearings on the situation in Iran before the Senate Committee on Foreign Relations, 96th Cong., 2d Sess. (May 8, 1980).

Hearings on the War Powers Resolution: Review of the Operation and Effectiveness of the War Powers Resolution before the Senate Comm. on Foreign Relations, 95th Cong., 1st Sess. (1977).

Report of the Senate Select Committee to Study Governmental Operations with Respect to Intelligence Activities (Church Committee Report), S. Rep. No. 94–755, 94th Cong., 2d Sess. (Apr. 26, 1976) (Books I–VI).

Report of the Senate Select Committee to Study Governmental Operations with Respect to Intelligence Activities (Church Committee Interim Report on Alleged Assassination Plots Involving Foreign Leaders), S. Rep. No. 94–465, 94th Cong., 1st. Sess. (Nov. 20, 1975).

Hearings on War Powers: A Test of Compliance relative to the Da Nang Sealift, the Evacuation of Phnom Penh, the Evacuation of Saigon, and the Mayaguez Incident, before the House Committee on International Relations, 94th Cong., 1st Sess. (May 7 and June 4, 1975).

Hearings on War Powers Legislation before the Senate Comm. on Foreign Relations, 93d Cong., 1st Sess. (1973).

Message of President Nixon vetoing House Joint Resolution 542, A Joint Resolution Concerning the War Powers of Congress and the President, 93d Cong., 2d Sess. (Oct. 24, 1973) (H. Doc. No. 93–171).

Hearings on War Powers Legislation before the Senate Foreign Relations Committee, 92d Cong., 2d Sess. (1972).

Powers of the President to Send the Armed Forces Outside the United States, Prepared for the Use of the Joint Committee Made Up of the Committee on Foreign Relations and the Committee on Armed Services of the Senate, 82d Cong., 1st Sess. (Feb. 28, 1951).

Hearings on Participation by the United States in the United Nations Organization before the House Committee on Foreign Affairs, 79th Cong., lst Sess. (1945).

Executive Branch Records

A Compilation of the Messages and Papers of the Presidents (J. Richardson, ed., 1897–1925).

Authority of the President to Repel the Attack in Korea, State Department Bulletin (July 31, 1950).

Office of Legal Counsel, U.S. Department of Justice, "Applicability of the Neutrality Act to Activities of the Central Intelligence Agency," memorandum from Larry L. Sims to Philip B. Heymann, Assistant Attorney General, Criminal Division (Oct. 10, 1979).

10 Op. Att'y Gen. 74, 79 (1861).

Report of the President's Special Review Board (1987) ("Tower Commission Report").

Constitutional Records

Records of the Federal Convention (Max Farrand, ed., 1911).

The Debates in the Several State Conventions, on the Adoption of the Federal Constitution (Jonathan Elliot, ed., 2d ed., 1836).

U.N. Documents

Report of the Secretary-General, An Agenda for Peace: Preventive Diplomacy, Peacemaking, and Peace-Keeping, A/47/277, S/24111 (June 17, 1992).

CASE LIST

Ange v. Bush, 752 F. Supp. 509 (D.D.C. 1990).

Baker v. Carr, 369 U.S. 186 (1962).

Bas v. Tingy, 4 U.S. 37 (1800).

Berk v. Laird, 317 F. Supp. 715 (E.D.N.Y. 1970), *aff'd*, 429 F.2d 302 (2d Cir. 1970).

Brown v. United States, 12 U.S. (8 Cranch) 110 (1814).

The Chinese Exclusion Case, 130 U.S. 581 (1889).

Committee of United States Citizens Living in Nicaragua (CUSCLIN) v. Reagan, 859 F.2d 929 (D.C. Cir. 1988).

Conyers v. Reagan, 578 F. Supp. 324 (D.D.C. 1984), *dism'd as moot*, 765 F.2d 1124 (D.C. Cir. 1985).

Crockett v. Reagan, 558 F. Supp. 893 (D.D.C. 1982), aff'd, 720 F.2d 1355 (D.C. Cir. 1983).

DaCosta v. Laird, 448 F.2d 1368 (2d Cir. 1971).

Dames & Moore v. Regan, 453 U.S. 654 (1981).

Dellums v. Bush, 752 F. Supp. 1141 (D.D.C. 1990).

Durand v. Hollins, 8 F. Cas. 111 (C.C.S.D.N.Y. 1860).

Fernandez v. Wilkinson, 505 F. Supp. 787 (D. Kan. 1980), *aff'd on other grounds*, 654 F.2d 1382 (10th Cir. 1981).

Fleming v. Page, 50 U.S. 603 (1850).

Goldwater v. Carter, 444 U.S. 996 (1979).

Haig v. Agee, 453 U.S. 280 (1981).

Immigration & Naturalization Service v. Chadha, 462 U.S. 919 (1983).

Inland Waterways Corp. v. Young, 309 U.S. 517 (1940).

In re Neagle, 135 U.S. 1 (1890).

Japan Whaling Association v. American Cetacean Soc'y, 478 U.S. 221 (1986).

Johnson v. Transportation Agency, 480 U.S. 616 (1987).

Kennedy v. Sampson, 511 F.2d 430 (D.C. Cir. 1974).

Kent v. Dulles, 357 U.S. 116 (1958).

Korematsu v. United States, 323 U.S. 214 (1944).

Little v. Barreme, 6 U.S. (2 Cranch) 170 (1804).

Lowry v. Reagan, 676 F. Supp. 333 (D.D.C. 1987).

McNary v. Haitian Centers Council, 969 F.2d 1350 (2d Cir. 1992), *rev'd*, 61 U.S.L.W. 4684 (June 21, 1993).

Martin v. Mott, 25 U.S. (12 Wheat.) 19 (1827).

Massachusetts v. Laird, 451 F.2d 26 (1st Cir. 1971).

Miller v. United States, 78 U.S. (11 Wall.) 268 (1870).

Mitchell v. Laird, 488 F.2d 611 (D.C. Cir. 1973).

Mitchell v. Laird, 476 F.2d 533 (D.C. 1973).

Mora v. McNamara, 389 U.S. 934 (1967).

The Nereide, 13 U.S. (9 Cranch) 388 (1815).

New York Times Co. v. United States, 403 U.S. 713 (1971).

Orlando v. Laird, 317 F. Supp. 1013 (E.D. N.Y. 1970), *aff'd*, 443 F.2d 1039 (2d Cir. 1971).

The Paquete Habana, 175 U.S. 677 (1900).

Powell v. McCormack, 395 U.S. 486 (1969).

The Prize Cases, 67 U.S. (2 Black) 635 (1863).

Process Gas Consumers Group v. Consumer Energy Council, 463 U.S. 1216 (1983).

Ramirez de Arellano v. Weinberger, 745 F.2d 1500 (D.C. Cir. 1984), *vacated on other grounds*, 471 U.S. 1113 (1985).

Resolution Trust Corp. v. Elman, 949 F.2d 624 (2d Cir. 1991).

Riegle v. FOMC, 656 F.2d 873 (D.C. Cir. 1981).

Sanchez-Espinoza v. Reagan, 568 F. Supp. 596 (D.D.C. 1983), *aff'd*, 770 F.2d 202 (D.C. Cir. 1985).

Shanghai Power Co. v. United States, 4 Cl. Ct. 237 (1983), *aff'd*, 765 F.2d 159 (Fed. Cir. 1985), *cert. denied*, 474 U.S. 909 (1985).

Sumitomo Shoji America v. Avagliano, 457 U.S. 176 (1982).

Talbot v. Seeman, 5 U.S. 1 (1801).

Telegraph-Oren v. Libyan Arab Republic, 726 F.2d 774 (D.C. Cir. 1984).

United States v. Belmont, 301 U.S. 324 (1937).

United States v. Curtiss-Wright Export Corp., 299 U.S. 304 (1936).

United States v. Humberto Alvarez-Machain, 504 U.S. ___, 112 S. Ct. 2188, 119 L. Ed. 2d 441 (1992).

United States v. Midwest Oil Co., 236 U.S. 459 (1915).

United States v. Nixon, 418 U.S. 683 (1974).

United States v. Smith, 27 F. Cas. 1192 (C.C.N.Y. 1806).

Youngstown Sheet & Tube Co. v. Sawyer, 343 U.S. 579 (1952).

Zemel v. Rusk, 381 U.S. 1 (1965).

Zuber v. Allen, 396 U.S. 168 (1969).

Index

About the Editors and Contributors

GARY M. STERN is Research Associate at the Center for National Security Studies, where he focuses on the war powers and other issues involving national security and civil liberties. In 1988, he co-authored an article on war powers and covert action in *Foreign Policy* and the American Civil Liberties Union's *amicus curiae* brief in *Dellums v. Bush*, 752 F. Supp. 1141 (D.D.C. 1990).

MORTON H. HALPERIN is a Senior Associate at the Carnegie Endowment for International Peace and serves as Chairman of the Advisory Board of the Center for National Security Studies. During the course of the war powers project, he was Director of both CNSS and the Washington Office of the American Civil Liberties Union. Among his many books are *Self-Determination in the New World Order* (1992) (with David J. Scheffer), *Nuclear Fallacy* (1987), and *Bureaucratic Politics and Foreign Policy* (1974). In 1988, he co-authored an article on war powers and covert action in *Foreign Policy*.

ELLEN C. COLLIER is a Specialist in U.S. Foreign Policy in the Foreign Affairs and National Defense Division of the Congressional Research Service of the Library of Congress. She edits the annual volume *Congress and Foreign Policy*, published by the House Foreign Affairs Committee, and has followed the War Powers Resolution since its enactment.

LOUIS FISHER is a senior specialist in separation of powers with the Congressional Research Service of the Library of Congress. His books include *President and Congress* (1972), *Presidential Spending Power* (1975), *The Constitution Between Friends* (1978), *The Politics of Shared Power* (1987), *Constitutional Conflicts Between Congress and the President* (1991), *Constitutional Dialogues* (1988), *American Constitutional Law* (1990), *Political Dynamics of Constitutional Law* (with Neal Devins, 1992), and a textbook in constitutional law entitled

Constitutional Structures: Separation of Powers and Federalism (Vol. 1) and *Constitutional Rights: Civil Rights and Civil Liberties* (Vol. 2).

HAROLD HONGJU KOH is a professor at Yale Law School, where he teaches the Constitution and Foreign Affairs, International Human Rights, Law and International Politics, International Business Transactions, among other subjects. He served as an attorney-adviser at the Office of Legal Counsel of the Department of Justice from 1983–1985. He has written numerous articles on international, foreign relations, and constitutional law, and is a member of the American Law Institute and the Board of Editors of *The American Journal of International Law*. He is the author of *The National Security Constitution: Sharing Power after the Iran-Contra Affair* (1990). He co-authored the law professors' *amicus curiae* brief in *Dellums v. Bush*, 752 F. Supp. 1141 (D.D.C. 1990).

JULES LOBEL is a Professor of Law at the University of Pittsburgh Law School. He has been counsel in several important cases challenging the Executive's use of force abroad, including *Dellums v. Bush*, 752 F. Supp. 1141 (D.D.C. 1990). He has written law review articles on war power issues for the *University of Pennsylvania Law Review* and the *Virginia Law Review*.

JOHN NORTON MOORE is the Walter L. Brown Professor of Law and Director of the Graduate Program at the University of Virginia School of Law. He also serves as Director of the Center for National Security Law at the School of Law. Professor Moore has written and testified extensively on the subject of war powers in the course of a professional life that has included five presidential appointments, most recently as Chairman of the Board of the U.S. Institute of Peace. He testified before the Senate Foreign Relations Committee and the House Subcommittee on National Security Policy during initial hearings on the War Powers Resolution, and worked on war powers issues while serving as the Counselor on International Law to the U.S. Department of State from 1972 to 1973. His books include *Law and the Indo-China War* (1972) and articles in *The ABA Journal* and *The Wall Street Journal*.

PETER RAVEN-HANSEN is the Glen Earl Weston Research Professor of Law at the National Law Center of George Washington University, where he teaches National Security Law, among other public law subjects. He is the editor of *First Use of Nuclear Weapons: Under the Constitution, Who Decides?* (Greenwood, 1987) and the co-author of *National Security Law* (1990), and *The Sword and the Purse in American Law* (1994).

JANE E. STROMSETH is Associate Professor of Law at Georgetown University Law Center, where she teaches Constitutional Law, International Law, and a seminar on the United Nations. She was formerly an attorney-adviser in the office of the Legal Adviser at the U.S. Department of State. Professor Stromseth is the author of *The Origins of Flexible Response: NATO's Debate over Strategy in the*

1960s (1988), and has written on war powers and on collective humanitarian intervention.

GREGORY F. TREVERTON is Vice Chairman of the National Intelligence Council. However, he completed his chapter before he joined the government, while he was Senior Fellow at the Council on Foreign Relations in New York, where he directed the Europe-America Project. He is the author, most recently, of *America, Germany and the Future of Europe* (1992) and *Rethinking America's Security* (1992) (with Graham T. Allison). His earlier books include *Covert Action: The Limits of Intervention in the Postwar World* (1987) and *Making the Alliance Work: The United States and Western Europe*. He has worked at both ends of Pennsylvania Avenue, serving the first Senate Intelligence Committee, and then the National Security Council during 1977–1979. He has also been director of studies at the International Institute for Strategic Studies in London, and a member of the faculty of Harvard University's Kennedy School of Government.